Barack Obama, the New Face of American Politics

Barack Obama, the New Face of American Politics

Martin Dupuis and Keith Boeckelman

Women and Minorities in Politics
Melody Rose, Series Editor

Westport, Connecticut
London

Library of Congress Cataloging-in-Publication Data

Dupuis, Martin, 1961–
  Barack Obama, the new face of American politics / Martin Dupuis and Keith
Boeckelman.
    p. cm. — (Women and minorities in politics, ISSN 1937–6510)
  Includes bibliographical references and index.
  ISBN 978-0-275-99160-9 (alk. paper)
  1. Obama, Barack. 2. Presidential candidates—United States. I. Boeckelman, Keith. II.
Title.
E901.1.O23D87 2008
328.73092—dc22   2007029124
[B]

British Library Cataloguing in Publication Data is available.

Library of Congress Catalog Card Number: 2007029124
ISBN: 978-0-275-99160-9
ISSN: 1937–6510

First published in 2008

Praeger Publishers, 88 Post Road West, Westport, CT 06881
An imprint of Greenwood Publishing Group, Inc.
www.praeger.com

Printed in the United States of America

♾™

The paper used in this book complies with the
Permanent Paper Standard issued by the National
Information Standards Organization (Z39.48–1984).

10 9 8 7 6 5 4 3 2 1

To my parents,
Don and Jan Dupuis,
who inspire me to follow my dreams,
and, in Barack Obama's words,
to have the audacity of hope.

To Sara,
At the dimming of the day.

Contents

Series Foreword		ix
Acknowledgments		xiii
1	From the South Side to Statewide	1
2	Will It Play in Peoria? The Primary Campaign	11
3	"Jesus Wouldn't Vote for Obama"—Alan Keyes: The General Election	25
4	"Money Is the Mother's Milk of Politics"— Raising Money and Spreading the Wealth	43
5	Overcoming a Funny Last Name: Media and the Vote	57
6	Barack Obama and Post-racial Politics	73
7	Mr. Obama Goes to Washington	89
8	"There Is No Red or Blue America": Obama's Message	101
9	Conclusion	117
Appendix A	*A Brighter Day, by Barack Obama*	127
Appendix B	*Full Text of Senator Barack Obama's Announcement for President*	133
Notes		139
Selected Bibliography		163
Index		165

Series Foreword

There could hardly be a more auspicious time to inaugurate a series on women and minorities in politics. The two Democratic frontrunners in the presidential race at press time are Barack Obama and Hillary Clinton. Condoleezza Rice is Secretary of State, the second woman (after Madeleine Albright) and first African American woman to hold the position. The nation is consumed with the immigration issue and with what higher population growth rates for "minorities"—whether achieved through fertility or immigration, legal or illegal—will mean for an evolving American identity. The "gender gap" in electoral politics is now a quarter century old. It would seem to be a good time to take stock.

Focusing on the roles played (and not yet played) by women and minorities in politics allows us to see the American political landscape through an exciting array of prisms, adding texture and richness to our understanding of America. This series has a simple but compelling purpose: to consider the impact of minorities' and women's involvement in all aspects of American politics.

This series is dedicated not only to women and minorities who are themselves directly involved in elected politics as politicians, candidates, or community leaders. We have taken a deliberate tack toward a broader definition of political action that includes but is not limited to electoral politics, social and political movements, interest group activities, and the role of voting blocs in American elections. Thus this series can claim the ambitious privilege of considering those who have gained access to institutional power, as well as constituents of that power.

At times, such as in this book, our view of the subject will be decidedly biographical, focusing deeply on a particular figure who strikes an impressive image. With other books in the series, we will consider whole movements, political trends, and significant advances in the political status of groups once considered political outsiders.

The current and future impact of minorities and women on American politics is tremendous. As women reach near-parity in some state legislatures, and ethnic minorities gain greater voice in political institutions, the implications for public policy, models of leadership, and electoral politics are transformative. The measure of these new voices in the American political realm is the objective of this series.

U.S. Senator Barack Obama makes a fascinating study for the political observer. As only the fifth African American to serve in the U.S. Senate, and one of the nation's most compelling voices on issues of justice and diversity, Senator Obama's story of service, leadership, and his meteoric rise to political fame create a multifaceted window into this series.

All good political stories are complex, and a series dedicated to diversity, as this one is, serves as a proper setting for exploring such complexities. The present book is no exception. As Dupuis and Boeckelman reveal, Senator Obama is both icon and enigma, which may explain his instant appeal in American culture. Dashing and cerebral, humble and self-assured, young and wise, this figure challenges many preconceived categories crafted for the American political class. This book does justice both to the man and to the country who watches him, by observing both his unique rise to power and his seemingly blithe transcendence of the expected.

Dupuis and Boeckelman's book stands out among a growing industry of books about this fascinating political star by documenting the rise of this unique individual. Through engaging prose, the authors have captured the early political career of Senator Obama, analyzing his race for United States Senate and the media's and public's assessments of his record in that chamber.

What is quickly apparent through this tale of rapid political success is that this man breaks down barriers. Born of mixed race, Senator Obama defies traditional racial characterization, preferring instead to identify widely with many Americans, and refusing to be defined by others. His politics favors traditional liberal public policy, while his considerable oratorical talent conveys a sentiment not unfamiliar to conservatives.

By observing the senator's early electoral habits, Dupuis and Boeckelman allow the reader to draw conclusions about his current presidential bid. The authors analyze Senator Obama's fundraising patterns and prowess, his willingness to engage new media, his distinctive rhetorical style, and public opinion poll data from both local and statewide races, allowing the reader to understand more clearly the senator's current election chances.

A relative newcomer to politics rarely wins the White House, and a person of color has not yet assumed the Oval Office. That fact is perhaps why this book and the series it initiates are so well timed: now, more than ever in American history, a minority just might ascend to the highest level of political office. *Barack Obama, the New Face of American Politics* conveys the appeal of the magnetic candidate who draws large numbers of donors to his campaign, and whose following has grown with a speed and enthusiasm unparalleled in recent elections. Whether this candidate can leverage his considerable talents and translate his pop-culture following and senate record into the Democratic presidential nomination remains to be seen. But to be the first African American candidate to become a viable contender for the nomination—and thus, for the presidency—speaks to the man, to the political moment, and the significance of our series.

Melody Rose, Ph.D.
Series Editor
Chair, Political Science
Founder & Director, NEW Leadership^{TM} Oregon
Portland State University

Acknowledgments

I thank my family and friends who have stood by me for more than a year as I researched, outlined, drafted, edited, researched some more, re-wrote, and re-edited this manuscript. Many thanks to my family— Jan and Don Dupuis; Alison, Mark, J. D., Samantha, and Ben Clemence; and the Thomas' for all your love and encouragement. Mike Dively, Tom and Ginny Helm, and Lisa Logan, thank you again for your support. Sara Boeckelman's research and writing skills are much appreciated, and her contribution to chapter 7 is especially noted. Elisa Rasmussen's editing efforts and Michael T. Callahan's computer expertise helped improve the text. Collaborating with my undergraduate research assistants was rewarding, and many thanks go out to them: Ashley Eberley, Jeremy Roth, and Jennie Zilner. Finally, thank you to my colleagues at the University of Central Florida; you demonstrate a dedication to learning and scholarship that is inspiring.

—Martin Dupuis

I thank my family for their support of and interest in this book, especially my wife Sara, who not only read and commented on the manuscript, but provided encouragement and love. I also thank my parents, Leroy and Jayne Boeckelman, my sister and brother-in-law Amy and Tim Hohulin, and my nieces Emma and Ellie Hohulin for their backing during this project. At Western Illinois University, Charles Helm, former chair of the political science department, supported my efforts, including helping me obtain a sabbatical leave for the fall semester of 2006. All of my colleagues in the political science department at Western Illinois University have provided encouragement, for which I am extremely grateful. I would particularly like to thank Richard Hardy, the current department chair, for his helpful advice on how to bring this book to fruition, Erin Taylor for reading part of the manuscript, and Janna Deitz for her input and willingness to talk through issues related to this project. Our department secretary, Debbie Wiley, helped facilitate manuscript preparation and communicating with the publisher in her usual efficient fashion. My graduate assistant Ruben Perta provided much-needed assistance in tracking down obscure facts and data. Bart Ellefritz helped me get prime access to key Obama events. I would like to thank the few Obama campaign aides and other Obama associates who did agree to be interviewed. Their insights enriched the book greatly.

—Keith Boeckelman

CHAPTER ONE

From the South Side to Statewide

At the beginning of 2004, Barack Obama was an almost unknown Illinois state legislator and a candidate for the U.S. Senate whom a mere 15 percent of likely voters in the state's Democratic primary favored. Among the many electoral challenges he faced, he had to make it clear to the public that, despite the similarity in their names, he was not Osama bin Laden. By the end of 2004, he had not only won his U.S. Senate election by the largest margin in Illinois history, but had become a "rock-star" politician who had captured the imagination of voters and the media nationwide. Thus, in less than a year he went from battling to gain name recognition to entertaining speculation that he would become the nation's first black president. On February 12, 2007, he took the next step in announcing his bid for the presidency in front of the Old State Capitol in Springfield, Illinois.

This book examines Barack Obama's rise to fame and what it means for American politics. Obama has captured America's imagination because his story reflects many of the most positive beliefs that permeate American culture: that plucky underdogs can triumph, that the American dream of success is open to immigrants and their children if they work hard, that racism is fading. He also appeals to Americans searching for common ground in an era of political division and hyperpartisanship and gives them hope that wealth, nepotism, and negative campaigning are not the only tickets to success in contemporary politics.

No one is perfect, and it is naïve to expect one person to "fix" American politics. In fact, we believe that institutional change is more likely to lead to political salvation than is changing the players. Nevertheless, we do believe that Obama's style of campaigning, his work in the

Senate, and his message inspire confidence and hope and are worth emulating for the sake of a healthy democracy. In contrast to the mudslinging and shrill and irrelevant messages voters have become used to, positive, issue-oriented campaigning and rhetoric help restore faith in democracy, particularly inspiring the poor and minorities to participate in politics.[1]

We wrote this book because we, too, find Obama's persona and message compelling. Like many, we have become disgusted with the pettiness of campaigns and the irrelevance of much contemporary political debate. Although we do not believe that he is the political messiah that some media coverage makes him out to be, we remember our own excitement when Obama visited Macomb, Illinois, the small college town where we lived and worked when this book began. People who are normally turned off by politics and politicians are drawn to Obama, which, we believe, is a healthy development.

Our analysis focuses almost entirely on Obama's public career and the events surrounding it, through his presidential announcement in early 2007, especially on his 2004 senate campaign and his first two years in the chamber. We have no doubt that there will be many accounts of his historic campaign for chief executive. Those searching for the "inner Obama" should read his own books, *Dreams from My Father* and *The Audacity of Hope*. That said, this chapter provides a brief overview of Obama's life before his 2004 U.S. Senate campaign. We provide a brief biographical overview and then focus more closely on his activities in his first elected position as an Illinois state senator. Chapter 2 considers the Democratic senate primary, where Obama pulled off a come-from-behind victory over formidable opponents. The wild general election race where Obama briefly faced off with Jack Ryan before defeating the inimitable Alan Keyes in the first U.S. Senate race between two African Americans is the focus of chapter 3. Chapter 4 delves into Obama's somewhat surprising ability to raise large amounts of money, while chapter 5 takes a closer at the role of the media in the campaign, including his innovative use of on-line technology. Chapter 6 examines how Obama's race has affected his political career. Chapter 7 explores Obama's first two years in the U.S. Senate, where he has tried to balance his instinct for bipartisanship with the demands of being a rising star in the Democratic Party, while also attending to the interests of his Illinois constituents. The following chapter takes a closer look at his message, both in the campaign and as he has refined it in office, focusing particularly on how he conceives the American Dream, his efforts to uplift politics and political rhetoric, and his "post-partisan" political stance. The concluding chapter analyzes the lessons of Obama's political career to date and examines his prospects for higher office.

BIOGRAPHICAL OVERVIEW

Barack Obama was born in Hawaii in 1961, the son of a Kenyan father, also named Barack, and a Kansas-born mother who met as students at the University of Hawaii. His parents divorced after his father left to pursue graduate work at Harvard when Obama was two years old. Father and son would meet only one more time before the elder Barack Obama died in a 1982 car accident after returning to Kenya. His mother remarried a native of Indonesia, where Obama lived between the ages of six and ten. Despite his youth, living in Indonesia made him aware of issues of poverty and inequality. In a newspaper interview many years later he noted, "It left a very strong mark on me living there, because you got a real sense of just how poor folks can get. You'd have some army general with 24 cars ... but on the next block you'd have children with distended bellies who just couldn't eat."[2] He later returned to Hawaii and attended a prestigious prep school, the Punahu Academy.

As he describes in his autobiography *Dreams from My Father*, he struggled with his racial identity throughout his high school years. Living with a white mother and grandparents and attending a predominantly white school, he found it difficult to navigate between black and white worlds. He endured racial slurs from a basketball coach, among others, leading him to conclude:

> We were always playing on the white man's court ... by the white man's rules. If the principal, or the coach, or a teacher, or Kurt, wanted to spit in your face, he could, because he had the power and you didn't.... Whatever he decided to do, it was his decision to make, not yours, and because of that fundamental power he held over you ... any distinction between good and bad whites held negligible meaning.... And the final irony: Should you refuse this defeat and lash out at your captors, they would have a name for that, too, a name that could cage you just as good. Paranoid. Militant. Violent. Nigger.[3]

Compounding his alienation, his African American friends did not consider him to be completely one of them, charging that he had to learn how to be black from books. His confusion led him to experiment with illegal drugs during his teenage years, writing that "pot had helped, and booze; maybe a little blow when you could afford it."[4] Later accounts by school contemporaries suggest that his alienation did not appear as outwardly pronounced at the time as he reported it to be in his autobiography.[5]

In 1979 he left Hawaii to attend Occidental College in Los Angeles. He continued to struggle with issues of identity, but became involved in political activity, protesting the university's investments in companies doing business in the apartheid-era government of South Africa. His efforts led him to realize that he was an effective public speaker, even as he felt ambivalent about whether his words had much impact. After two years, he transferred to Columbia University in New York, where he majored in political science. During his time there, he became more academically focused, to the extent that some of his friends concluded that he was becoming a "bore."[6]

Obama graduated from Columbia in 1983. After a stint at a multinational consulting firm in New York, he moved to Chicago in 1985 to work as a community organizer for the Developing Communities Project, focusing on issues like jobs and public housing in the inner city. His decision to pursue community activism reflected his belief, inspired by the civil rights movement, that grassroots, bottom-up efforts were the key to social change.[7] Obama's immersion in street-level community organizing taught him valuable, if sometimes frustrating, lessons about politics.

Perhaps most importantly, he found that achieving the "common good" was an elusive goal. As he began his work, he embraced a populist ideal of the concept, believing that it is possible to solve problems if "you could just clear away the politicians, and media, and bureaucrats, and give everybody a seat at the table."[8] Of course, he found that removing these annoyances is impossible. Those with power blocked his efforts and he discovered that approaching the table in the first place is not that appealing or interesting to most citizens. He became increasingly aware of the slow pace of change and the systematic and psychological obstacles to achieving his progressive vision. In a rumination on Harold Washington, Chicago's first black mayor, he described inner-city life as a "trap" with a "sad history, part of a closed system with few moving parts, a system that was losing heat every day, dropping into low-level stasis."[9]

He described the frustrations of overcoming seemingly petty individual agendas driven by "fear and small greeds." He lamented the public housing complex manager who lied about potential asbestos dangers in tenant apartments and a high school principal who would only support a program for schools if Obama would consider his wife and daughter for jobs. As another example, he pointed to the housing project official who "spent most of her time protecting the small prerogatives that came with her office: a stipend and a seat at the yearly banquet; the ability to see that her daughter got a choice appointment, her nephew a job in the CHA bureaucracy."[10]

These experiences led him to realize the ineffability of the concept of the common good and that conflict and differing world views are the essence of politics. With a degree of resignation, he noted in his autobiography that "in politics, like religion, power lay in certainty, and that one man's certainty always threatens another's."[11] In his frustration, he began to feel like a "prisoner of fate." Ultimately, however, he came to appreciate the small victories, such as cleaning up a park or creating a jobs program. His immersion in the larger Chicago political milieu of corruption and racial conflict helped him develop a pragmatic approach to politics that has been evident in his subsequent career.[12] Objectively, he also succeeded in building the organization itself, increasing its budget from $70,000 to $400,000 and its staff from one to thirteen people.[13]

In 1988 Obama left Chicago to attend Harvard Law School, where he became the first African American president (editor) of the university's law review. Foreshadowing his later political career, he won election, in part, by reaching out to conservatives.[14] After graduating, he returned to Chicago to practice civil rights law, and he later began teaching constitutional law at the University of Chicago. In 1990, he married Michelle Robinson, whom he had met when he was a summer intern at the law firm of Sidley and Austin.

He remained active in community affairs, working, for example, with the Annenberg foundation to improve public schools. In 1992, he headed a voter registration effort called "Project Vote" that registered 150,000 new African American voters for that year's election, helping Bill Clinton win Illinois and also generating votes for Illinois' first African American U.S. Senator, Carol Moseley-Braun.[15] In the midst of this effort he commented, "today we see hundreds of young blacks talking 'black power' and wearing Malcolm X T-shirts, but they don't bother to register and vote. We remind them that Malcolm once made a speech entitled 'The Ballot or the Bullet,' and today we've got enough bullets in the streets but not enough ballots."[16]

STATE SENATOR

Obama entered elective politics with his successful run for the state senate in 1996. He represented District 13, on the south side of Chicago, an area with some racially integrated middle class neighborhoods around the University of Chicago, as well as poorer African American areas to the west. (After the 2001 redistricting, it became a somewhat more affluent and racially mixed district that stretched along the southside lakefront.) His bid began with a small controversy. The incumbent state senator, Alice Palmer, had decided not to run for reelection, opting to run for a Congressional seat that was vacated in mid-term and supporting Obama as her successor. After losing in the primary, she attempted to reenter the race for her old seat. Because of her late decision, there were questions about whether some of the signatures on her nominating petitions were valid. After Obama challenged the petitions, she withdrew from the race and later withdrew her support from Obama as well. In a similar fashion, he knocked his three other Democratic rivals out of the race. His aides questioned the validity of their petitions, a move that some attributed to Obama's mastery of the "bare-knuckle arts of Chicago electoral politics," although he appears to have had some misgivings about such hardball tactics at the time.[17]

After eliminating his primary opposition, he faced only two weak opponents in the general election. Nevertheless, some on the left criticized him as a candidate with "impeccable do-good credentials and vacuous-to-repressive neo-liberal policies."[18] At the same time, Obama complained that Democratic Party officials who supported his campaign were too concerned about the "business" side of politics, such as whether he would be able to raise money, rather than where he stood on issues.[19] He went on to serve in the Illinois Senate through 2004, easily winning reelection in 1998 and running unopposed in 2002.

Despite its obscurity, Obama found service in the state legislature appealing because of the ability to achieve concrete results on issues he cared about, such as health insurance for the poor. He later wrote that "within the capitol building of a big, industrial state, one sees every day the face of a nation in conversation: inner city mothers and corn and bean farmers, immigrant day laborers alongside suburban investment bankers—all jostling to be heard, all ready to tell their stories."[20] In his early years, he was viewed as a promising legislator, but one who also sometimes found it difficult to stomach the slow pace of the legislative process and the necessity for compromise.[21] Even Republicans, however, recognized his potential. His colleague Kirk Dillard said, "I knew from the day he walked into this chamber that he was destined for great things.... Obama is an extraordinary man, his intellect, his charisma ... he can really work with Republicans."[22] He was known for his ability to master the details of legislation, as well as for his phenomenal memory. The latter quality enabled him to anticipate problems with bills because of his familiarity with how similar initiatives had fared in the past.[23] He benefited from an important mentor, then minority leader (later senate president) Emil Jones, who promoted Obama's prospects by assigning one of his legislative assistants to help the new senator with press relations and to position him for higher office.[24]

A turning point in his career occurred in 1999. During the fall veto session he missed a vote on a highly publicized, and ultimately narrowly defeated, anticrime measure supported by Governor George Ryan and Chicago Mayor Richard M. Daley that would have made illegal possession of a gun a felony. His absence occurred when he prolonged a family vacation to Hawaii after his daughter fell ill with the flu, despite pleas to return and the offer of a state plane to come pick him up. After enduring widespread criticism for this incident, Obama seems to have rededicated himself to becoming an effective legislator, especially after the

Democrats took over the body in 2003.[25] He was widely praised, for example, for his work on death penalty reform and his ability to bring reluctant prosecutors and police to the table and persuade them to support mandatory recording of murder suspects' interrogations.[26]

During his time in the U.S. Senate, he served on the Public Health and Welfare (later Health and Human Services) and Judiciary Committees, rising to chair the former during his last two years. As a committee chair, he was known as someone who was open to ideas from all committee members, including Republicans.[27] As an example, he supported emphasizing tax credits as a way to help the needy. In 2000 he cosponsored a plan to create a tax credit for donations that helped build or rehabilitate affordable housing.

A good deal of the legislation he authored during his time in the state legislature reflected interests related to these two committees. In the area of health, he sponsored the unsuccessful Bernadin amendment, named after the popular Cardinal of Chicago, which would have provided a constitutional guarantee of health insurance to all Illinois residents. Regarding welfare, he sponsored legislation creating an earned income tax credit for Illinois and bringing welfare reform to the state. In the criminal justice area, in addition to his work on the death penalty, he was able, after several tries, to pass legislation monitoring racial profiling.

Another area of emphasis was political reform. During his first term, he successfully sponsored ethics legislation developed by former U.S. Senator Paul Simon that limited political fundraising during legislative sessions and on state property, while restricting the personal use of campaign funds. Other legislation in this realm includes his unsuccessful efforts in the wake of the 2000 election to improve voting systems by allowing voters to replace spoiled ballots and to implement electronic voting systems. He was successful, however, in passing legislation requiring local governments to tape closed meetings.[28]

His legislative voting record was generally liberal, perhaps reflecting the nature of his district as much as his own ideological makeup.[29] In his first two-year term, for example, he had received a 100 percent rating from the American Civil Liberties Union and Planned Parenthood. During this period, he also supported the Democratic Party 100 percent of the time on votes that entailed partisan divisions.[30] Nevertheless, he also showed an independent bent, sometimes going against the well-funded lobbying groups that dominate the Illinois legislature. For example, he voted against major legislation to expand gambling in the state and opposed a successful effort, later declared unconstitutional, to provide a monopoly on liquor distribution that benefited a few powerful wholesalers.[31] Admittedly, this independence probably came easier to him than to some other members, given the "safe" district he ran from and the fact that he had little need to raise money to protect against a well-funded opponent. In his 1996 campaign, he spent $23,493, compared to over $400,000 for four other first-time senators.[32]

Although he often opposed legislation that would subsidize one firm or industry, Obama compiled a somewhat more pro-business voting record than one might expect. In his first term he received a 91 percent support score from the Illinois Farm Bureau and a 75 percent rating from the Illinois Chamber of Commerce.[33] This compares to 67 percent support for the Farm Bureau and 61 percent for the Chamber among thirteen other senators whose districts were primarily in Chicago. In fact, only one city-based senator had a more pro-Chamber of Commerce voting record, and none supported the Farm Bureau more than Obama. The six other black senators, on average, supported the Farm Bureau 71 percent of the time and the Chamber of Commerce 56 percent of the time. Obama's relatively pro-business record continued throughout his term. In his last two years in the state senate (2003–2004), he supported the Chamber of Commerce more than any other Democrat from the city of Chicago, albeit less than any Republican.[34] Although he voted with them only 20 percent of the time, a mere two other senate Democrats, out of thirty-three statewide, supported the Chamber more.

Obama also sometimes voted "present" on controversial social issues such as abortion and gun control. Fellow state senators attributed this strategy to a "calculating" streak in Obama and see it as early evidence of his ambitions for higher office.[35] These votes had the same impact as a "no" vote, but provided more political "cover." A "present" vote during his second term on legislation requiring parental notification of abortion would later become an issue in his U.S. Senate race.

Early in his state legislative career, Obama began to set his sights on higher office. After his first year as a state senator, he toured southern Illinois to test the waters for a possible statewide candidacy. In 2000, he challenged Congressman Bobby Rush for his seat representing Illinois' First Congressional District. The district has a storied history, as it has had a black Representative since 1929 when Oscar DePriest took office, the longest continuous representation by an African American of any district in the country.[36] Harold Washington, Chicago's first black mayor and a hero to the city's African American voters, also represented the district. Primarily rooted in the south side of Chicago, the district also included some voters from the southwest suburbs, and its makeup was about 30 percent white.

Although he had few issue differences with the incumbent, Obama argued that Rush had failed to provide leadership for the district, did not deliver government benefits effectively, and was "out-of-touch." Obama intimated that he represented a new generation of black politicians, focused on progress rather than protest.[37] For his part, former

Black Panther Rush challenged Obama's authenticity to represent the predominantly African American district by labeling him a "Harvard-educated carpetbagger."[38] This line of attack seemed to work, as some voters thought Obama "a bit too exotic for the district," whereas Rush's more humble background was a better fit.[39] Obama obtained the support of some black ministers, some white elected officials in the suburban part of the district, an organization representing liberal independent voters, and the *Chicago Tribune*. Rush, however, benefited from the endorsements of high-profile political figures such as Jesse Jackson and Bill Clinton. The African American newspaper, the *Chicago Defender,* also endorsed Rush, arguing that "Representative Rush deserves another term to further his agenda ... and use his blooming clout in D.C. His opponents Barack Obama and Donne E. Trotter are both highly qualified, but ... a U.S. Congressional run might be better advised for another time in the future."[40] In the March primary, which was the key race in the overwhelmingly Democratic district, Rush crushed Obama, winning 61 percent to Obama's 30 percent, with two other candidates taking the remaining votes. Obama ran well in the suburban part of the district, winning nearly two-thirds of the vote, as well as three-fourths in the far southwest-side Nineteenth Ward, foreshadowing his ability to attract white voters.[41]

Despite his somewhat humbling loss, Obama maintained his reputation as a rising political star, who was viewed as a potential candidate for statewide office or a future mayor of Chicago. His support among African Americans, liberal voters, and independents formed the basis for a potentially potent political coalition.[42] At the same time, he began to find his work as a state senator less satisfying, too removed from the power to address major national issues such as jobs, health care, and national security.[43] In running for the U.S. Senate, he developed an "up or out strategy," whereby if he failed to achieve higher office, he would pursue a more family-friendly-career.[44]

CHAPTER TWO

Will It Play in Peoria? The Primary Campaign

D uring his primary campaign, Obama played the role of the underdog, the "skinny guy from the South Side with a funny name." Indeed, there is no doubt that he faced an uphill battle against better known and better-funded opponents. This chapter will show how Obama beat the odds with his remarkable charisma, an effective campaign strategy, and some luck to move from obscure state senator to victor in the Democratic primary for U.S. Senate. After providing some background on Illinois politics, we will look at the major primary candidates. Next, we will examine how the race played out and explore the factors that accounted for Obama's victory.

BACKGROUND

Barack Obama's U.S. Senate victory occurred in a state with a tradition of pragmatic, individualistic, even corrupt politics. Illinois politicians are often "professionals," who engage in politics for personal gain, rather than to pursue an abstract public interest, as is true in some other midwestern states, such as Wisconsin, Minnesota, or Iowa.[1] Kent Redfield, an expert on the state's political culture, said during the campaign, "Our politics tend to be pretty pragmatic. We'd rather fight about roads and bridges ... than whether we should have gay marriage."[2] This pragmatism sometimes edges into malfeasance. Of the last six elected governors, excluding the current incumbent, half faced criminal punishments after leaving office. Most recently George Ryan (1999–2003) was convicted in 2006 on various corruption charges stemming from trading state contracts for vacations and other perks.

There is a strong tradition of regionalism in Illinois politics. In the past, this dynamic has pitted Chicago against the more rural "downstate" region. Culturally and geographically, far southern Illinois is closer to the South than to the city. In recent years, the Chicago suburbs have emerged as a major power base as well. This area accounts for between 42 percent and 44 percent of Illinois' population, depending on how one defines suburban, while roughly one-third of Illinoisans live downstate.[3] Moreover, surveys show that residents of one region generally distrust politicians representing the others.[4] These geographical divisions make it a challenge to develop a style and issue repertoire that works in these vastly different venues. It is a rare politician who can appeal to a majority of voters in all parts of the state.

Over 40 percent of Illinois' population lives in Cook County, with the city of Chicago accounting for slightly over half of that total. The city has a colorful political history, due in large part to the operation of the Chicago political machine, often considered the last of its kind in a major U.S. city. By trading jobs and other favors for votes, the Democratic Party largely controlled city elections and often exerted great influence in statewide contests as well, especially in its heyday under Mayor Richard J. Daley, who served from 1955 to 1976. The machine's electoral advantage stemmed from its ability to slate candidates in Democratic primaries and then deliver enough votes for them on election day that they usually won.

The relationship between the machine and African Americans has been somewhat uneasy, however. Its vaunted ability to provide public services often fell short in black neighborhoods. Although black precincts turned out some of the highest vote totals for Democratic candidates, African American politicians were allowed to ascend only so far. When Harold Washington (1983–1987) ran to become the city's first black mayor, the machine not only opposed him in the primary, but supported his Republican opponent in the general election.

Today, under Mayor Richard M. Daley, the machine's power is weaker due to limits on the use of patronage, as well as Daley's reluctance to get directly involved in many primary contests. Nevertheless, it still can turn out voters, especially in white and Hispanic areas of the city. Thus, the machine still carries some freight in Democratic primaries, where Chicago typically accounts for more than one-third of the statewide vote.

In this milieu, Illinois has a somewhat surprising history of electing idealistic liberals to the Senate, such as Paul Douglas (1949–1967) and Paul Simon (1985–1997). Both struggled to balance their ideals with the compromises often necessary to legislate successfully. Douglas was described as "long on principle, short on votes," and "an idealist who followed no one and led only a few liberals."[5] Simon was somewhat less rigid, but he, too, was never considered a power in the Senate.[6] Still, the latter is sometimes viewed as a forerunner for Obama, given their similar abilities to engender trust in voters, even those who were considerably more conservative.[7] As discussed more fully in chapter 6, the state has elected several blacks to statewide office, including Carol Moseley-Braun to the U.S. Senate in 1992, Roland Burris as Attorney General and State Comptroller, and Jesse White as Secretary of State. According to David Bositis, an expert on black politics, "Illinois has probably elected more black statewide officials than any state in the country."[8]

Often considered a political bellwether through the 1980s, with two competitive, evenly matched parties, Illinois has trended Democratic in recent years. In part, this trend reflects a divided Republican Party struggling to reconcile conservative and moderate factions. In addition, the scandals surrounding former governor George Ryan have hurt the state GOP. The most notorious controversy occurred when Ryan was Illinois secretary of state and his office allegedly sold commercial drivers' licenses to unqualified drivers to generate political contributions. In a highly publicized incident, six children died in an accident involving one such trucker. National Republicans have also fared poorly in Illinois in recent years. Although President Reagan won the state twice and George H.W. Bush did so in 1992, George W. Bush lost to Al Gore by twelve points in 2000 and to John Kerry by ten in 2004.

Since 1940 most of Illinois' U.S. Senators have served multiple terms.[9] The open seat in 2004, however, had been occupied by two one-term senators, after Democrat Alan Dixon held it from 1981 to 1993. In 1992, Carol Moseley-Braun, an African American former state legislator and Cook County Recorder of Deeds, mobilized African Americans, white liberals, and some suburban women to upset Dixon in a three-candidate Democratic primary, winning a close race with a plurality of 38 percent. Moseley-Braun got 82 percent of the black vote and benefited from a higher than expected black turnout, but she polled only about 26 percent of the white vote.[10] She benefited from $5 million that candidate Al Hofeld spent on attack ads against incumbent Alan Dixon, spending that seemed to hurt Hofeld too, as well as from a backlash against Dixon's vote in favor of Clarence Thomas's Supreme Court appointment.[11] She went on to defeat a relatively weak Republican opponent, Richard Williamson, who had not previously held elective office.

Controversy surrounded Moseley-Braun's term in office, however, limiting her prospects for reelection. Early in her term, she engaged in heated battles over the Confederate flag, among other things, with conservative icon Senator Jesse Helms of North Carolina. These highly publicized incidents cast her more as a symbol for African Americans than as a Senator focusing on Illinois' problems.[12] Her 1996 visit to Nigeria and praise of its dictator, General Sani Abacha, also hurt her credibility with voters. Further, allegations that her sister had used her state job to help fundraising efforts for Moseley-Braun undermined her good government persona. These controversies led to her defeat in 1998 by state senator Peter Fitzgerald.[13]

Despite crusades to clean up Illinois politics and limit the expansion of O'Hare Airport, Fitzgerald never achieved broad support among voters or leaders of his own party. As his reelection year approached, he was viewed as the most vulnerable Republican senator up for reelection in 2004. He was at odds with many prominent Illinois Republicans, including U.S. House Speaker Dennis Hastert, who was trying to organize a primary challenge, when Fitzgerald dropped out of the race in April 2003, citing family concerns.[14]

CANDIDATES AND ISSUES

With a weak incumbent, and, later, an open seat in play, both parties attracted a large number of candidates, fifteen in total, including seven millionaires. For the Democrats, five candidates were viewed as having a realistic chance of winning: Dan Hynes, Blair Hull, Maria Pappas, Gery Chico, and Barack Obama. In general, their strategies focused on building coalitions of voters, hoping to put together a plurality, rather than attempting to appeal to all voters statewide.[15] A brief sketch of each candidate appears below.

Dan Hynes, the state comptroller, was the candidate of the Democratic organization and organized labor. A proven vote-getter, he received the most votes of any Democratic statewide candidate in 1998. When elected comptroller that year, at age thirty, he was the youngest person to win a statewide office in Illinois since the 1940s.

For his senate campaign, he garnered the support of many establishment politicians, such as Illinois House Speaker and State Democratic Party chair Michael Madigan, and the remnants of the Chicago Democratic political machine.[16] His father Thomas Hynes was a prominent machine figure, who had been a former Cook County assessor and state senate president. Aldermen or committeemen in twenty-three of Chicago's fifty wards supported him, primarily those in white and Hispanic areas.[17] Cook County Board President and Eighth Ward boss John Stroger, an African American with strong ties to the machine and to Hynes's father, also endorsed him. In addition he received the backing of major unions, including the AFL-CIO, the state's largest, and the vast majority of Democratic county chairs. Supplementing his organizational advantages, Hynes assembled a network of trial lawyers to raise money.[18] Dan Hynes enjoyed a favorable reputation as a competent public official. Nevertheless, he failed to develop a compelling political persona, often appearing plodding and cautious, resembling machine politicians of the past, who believed organization was more important than charisma.

Blair Hull was a multimillionaire newcomer to politics with a background in computerized options training. He garnered criticism for his sporadic voting record, including failure to vote in the 2000 presidential election. His wealth allowed him to far outspend his competitors, and he ultimately devoted about $29 million of his own money to his campaign. With no natural base, and all the Democratic candidates from the Chicago area, Hull sought votes by saturating downstate TV markets with commercials and spending a great deal of money on organizing the region. This strategy was inspired by the 2002 Democratic gubernatorial primary, which Rod Blagojevich was able to win with a strong downstate showing, while losing in the Chicago area. Hull also courted women and black voters. To appeal to the former, he emphasized his membership on the boards of pro-choice political organizations, such as the National Abortion Rights Action League, and his support for Title IX, which promotes varsity sports opportunities for girls and women at the high school and college levels.[19] Challenging Obama's perceived base, Hull attracted the support of some prominent African American politicians, most notably Congressman Bobby Rush, who endorsed him in ads on black radio stations.[20]

Hull advocated a national health-care program as a central campaign issue and funded several trips to Canada with senior citizens to buy cheaper prescription drugs. In a populist vein, he promised to eschew contributions from political action committees or "special interests" and not draw a senate salary if elected. He had difficulty connecting to average voters on the stump, however, and perceived political strategy in largely quantitative terms. He described his approach to a reporter as follows: "You'd create a persuasion model based on canvassing that says 'the probability of voting for Hull is ...' plus some variable on ethnicity ... with a positive coefficient on age, a negative coefficient on wealth, and that gives us an equation."[21]

Maria Pappas, one of three female candidates running for the Democratic nomination, was the only one considered to have a realistic shot at winning. A psychologist and lawyer, she entered politics when she won a seat on the Cook County board in 1990. Later she served as Cook County treasurer. Her political base included ethnic whites in Chicago and residents of suburban Cook County. Her popularity stemmed in part from her reputation as a watchdog on spending while on the Cook County board, as well as from reforms she initiated as county treasurer, such as allowing people to pay property tax bills at some bank branches.

Known as somewhat quirky, she had campaigned in the past with her dog in her purse and reportedly decided which constituent mail to answer on the basis of handwriting analysis.[22] Her campaign style reflected a fluid schedule focused on person-to-person contact and stunts, such as appearing with a Hummer sports utility vehicle in front of a Hooters restaurant to protest congressional pork barrel policies.[23] Like Obama and Gery Chico, she had little name recognition downstate and lacked the funds to match Blair Hull's advertising efforts. She was never able to recover from a late-starting campaign, and her support in the polls generally declined throughout the contest.

Gery Chico, although mired in single digits in the polls throughout most of the campaign, was the first candidate to enter the race. He had served as Chicago Mayor Richard M. Daley's chief of staff and later president of the city's school board, overseeing school reforms supported by the mayor. As the son of a Mexican American father and grandson of Mexican immigrants, he tried to appeal to Hispanic voters with Spanish-language speeches at some rallies. He was backed by the bosses of a few Chicago wards with heavily Hispanic populations. His issue-oriented campaign emphasized education concerns, such as reforming the No Child Left Behind law and providing free college tuition for future teachers. He was also the only candidate to back gay marriage. Despite his widely acknowledged command of the issues and strengths as a debater, he was not viewed as a charismatic candidate.[24] Questions about his role in the collapse and bankruptcy of his former law firm also dogged Chico's campaign.

Barack Obama was the second candidate to enter the race. Initially, his strategy consciously reflected an attempt to rebuild the coalition that led to Carol Moseley-Braun's 1992 senate primary victory, as the race shaped up with somewhat similar dynamics. Admittedly, there were only three candidates in the 1992 race, instead of the seven in 2004. Nevertheless, Moseley-Braun faced one opponent, incumbent Senator Alan Dixon, who had strong support from the Democratic Party organization, and another, Al Hofeld, who ran as a wealthy self-funded "outsider." About a month before the primary, one observer drew an explicit connection between the two races. "There are distinct parallels, with Blair Hull being Al Hofeld and Dan Hynes being Dixon and Obama being Carol. The difference is Carol was not a serious candidate and thought this would be an interesting thing to do. I don't think it ever entered her head that she would win."[25] Dixon and Hofeld ended up spending much of the campaign attacking each other, allowing Moseley-Braun to eke out a narrow victory.

Initially, Obama focused on building a base coalition of African Americans and liberal suburban whites, especially in Chicago's northern suburbs and in downstate university communities. Early in the campaign, he worked to line up endorsements from leading black Chicago aldermen, Toni Preckwinkle and Leslie Hairston, and built strong support among African American clergy in the city.[26] Antiwar activists rallied around Obama due to compelling speeches he had given in 2002 and 2003 opposing intervention in Iraq.[27] Although Hynes had the support of "organization" Democrats, Obama built his own network among some African American office holders, as well as those in the more liberal suburban wing of the party, including some he had supported in previous campaigns. He was also endorsed by four Illinois members of Congress—Jesse Jackson, Jr., Danny Davis, Lane Evans, and Jan Schakowsky—the most of any candidate. The Evans endorsement was particularly important in giving Obama credibility with downstate voters.[28]

As the campaign progressed, he widened his appeal beyond this initial base of African Americans and liberals to make significant inroads with more moderate white Democrats. In addition, he picked up most of the labor union support that didn't go to Dan Hynes. He was especially successful with public service unions, earning the endorsements of groups such as the American Federation of State, County, and Municipal Employees and the Illinois Federation of Teachers.[29] Major environmental groups, including the Sierra Club and the League of Conservation Voters, also endorsed him.

Like other candidates, Obama brought strengths and weaknesses to the race. On the negative side, he was unproven as a candidate for higher office, as his failed challenge to Congressman Bobby Rush, discussed in chapter 1, showed. Also, there was some doubt whether he was "black" enough to appeal to African Americans. A columnist for the *Chicago Sun-Times* explained the challenge facing Obama six months before the primary:

> Low income and working class blacks don't think Obama is "down enough." It's a cultural phenomenon, and it's rooted in an unfortunate strain of anti-intellectualism and distrust of those with close association with the white power structure.... Some of the black nationalists are whispering that "Barack is not black enough." He's of mixed race. He hangs out in Hyde Park, and is the darling of white progressives: he's not to be trusted. And there are the black Machine Democrats. They're all crabs in a barrel, trying to get to the top. And they don't want Obama to get there first.[30]

In addition, his name appeared to be a disadvantage. Both first and last were unusual, and his surname differed by one letter from the moniker of 9/11, mastermind Osama bin Laden. For a brief period, a

Republican political operative created a website that superimposed Obama's face over Osama bin Laden's, although he later apologized and took it down.[31] In a widely reported incident, President Bush appeared briefly to mistake an Obama campaign button that U.S. Representative Jan Schakowsky wore to a meeting as an endorsement of the terrorist leader.

Obama came into the race with several advantages, as well. Following the advice of political commentator Chris Matthews to "hang a lantern on your problem," or turn perceived weaknesses into strengths, Obama turned his name into a positive.[32] On the stump, he joked about it, jesting that people called him "Alabama" or "Yo Mama." In a more serious vein, he used his name to mark his authenticity, pointing out that he resisted attempts by his political consultants to use something more "mainstream," such as Barry, as he was sometimes called growing up. Moreover, his name may ultimately have helped attract some white voters, who tend to view African immigrants more favorably than native-born African Americans.[33] Combined with a campaign image that emphasized a record of accomplishment, such as being the first black president of the *Harvard Law Review*, Obama was able to bridge a gap bedeviling many African American candidates who find it difficult to appeal to both blacks and moderate and working class whites. As Noam Scheiber put it in an article in the *New Republic* magazine, "Free of the burden of reassuring culturally moderate whites that he wasn't threatening, Obama could appeal to their economic self-interest while also exciting his African American and progressive white base."[34]

If Hull had money and Hynes had the support of much of the Democratic organization, Obama's personal charisma and speaking ability played to his advantage. A reporter for the *Chicago Tribune* captured his appeal as follows:

> His clear voice resonating through the auditorium, state Sen. Barack Obama was reciting his mantra about how Americans are intrinsically good people linked by decency and hope when an aide to another political candidate shrugged his shoulders. "He is without a doubt the most dynamic speaker up there," the aide said, referring to Obama amid the six Democratic candidates for the U.S. Senate on hand for a joint appearance. "I wish my candidate had half of that." After the forum, a small gaggle of fawning supporters surrounded Obama, shoving campaign literature at him to be autographed. Meanwhile, several other candidates looked almost lonely, searching the crowd for someone to chat up.[35]

His personal magnetism helped him recruit many supporters who normally paid little attention to politics.[36]

While there were some differences in emphasis discussed above, in general, there weren't big issue differences among the candidates. One reporter compared the issue content of the campaign to "a political version of a 'Seinfeld' episode," in the sense that it was about nothing.[37] In most of the multitude of campaign debates, especially the early ones, the candidates largely avoided attacking each other, instead focusing their ire on Bush administration policies.[38] All five major candidates, for example, criticized the president's tax cuts and advocated tax relief for middle income workers.[39] All also slammed the administration for underfunding the No Child Left Behind law. Obama took a slightly more pro-gun control stance than the other candidates and staked out a somewhat more forceful position against the Iraq War. While all candidates spoke against it, only Obama and Chico opposed the $87 billion funding request to rebuild Iraq.[40] In downstate appearances, Obama often emphasized bread-and-butter issues, such as protecting American jobs.[41] He also specialized in one-liners attacking the Bush administration, such as "The problem with No Child Left Behind is Bush left all the money behind," or "The president says the economy is in a jobless recovery, but there is no recovery without jobs."[42]

THE PRIMARY RACE

The senate race played out in three distinct phases, with Hynes leading the first, Hull the second, and Obama the third. In the first phase, which ran through mid-January of 2004, Hynes led in the polls, in part because of his name recognition and organization.[43] Obama entered the race in January 2003, before Hynes, Hull, or Pappas had officially announced. Aware that achieving about a third of the vote might be enough to win a multicandidate race, his campaign kickoff showed that he was following Carol Moseley-Braun's strategy, discussed above, of putting together a coalition of African Americans and white liberals. Many of the figures spotlighted in Obama's announcement were leading African American politicians, such as Illinois Senate President Emil Jones and Congressmen Jesse Jackson, Jr., and Danny Davis. He also cited Moseley-Braun's decision to forgo the race as a factor in his own decision to enter.[44] In his primary campaign kickoff speech, he repeatedly claimed the mantle of Dr. Martin Luther King. He also touched on themes appealing to liberals, such as criticizing tax cuts for the wealthy as a violation of the fundamental American value of fairness.[45]

During this phase of the race, Obama worked to build name recognition. After his announcement, he made the usual rounds of county Democratic Party dinners and other speaking engagements and traveled the state with luminaries who had endorsed him, such as downstate congressman Lane Evans. He spent much of his time working the Chicago area, however, recognizing that there were more Democratic votes available there.[46] Foreshadowing his strengths, Obama had a strong showing in the first televised debate in October 2003, showing "presence" and "command."[47]

By the summer of 2003, he had pulled into a second place tie with Pappas at 14 percent with Hynes, the leader at 21 percent, with 41 percent undecided. This poll revealed that Obama trailed Hynes and Pappas in name recognition, at one-third, compared to over 50 percent for the other two candidates. However, he also had the highest favorable rating at 10 to 1 in favor and did the best among the most well-informed voters.[48] He surprised some with his success at raising money during this period, falling just short of Hynes's totals.

The campaign entered a second stage in mid-January 2004, as Blair Hull's $19 million spending spree on campaign commercials began to pay off and he emerged as the frontrunner. A *Chicago Tribune*/WGN news poll conducted February 11–17 showed Hull in the lead with 24 percent, followed by Obama at 15 percent, Hynes at 11 percent, Pappas at 9 percent, and Chico at 5 percent. Hull's fourteen-point boost from a poll conducted the previous month was due to TV ads shown both in Chicago and downstate. Hull's support increased at the expense of every candidate except Obama. His backing was shaky, however, as 40 percent of likely Democratic primary voters surveyed thought that Hull's advantage over his opponents in resources was unfair.[49]

During this stage, Obama continued to struggle to get people to know who he was and to solidify his position with black voters. With respect to name recognition, the poll showed him in last place of the five major candidates among likely primary voters at slightly under a third, compared to 60 percent for Hull and over 50 percent for Hynes and Pappas.[50] Although Obama ran strongly among black voters compared to other candidates, he was favored by less than a majority at 38 percent. Obama's relatively weak showing in previous polls worked to his advantage at this stage of the campaign in one sense, just as Moseley-Braun's similar position had in 1992. Anticipating that Dan Hynes would be his main rival, Hull attacked the state comptroller, who responded in kind, allowing Obama to build support relatively unscathed.[51]

Hull's lead turned out to be short-lived, however. His campaign began to self-destruct, just as his poll numbers surged, allowing Obama to emerge as the frontrunner, a position he would hold until election day and his dramatic win. In mid-February the *Chicago Tribune* reported that Hull's ex-wife had taken out an order of protection against him in 1998. Hull initially refused to explain the incident, arguing that it was irrelevant to his ability to perform as a senator. This stance undermined his ability to appeal to women voters, however, as the head of the Illinois chapter of the National Organization for Women publicly condemned his silence.[52]

The media did not let the issue slide, either. Responding to pressure, Hull and his ex-wife agreed to make previously sealed divorce records public. The records revealed that police accused him of hitting his wife in the leg in an argument surrounding their stormy separation. The divorce file also showed Hull using profane and abusive language, issuing death threats, and resorting to fake punches designed to make his ex-wife "flinch."[53]

Of course, Hull's opponents did all they could to fan the flames of the divorce story. A newspaper columnist speculated that Dan Hynes had a hand in orchestrating the scandal, hoping not only to undermine Hull, but to disgust enough voters to drive down turnout, which was to his advantage.[54] Hynes and Maria Pappas attacked Hull on the issue in a statewide radio debate on February 23. Pappas cited her training as a psychologist to urge Hull to seek further counseling with his ex-wife and children.[55] Hull himself made some strategic miscalculations that kept the story alive longer than it might otherwise have been. He charged that his ex-wife exaggerated the situation described in the divorce files to increase her monetary settlement, guaranteeing another day of coverage after her very public denial. Then, he ran television commercials denouncing the attacks as unfair and pointing out that the domestic battery charge against him was thrown out by a judge. These ads did little to help the situation, but, again, kept the story in the public eye for another few days and distracted the Hull campaign from emphasizing other issues.[56]

By late February, the divorce story had begun to take its toll, and Obama emerged with a lead over Hull.[57] One week before the primary, a *Chicago Tribune* poll showed that Obama had surged to 33 percent, while Hull had fallen back to 16 percent. Hynes also gained eight points, rising to 19 percent.[58] Obama's support among black voters rose particularly dramatically, to 63 percent from 38 percent in the mid-February poll discussed above. In the *Tribune* survey, 50 percent of Democratic voters responding believed that Hull's divorce would affect his chances of winning "a lot" or "some."

Obama also began to run TV ads in the last three weeks in the campaign, starting in Chicago and moving downstate in the last week.[59] His advertising appealed to both his black-liberal base and to more moderate whites by citing both his race and "establishment" credentials. In one ad, Obama spoke to the camera, saying, "They said an African American had never led the *Harvard Law Review*—until I changed that. Now they say we can't change Washington, D.C.... I approved this message to say 'Yes we can.'"[60] Another ad that he ran downstate featured an endorsement of the popular late Senator Paul Simon's daughter, who claimed that Obama was "cut from the same cloth" as her father. Other television ads and targeted mailings focused on appealing to women and the elderly by playing up Obama's accomplishments on issues like health care.[61]

In the waning days of the race, Hynes and Hull went on the attack. Hynes accused Obama of failing to challenge state pork barrel spending under former Governor George Ryan. In the last Democratic primary debate on March 10, Hynes charged, "When George Ryan was leading our state into a fiscal ditch, I took him on.... Barack Obama took a different course. He stayed silent. He didn't do anything."[62] Meanwhile, Hull publicized Obama's "present" votes on abortion legislation requiring parental notification, arguing that they undermined his pro-choice credentials. A Hull mailing in early March showed an illustration of a duck with the headline "He ducked," referring to Obama.[63] In response, Obama aides attacked Hull's admission that he had rarely voted in previous elections. Pro-choice groups also defended Obama, arguing that "present" votes had the same impact as voting "no" and that Hull did not understand the legislative process.[64] Controversy also resurfaced about Obama's admissions of drug use as a young man. Obama tried to remain above the fray, calling it "depressing" that the campaign focused on "drugs and divorces."[65]

RESULTS

Obama won the primary with nearly 53 percent of the vote. In second place, Dan Hynes received slightly under 24 percent, followed by Hull at 11 percent, Pappas at 6 percent, and Chico at 4 percent. Although Hynes won eighty-one counties to Obama's fourteen and Hull's seven, Obama won the largest Chicago area counties. In Cook County, which accounted for slightly over 60 percent of the statewide Democratic primary vote, he beat Hynes 64 percent to 17 percent. Hynes failed to do as well as expected in white and Latino areas of Chicago where the machine still holds sway.[66] Of twelve majority white wards with a strong machine presence, Obama won eight, reversing a long-term pattern in areas of the city that had previously been hostile to black candidates.[67] In fact, Hynes won his father's Nineteenth Ward by less than 2,000 votes. Observers attributed this failure to the machine's weakness in a less patronage-rich environment, Mayor Daley's decision to stay on the sidelines, and Obama's excellence as a candidate.[68] In an interview after the primary election, Dan Hynes mused, "Three days before the primary, I opened the newspaper and looked at the picture from the St. Patrick's Day Parade ... that's my day! And there was Barack Obama surrounded by every single Irish politician in town. I'm cropped out of the picture. And I thought to myself 'That's not good.'"[69]

Obama won all of the Chicago suburban "collar counties," that is, DuPage, Kane, Lake, McHenry, and Will. He also did well in the counties containing state universities, winning Champaign (University of Illinois), DeKalb (Northern Illinois University), Jackson (Southern Illinois University), and McDonough (Western Illinois University) counties. Sangamon County, which contains the state capital Springfield, went into Obama's column as well. In most of the downstate counties, he finished third, behind Dan Hynes and Blair Hull, although he managed to come in second in some of the more urban counties of the region, such as Macon and St. Clair. By some estimates, Obama won around 90 percent of the black vote, exceeding Carol Moseley-Braun. In addition, turnout in heavily African American areas of Chicago was up to 30 percent higher than in other recent elections.[70]

Table 2-1 breaks down Obama's vote in various parts of the state. For the sake of comparison, it also shows vote percentages for prior Democratic primary victors Paul Simon in 1984's five-candidate race and Carol Moseley-Braun in 1992. The table breaks down the vote in Chicago, suburban Cook County, the five collar counties (DuPage, Kane, Lake, McHenry, and Will) that traditionally contain Chicago's other suburban areas, the Illinois portion of the St. Louis suburbs, and seven other metropolitan areas in the state. Votes from four rural counties with state universities—Coles, DeKalb, Jackson, and McDonough—are also compiled, because these areas were among Obama's few bastions of strength

Table 2-1   Votes for Obama (2004), Moseley-Braun (1992), and Simon (1984) by Region of Illinois

	Obama	Moseley-Braun	Simon
City of Chicago	67% (1st)	51% (1st)	21% (3rd)
Suburban Cook County	61% (1st)	39% (1st)	36% (1st)
Collar Counties	56% (1st)	38% (1st)	41% (1st)
St. Louis Metro	28% (3rd)	13% (3rd)	71% (1st)
Rockford Metro	30% (3rd)	35% (2nd)	38% (1st)
Peoria Metro	27% (3rd)	20% (3rd)	36% (2nd)
Quad Cities Metro	15% (3rd)	21% (3rd)	39% (1st)
Springfield Metro	40% (1st)	26% (2nd)	55% (1st)
Bloomington Metro	35% (2nd)	44% (1st)	54% (1st)
Champaign Metro	63% (1st)	49% (1st)	64% (1st)
Decatur Metro	29% (2nd)	24% (3rd)	50% (1st)
Rural State University Counties	47% (1st)	32% (2nd)	67% (1st)
Rural Illinois	18% (3rd)	16% (3rd)	36% (1st)
Statewide Total	53% (1st)	38% (1st)	36% (1st)

Source: Author calculations based on Illinois State Board of Elections, *Official Vote at the Primary Election*, March 16, 2004.

downstate in the primary. The final category includes the rest of the state, loosely characterized as "rural Illinois." In addition to the vote percentage, the table shows the candidates' place ranking for each region.

Table 2-1 shows that Obama generally did well in the same places that Carol Moseley-Braun did, following in her electoral footsteps to a degree. He did better in several key locales, however, especially Chicago and its suburbs, because of his ability to attract more white voters in these areas than Moseley-Braun did. The Paul Simon comparisons notwithstanding, Obama fell short of his predecessor among downstate voters, but far exceeded him in the Chicago area. The table also shows that Obama did relatively well in the more economically vibrant "post-industrial" parts of downstate, such as Bloomington, Champaign, and Springfield, compared to the more industrial regions of Rockford, Peoria, the Quad Cities, and Decatur. Finally, the historical comparison illustrates the magnitude of Obama's victory, as he was able to get far more of the vote than either Moseley-Braun or Simon in a race with more candidates than either of his predecessors faced.

Of course the question remains whether Obama would have won if it had not been for Hull's divorce scandal. This event led many people to rethink their preferences and take another look at the candidates.[71] Clearly Obama benefited, but it is impossible to know what would have happened absent the scandal. Given the magnitude of his victory, we think Obama would have still won, albeit by a narrower margin. To begin with, Hull was clearly a weak candidate with few passionate backers. Other candidates were primed to go negative against him, and if not for the divorce, he would have had to fend off another line of attack, something he appeared unprepared to do effectively. Downstate, an area he targeted and where the divorce issue was covered less extensively, Hull still lost to Hynes. Furthermore, at his peak, his standing in the polls was only 24 percent, with one-third undecided and 55 percent not paying much attention to the race.[72] It's questionable whether voters would have gone his way with Obama and others running TV commercials at the end of the campaign. Finally, Obama had an effective "Get Out the Vote" operation, staffed by the public employee unions who had endorsed him, as well as passionate volunteers who came to see his campaign as something akin to a crusade.[73]

In his victory speech, Obama harkened back to the underdog theme, perhaps the last time he could realistically do so. Echoing the themes of the campaign, he said, "I think it's fair to say that the conventional wisdom was that we could not win. There's no way that a skinny guy from the South Side with a name like Barack Obama could ever win a statewide race. Sixteen months later we are here, and Democrats from all across Illinois … black, white, Hispanic, Asian have declared: Yes we can! Yes we can! Yes we can!"[74]

CHAPTER THREE

"Jesus Wouldn't Vote for Obama"— Alan Keyes: The General Election

After the primary, the *Chicago Tribune* editorialized that Illinoisans were in for the "Senate race of a generation," promising an "uncommon gift waged by uncommon candidates."[1] The description of the contest as "uncommon" turned out to be an understatement, with "bizarre" or "wacky" better characterizing it in the end. As for the "gift" part, it ended up being something of a white elephant, with Obama facing flawed, and, at times, no opponents, rendering the outcome a foregone conclusion and lowering the level of issue debate.

After the March primary, promising Republican primary victor Jack Ryan proved somewhat unready for a high-profile statewide campaign. Then, after material in his previously sealed divorce records came to light, he withdrew from the race entirely. His exit threw the Illinois Republican Party into an increasingly frantic process to choose a successor that combined elements of comic opera and contemporary TV dating shows. Potential candidates entered and exited the stage almost too quickly for the voting audience to keep track of them. After being rejected a number of times, by more desirable candidates, a desperate Republican Party finally courted conservative African American media personality Alan Keyes. After a largely self-destructive campaign, Keyes endured a record-setting loss to Obama in November.

This chapter looks at the unusual general election campaign leading to Obama's victory. It examines the campaign during its three stages: Obama v. Jack Ryan, Obama v. no one, and Obama v. Alan Keyes. We conclude by examining the results of the race and the factors that led to Obama's win.

OBAMA v. JACK RYAN

The Republican primary field featured eight candidates, including wealthy businessmen James Oberweis and Andrew McKenna, State Senator Steve Rauschenberger, and retired Air Force General John Borling. All except Borling ran on conservative platforms.[2] The winner, Jack Ryan, grew up as one of six children in the wealthy Chicago suburb of Wilmette. He attended Dartmouth, where he played football, and then received his law degree and an MBA from Harvard. After pursuing a highly lucrative career in investment banking, in 2000 he became a teacher at Hales Franciscan, a predominantly black Catholic school on Chicago's South Side. He won the primary with 35 percent of the vote, leading Oberweis with 24 percent, Rauschenberger with 20 percent, and McKenna with 15 percent. Although his victory was not as large as Obama's, he did better than his opponents in terms of statewide appeal, winning 83 of the state's 102 counties, including all but two with populations over 100,000 (Kane and St. Clair). His decision to air TV ads before any of the other Republican candidates helped ensure his victory.[3]

His win in the Republican primary drew national media attention to the Illinois senate race as a contest of "two, young, charismatic Harvard graduates."[4] Given Ryan's background as an inner-city teacher, his general election strategy emphasized reaching out to minority voters and social moderates. Shortly after the primary, Ryan said, "I spent a lot of time in the Republican primary speaking at churches on the south side of Chicago or south Peoria or communities that the Democrats think are theirs. Our basic premise is that whether you are a Democrat or Republican, rich or poor, we have ideas and plans that make America better for everybody."[5]

In contrast to the primary, where issue differences between the candidates were miniscule, Jack Ryan offered a clear ideological contrast to Obama. His campaign emphasized free market economic approaches, including low taxes, deregulation, and school vouchers, as well as support for President Bush's policies in Iraq. He also tried to attack Obama's voting record as a state senator to paint him as too liberal for Illinois. For example, he criticized Obama's sponsorship of the Bernadin amendment, which would have guaranteed universal affordable heath insurance in the state. Citing an estimated cost of $4 billion to accomplish this goal, Ryan tried to link Obama to the failed Clinton healthcare plan of the early 1990s and charged that his views on the issue were "outside the mainstream."[6] Ryan also attacked Obama's senate voting record as "anti–gun owner."

His campaign created a "Barack Obama Truth Squad" to issue e-mail press releases to "correct" any Obama misstatements.[7] His attacks sometimes overreached, however, and he struggled to find his footing as a candidate. For instance, as part of efforts to paint Obama as a tax-and-spend Democrat, Ryan charged that he had supported tax and fee increases 428 times as a state senator. It turned out, however, that these alleged "tax hikes" were all part of only two bills, one of which was the Fiscal Year 2004 state budget, which Obama had in fact voted against, reducing his "support" for tax increases by 280.[8] In another attempt to tie Obama to bloated government, Ryan falsely claimed that the state government employed more people than manufacturers did in Illinois, citing a figure of 846,000, compared to an actual count of around 112,000.[9] Media outlets were quick to correct Ryan's errors, which made him look somewhat unprofessional as a campaigner.

The Ryan campaign also ignited controversy in May with its decision to assign an aide, Justin Warfel, to follow Obama around and film everything he did. Supposedly designed to ensure that Obama's message was consistent throughout the state, the move engendered criticism when Warfel followed Obama into restrooms and recorded personal telephone conversations with his wife and daughters. Newspaper editorials condemned Ryan's stunt, and prominent members of his own party also chastised him. For example, Peoria Republican Congressman Ray LaHood called the move "about the stupidest thing I've seen in a high-profile campaign."[10] After ten days, Ryan ordered Warfel to back off, but the ploy only diminished his stature and enhanced Obama's.

Allegations about Jack Ryan's divorce began to appear in the primary, as the one-time campaign manager of opponent John Borling claimed to know sordid details about Ryan's 1999 split from actress Jeri Ryan. On the day after the primary, Republican State Party Chair Judy Baar Topinka claimed that Ryan's victory meant that voters found the issue irrelevant.[11] Rumors swirled until June 21 when, in response to a lawsuit by the *Chicago Tribune* and a Chicago TV station, a California judge unsealed the Ryans' divorce records. They revealed that Jack Ryan had taken his ex-wife to sex clubs in New York, New Orleans, and Paris, complete in one instance with cages and whips, and asked her to perform sex publicly. When she became upset, the records revealed, Ryan complained that it was not a "turn on" for her to cry.[12]

Initially Ryan denied most of the allegations, admitting only that the couple had visited one "avant-garde" Paris nightclub that made both him and Jeri Ryan uncomfortable.[13] By the scandal's second day, Ryan had shifted his message somewhat, arguing that he had not broken the law or the Ten Commandments. Although Ryan vowed to stay in the race, leading Republicans gradually turned against him. Party Chair Topinka and former governor Jim Edgar expressed anger that Ryan had not been forthcoming with them when he claimed, before the March primary, that there would be nothing embarrassing in the divorce files.[14] A member of the Republican National Committee expressed a sense of betrayal that Ryan implied there was nothing detrimental in the records. "I don't think he was protecting his son; I think he was protecting his political aspirations."[15]

By the end of the week, many other Republican officials had turned against him. Although some State Central Committee members continued to support him, others described the situation in terms ranging from "black eye" to "train wreck."[16] On Thursday, June 24, three days after the scandal broke, the Republican members of the Illinois congressional delegation unanimously asked House Speaker Dennis Hastert to try to persuade Ryan to get off the ballot.[17] Several GOP county chairmen also weighed in against Ryan. For example, the chairman of the Jefferson County Republican Party commented that his actions were "repulsive and alien for people in southern Illinois." DuPage County Chair Kirk Dillard commented that "only in the Land of Oz would people think that Jack Ryan can beat Barack Obama after this week's activity."[18]

Responding to pressure from the media, especially the *Chicago Tribune*, and a backlash among Republican voters and party leaders, Ryan said he would withdraw his name from the ballot on June 25. In pulling out, he said he did not want to run a brutal, "scorched-earth campaign that has turned off so many voters, the kind of politics I refuse to play."[19] Some wondered at the time whether this was a good move or whether the party should have waited for voters' reactions. One Illinois political observer noted that "He [Ryan] got in trouble for having sex with his wife. Given Illinois' history that is not even a fig leaf on the tree of corruption."[20] Meanwhile, Senator Peter Fitzgerald accused State Party Chair Judy Baar Topinka of dumping Ryan to undermine his potential gubernatorial bid in 2006.[21]

While most media attention focused on Ryan, Obama continued to campaign. He tried to tie his opponent to President Bush's policies, which were relatively unpopular in Illinois, but he took the high road on the question of Ryan's divorce, vowing not to make it an issue and calling on Democratic party leaders not to do so as well. In contrast to the primary, where he focused most of the attention on the Chicago area, the general election campaign was clearly a statewide effort. The day after the primary, he traveled to Alton, in southern Illinois, followed by visits to Peoria, Rock Island, and Galesburg in the western part of the state the following day.

OBAMA v. NO ONE

Ryan's exit set the stage for the nineteen-member Republican State Central Committee to come up with a replacement. The process turned out to be lengthy and difficult, with many of the most desirable candidates saying "no thanks," while several of the losers from the primary found themselves rejected again. To replace Ryan, Republicans flirted, in varying degrees of seriousness, with candidates ranging from Federal Prosecutor Patrick Fitzgerald to three former Chicago Bears players to 70s rocker Ted Nugent. Finally, they settled on media personality and failed presidential and Maryland Senate candidate Alan Keyes.[22]

Almost immediately after Ryan's withdrawal, prominent Republicans such as former governors Jim Thompson and Jim Edgar refused to enter the race. Initially, attention turned to Ron Gidwitz, a wealthy businessman, former state Board of Education chairman, and leading Republican fundraiser. Gidwitz dropped out on July 1, saying he did not want to leave Illinois. Next in line was primary candidate state senator Steve Rauschenberger, but he also declined to run due to doubts that he could raise enough money to run a viable campaign.[23] Meanwhile, second-place primary finisher Jim Oberweis, who appeared to actually want the nomination, was not considered seriously. His campaign ads opposing immigration, and, by implication, President Bush's policies, alienated prominent national Republicans.

Former Chicago Bears coach Mike Ditka then intimated that he might enter the race. His candidacy began when staffers for Illinois House Minority Leader Tom Cross started a half-serious website encouraging him to run.[24] Somewhat surprisingly, he expressed interest in the race, with his high profile and name recognition raising Republican hopes. He was serious enough to meet with Republican Senatorial Campaign Committee head Senator George Allen of Virginia and State Party Chair Topinka, before abruptly pulling out on July 14. In withdrawing, Ditka expressed concern about how he would react to increased media scrutiny, the loss of lucrative endorsement deals, and the prospect of having to play golf on unfamiliar courses.[25]

After missing their self-imposed July 16 deadline, the Republicans experienced continued frustration as they searched for a candidate. Next to turn the party down was State Senator Kirk Dillard, who rejected the offer to run due to concerns about fundraising and leaving Illinois. Obscure Cook County board member Elizabeth Doody Gorman, whose Republican credentials were in some doubt, but who nevertheless supposedly appealed to suburban women, eventually spurned the party, citing time and money concerns.

Throughout this time, Obama campaigned as if he did have an opponent, traveling the state and giving speeches. At an event in downstate Lincoln, he quipped, "At this point, even if you don't like me, you don't have much of a choice."[26] Of course, he remained in office as a state senator, where he sometimes took centrist positions to bolster his statewide appeal. For example, despite being a strong advocate of gun control laws in the past, he voted for legislation allowing retired police officers to carry concealed weapons.

Obama's stature rose dramatically during this period, as he began to receive attention outside the state of Illinois. He was the subject of profiles in the national media that viewed him in "near-Messianic" terms.[27] Obama's appearances on Sunday morning talk shows before the Democratic National Convention led Bob Schieffer of CBS to label him a "rock star." He also continued to raise large amounts of campaign money, including a great deal from celebrities ranging from Barbra Streisand to Michael Jordan. Probably the most significant event in his entire campaign occurred when he delivered a highly acclaimed keynote speech to the Democratic National Convention on July 28.

Still largely unknown outside Illinois before the convention, Obama was probably one of the most obscure choices to deliver a keynote address in modern convention history. Past notables chosen included New York Governor Mario Cuomo, Texas Governor Ann Richards, and future president Bill Clinton. Obama's selection reflected an effort by the Kerry–Edwards campaign to reach out to black voters and to mollify critics who said there were not enough African Americans in top campaign jobs.[28]

Obama began the speech by telling his personal story of humble origins, explaining how his father grew up herding goats and his grandparents enjoyed the benefits of federal programs, such as the GI Bill and Federal Housing Administration. He tied the narrative to the American Dream, saying, "In no other country is my story even possible." He also stressed communal themes, implicitly criticizing excessive individualism.

> If there's a child on the South Side of Chicago who can't read, that matters to me, even if it's not my child. If there's a senior citizen who can't pay for their prescription … that makes my life poorer, even if it's not my grandmother. If there's an Arab-American family that's being rounded up … that threatens my civil liberties. It's that fundamental belief—I am my brother's keeper, I am my sister's keeper—that makes this country work.[29]

The speech tried to achieve a centrist tone, stressing what unites Americans. After criticizing pundits and negative campaigning, he said, "We worship an awesome God in the blue states, and we don't like federal agents poking around our libraries in the red states. We coach little league in the blue states and have gay friends in the red states. There are patriots who opposed the War in Iraq and patriots who supported it. We are one people."[30]

The speech received almost universal acclaim and made Obama an overnight sensation. Some political consultants described it as the best keynote address in many years, and the *New York Times* reported that Obama "owned the town" the following day.[31] *Time* magazine described it as "one of the best speeches in convention history," and the *Pittsburgh Post-Gazette* labeled it "a trenchant and vivid piece of oratory delivered in a melodic voice."[32] Even some Republicans were complimentary. Bob Winchester, a member of the Illinois Republican State Central Committee that was trying to pick Obama's opponent praised the speech and added, "I just wish he was a Republican."[33] In another indicator of the impact of his speech, his autobiography rose from six hundred seventy-six to the top ten on Barnesandnoble.com during the week of the convention.[34]

While clearly benefiting from this media attention, Obama tried to downplay the suddenly heightened expectations, including predictions that he would be America's first African American president. He noted, "I've spent seventeen months as David and one month as Goliath. I tend to distrust hype."[35] Nevertheless, a reporter covering post-convention campaign events described Obama fever running at a "scorching temperature."[36]

Immediately after his triumphant return from the Democratic National Convention, he took a five-day, thirty-county tour of downstate Illinois. Befitting his new celebrity, crowds at his appearances that once numbered in the dozens now were in the hundreds. In some cases, events had to be moved to larger venues at the last minute to accommodate his increased fan base. He assured these adoring crowds that he had not "gone Hollywood" despite his newly found acclaim as a national star.[37] In many of these appearances, he stressed local issues, such as increasing markets for ethanol and bringing broadband Internet access to rural areas.[38]

Meanwhile, Obama's sudden fame and adulation made the Republicans' task in finding a replacement even more difficult. Senator Peter Fitzgerald, the man the nominee would try to replace, commented that "you wouldn't have thought this search could be any harder than it was a week ago but it just got harder because of the rollout of Barack."[39] He further compared accepting the Republican nomination to willingly contracting cancer. Potential nominee State Senator Kirk Dillard expressed relief that he had not entered the race against Obama, commenting that the hoopla surrounding his speech "would have made my uphill climb even tougher."[40]

An increasingly desperate Republican State Central Committee met on August 3 to interview and discuss remaining candidates. Fourteen contenders were interviewed that day, including four of the original primary candidates, most prominently second-place finisher Oberweis. Also among those considered was a candidate wearing a white colonial wig who lived in his car. The previous day, committee members had contacted Alan Keyes about his interest in running. Although unable to attend, Keyes agreed to fly to Illinois later in the week for an interview.

After hours of interviews and heated discussion, State Central Committee members narrowed the field to two African American candidates with tenuous connections to Illinois, Keyes and Andrea Grubb Barthwell. Keyes, a former candidate for U.S. Senate from Maryland and two-time contender for the Republican presidential nomination, was an outspoken social conservative. Barthwell had quit her job as a deputy drug czar in the Bush administration's National Office of Drug Control Policy a few weeks earlier to become eligible to run for the Senate. Her potential effectiveness as a candidate suffered from reports that she had been the subject of an internal sexual harassment investigation. Among other things, she allegedly had pretended a kaleidoscope was a male sex organ at an office party and placed it on an employee's chair for him to sit on.[41] As if this were not enough potential bad publicity, she also had a history of alcohol and drug addiction. The decision to pick Keyes or Barthwell was contentious. Reporters were removed from the floor where the meeting was held at one point, because of concerns that they would overhear the yelling going on inside. Upon leaving, one committee member was described as "ashen-faced," and another said she was "not happy."[42]

The following day, after interviewing Keyes, the State Central Committee chose him. After taking a few days to think about it, he accepted. Although the choice excited conservatives, early reviews from parts of the GOP establishment were somewhat tepid. One GOP insider commented, "I think we're like alcoholics, we've finally hit bottom."[43] U.S. House Speaker Dennis Hastert, while nominally endorsing Keyes, compared the decision to a football coach who must go deep into his depth chart to find a replacement player.[44] Supporters believed that even in the likely event of Keyes's loss, he would bring conservatives to the polls, helping Republicans regain control of the state senate.[45]

OBAMA v. KEYES

Keyes's campaign focused largely on issues related to his religious and moral beliefs, particularly abortion. By contrast, Obama tended to emphasize bread-and-butter concerns, such as the economy and health care. Keyes also adopted, or at least displayed, the campaign persona of an angry preacher, which turned out to be no match for Obama's rockstar charisma. Although anyone facing Obama would have faced an uphill battle, Keyes did little to improve his chances.

As the campaign began, Keyes wasted no time in aiming his rhetorical guns at Obama. On his first official day of campaigning, he compared Obama's pro-choice stance on abortion to the "slave-holder's" position on slavery. This was to be the first of several widely publicized, provocative statements that Keyes uttered in the campaign. A week later, he told a crowd in Aurora that Obama's views on abortion resembled terrorists, "who are willing to use force to destroy the lives of innocents."[46] At the Republican National Convention Keyes labeled Vice President Dick Cheney's daughter and all gays "selfish hedonists."[47] After returning to Illinois in early September, Keyes claimed that Jesus would not vote for Obama, due to his vote in the Illinois senate against legislation requiring abortion doctors to save viable fetuses. In mid-October, Keyes told an anti–gay marriage rally that incest was inevitable for the children of homosexual couples, because they would not know who their biological brothers and sisters were. In the campaign's final days, he compared free trade to "gang raping" the American economy.

Keyes's rhetorical outbursts dismayed many Republican officeholders, who felt they undermined the party's chances in other races.[48] State party chair and Illinois treasurer Judy Baar Topinka, for example, described Keyes's Republican convention comments as "idiotic" and did her best to avoid being seen or photographed with him. A downstate conservative activist criticized Keyes's campaign as "not your typical folksy Midwestern campaign. It can be off-putting at first."[49]

His over-the-top rhetoric appeared to reflect a strategic decision that would allow Keyes's relatively underfunded campaign to get free media, as his finances kept him from running paid TV commercials until the contest's last week. In a meeting with top Republican donors in September, Keyes reportedly said that he would make "inflammatory" comments "every day, every week," until the election.[50] Keyes's media adviser commented that "where traditional candidates do their best to avoid controversy, Alan seeks it out."[51] His embrace of conflict turned more people off than on, however. Even when he emphasized less incendiary issues, they seemed unlikely to appeal to voters much. For example, he identified repeal of the Seventeenth Amendment to the Constitution, which mandates that U.S. Senators be elected by the people rather than state legislatures, as a "critical" issue in his campaign.[52] He also promoted a plan to exempt the descendents of slaves from taxation as a method of reparations.

By contrast, Obama's campaign focused largely on issues such as the economy and health care, while he criticized Keyes for emphasizing abortion at the expense of matters that were more salient to Illinois voters. Obama placed his ideas in the context of the struggles of ordinary families to make ends meet as the Bush administration focused on tax cuts for the wealthy. In doing so, he occasionally violated the conventional wisdom that politicians must be optimistic and avoid "class warfare." In an October appearance, he argued, "We may be the first generation in a very long time to pass along a world to our children that's a little bit meaner, and a little bit poorer than the one we inherited, and that's unacceptable, and it's un-American."[53]

In the realm of economic policy, Obama advocated eliminating tax incentives for businesses that move jobs overseas, enforcing U.S. trade agreements, and improving education and job training. On health care, he proposed expanding coverage to children and those over fifty-five and creating a health insurance pool for small business owners to insure their workers. He also advocated a plan that would give a tax credit to families earning under $50,000 annually who saved for retirement through an IRA or 401K.

Although he emphasized them less, his view on social issues generally fit the traditional liberal mold. He advocated the pro-choice position on abortion, supported stem cell research, and essentially supported gay marriage without doing so explicitly. Nevertheless, he rejected the "liberal" label as a Republican-created caricature that poorly fit his views. Instead, he preferred the term "thoughtful progressive," combining a belief in government action to solve problems with a commitment to fiscal responsibility.[54]

In the foreign policy arena, Obama advocated political and economic initiatives to promote democracy in autocratic nations, thereby stopping terrorism at its source.[55] He argued that the use of "soft power" was preferable to military action in addressing the root causes of terrorism. He did leave the door open for military action in Iran, if sanctions failed, identifying the threat of nuclear weapons there as the United States' biggest foreign policy challenge.

In his campaign, Obama also stressed larger themes of citizenship and political engagement, arguing that citizens had a civic responsibility to go beyond voting and gain a deeper understanding of issues. He argued that voters must be aware of obligations to future generations, saying, "We don't just inherit the world from our parents, we borrow it from our children. So we have an obligation to give them clean air and water and a Constitution that's not poked full of holes."[56] Similarly, he stressed the need to uplift political debate in the United States. In a speech in southern Illinois, he said, "People are tired of hearing politicians attack each other when they wish someone was attacking their problems.... We need to raise the complexity of this country, not simplify it into 30-second slogans."[57] Late in the campaign, at an appearance in Peoria, he criticized Keyes directly for debasing political discourse, accusing him of a "scorched-earth, slash and burn, say anything, make-up anything approach to politics." He added, "Think about if you were on the job and lied all the time ... and you sent out brochures saying 'Jim in the cubicle across from me is a terrible person.' Think how productive that company would be."[58]

One of the biggest challenges the Obama campaign faced with Keyes was trying to "keep their eye on the ball," by not letting Keyes goad them into arguing.[59] Despite this awareness, Keyes did occasionally succeed in setting the terms of the debate, focusing it on moral concerns, thus undermining to a degree Obama's ability to frame it around issues such as jobs and health care. He forced Obama to explain and defend his own religious beliefs and to lay out his interpretation of the Bible on the campaign trail. In a forum at Illinois Benedictine University, Obama claimed that "his Christianity had been challenged" and explained his own views on the relationship between religion and public policy, contending that when faith guides decisions it can lead to absolutism.[60] He argued that "politics is the art of compromise. Faith is, by definition, not open to compromise."[61] In addition, Keyes appeared to get under Obama's skin in at least a few instances. For example, in an appearance in southern Illinois, Obama said "I don't just want to win. I want to give this guy who is running against me a spanking."[62] Keyes responded in a typically provocative fashion that Obama's language was "the language of the master, who, when he is displeased with the slave gives him a whipping."[63]

At the same time, Keyes's bombastic campaign style probably allowed Obama to avoid explaining or justifying some of his more nuanced positions. For example, he claimed to support both free trade and the repeal of the North American Free Trade Agreement.[64] Moreover, he was not forced to explain how some of his positions had changed since the primary campaign. In the primary, for instance, Obama took a strong anti–Iraq War stance. In the general election, he continued to oppose the war, but also argued against an immediate pullout. Although such position shifts are typical as candidates move from primaries to general election campaigns, Keyes probably could have done more to force Obama to explain them. The exception concerned some social policy questions like gay marriage. Keyes's focus on the issue forced Obama to elucidate his fairly complicated position that combined opposition on religious grounds, support for civil unions, and a belief that individual states should ultimately decide the matter. Critics blasted Obama's position as "impossible to take seriously," viewing it as a smokescreen behind which he supported gay marriage without really appearing to do so.[65]

If Keyes was able to neutralize Obama somewhat in the realm of issues, the frontrunner clearly won the contest of style and personality. In contrast to Keyes, who usually resembled a preacher in his campaign appearances, Obama tailored his style and use of language to different audiences in different settings.[66] For example, he sprinkled appearances in southern Illinois with the word "y'all," while using "precise, polished" language in speaking to upper-class suburbanites and inserting black slang into speeches before African American audiences.[67] At the same time, he emphasized his political independence and leadership qualities by supposedly telling people what they "didn't want to hear."[68] For instance, he would inform fiscal conservatives that he would raise their taxes, liberals that government was not the answer to all their problems, and union leaders that they really believed in free trade.[69]

His combination of honesty and adaptability clearly worked for him. After an Obama campaign appearance at the State Fair, the Mayor of Rockford commented, "There were a lot of Republicans in the crowd that just said 'I like this guy. I believe in this guy.' It almost has a Paul Simon feel. You know I don't really agree with this guy on a lot of issues, but I believe what he says. I believe he is sincere."[70] Like Simon, voters gave Obama high marks for integrity and appreciated the fact that he did not engage in "smear politics."[71] Further enhancing his appeal, Obama mastered the nonverbal techniques of connecting to people in speeches, such as opening his hands with fingers slightly spread, indicating inclusion, or using eye contact in a way that showed he was "tuned into" his audience.[72]

Ultimately, Keyes was unable to appeal to voters, other than a small core of strong conservatives who turned out enthusiastically at his rallies. A poll in September showed Keyes with a 22 percent favorable rating, compared to 60 percent for Obama.[73] The same survey showed that the "carpetbagger" issue hurt Keyes, making at least one-third of those responding less likely to vote for him. In an October poll, 39 percent of voters labeled Keyes as "extremist" compared to 11 percent for Obama.[74] As the campaign wore on, Keyes continued to lose the support of many in the Republican establishment, especially moderates. Republican critics charged that Keyes was not doing enough to attack Obama's record as a state senator and focused too much on morality issues, at the expense of taxation and budget matters.[75] In fact, Obama was able to use his state senate experience as a positive in his campaign, arguing that it prepared him well to understand the legislative process. A mid-October statewide mailing sent out by the Republican Party promoting the "Republican team" conspicuously left off teammate Keyes. Meanwhile, the Democrats paid to have their own fliers sent out that linked Keyes explicitly to Republican state legislative candidates they were trying to defeat.[76] In an unusual move, the Obama campaign also promoted Keyes's campaign events to reporters, in the apparent belief that "the more exposure Keyes gets, the better it is for Obama."[77] Referring to Keyes, one Obama staffer commented, "You couldn't have paid him to say some of the things he said."[78]

Despite Keyes's efforts to keep him on the defensive, Obama's vast lead in the polls provided him the time and opportunity to attend out-of-state fundraisers to help other candidates in New York, Minneapolis, Birmingham, Washington, D.C., Martha's Vineyard, and elsewhere.[79] By early October he had already helped raise $850,000 for the Democratic Senatorial Campaign Committee and $260,000 for individual candidates in thirteen states.[80] In addition, he contributed $283,000 to other candidates running in 2004.[81] Early in the campaign, Obama attracted prominent out-of-state supporters, such as one-time presidential candidate and future Democratic National Committee Chair Howard Dean and former Georgia Senator Max Cleland to campaign with him. He later returned the favor, using his star power and fundraising ability to help other Democratic candidates. Even the Kerry–Edwards presidential ticket recruited him to campaign in battleground states and mobilize black voters.[82] By September, Obama was traveling out of state so much that his campaign tried to keep his movements secret.[83] Late in the campaign, with victory a foregone conclusion, Obama diverted some of his volunteer workers to assist the campaign of northwest suburban Chicago Democratic congressional candidate Melissa Bean.

Reflecting his now-abundant campaign funds, Obama began running TV commercials in mid-August during the Olympics. The initial ads were designed to "reintroduce" Obama downstate and emphasized his ability to work in a bipartisan fashion on issues like tax relief and health care.[84] In the last three weeks before the election, he spent about $2 million on additional statewide advertising.[85] He was also able to get a great deal of free media. Even a top-twenty single promoted his political efforts, as an all-star group of rappers posed the question, "Why is Bush acting like he trying to get Osama? Why don't we impeach him and elect Obama?"[86] Obama was endorsed by all of Illinois' major newspapers, and an Associated Press survey of daily newspapers found that none reported endorsing Keyes.[87]

As noted above, Keyes was unable to run television ads until the last week or so of the campaign when he unveiled spots where various luminaries from President Reagan to radio talk show host Rush Limbaugh spoke on his behalf. Keyes may have benefited from some indirect spending, however. Radio and TV ads paid for by a 527 group called "Empower Illinois" criticized Obama's state senate votes in favor of abortion, against tougher sentences for gang crimes, and in favor of sex education programs for kindergartners.[88] Although supposedly independent of Keyes's campaign, these ads did reflect some of his major themes. The Obama campaign responded that these votes were taken out of context.

The campaign culminated in three debates, disappointing Keyes, who needed the platform and was never at a loss for words. Originally, Obama had agreed to six encounters with Jack Ryan, but offered fewer to Keyes, joking that the original offer was for in-state residents only. Keyes compared Obama's refusal to schedule more debates to a boxer who talks big when the ring is empty, but bolts when facing actual competition.[89] This was one of the few cases where the Obama campaign received sustained criticism in the media. Critics charged Obama with hypocrisy for calling for many debates when he was an unknown, but changing his mind as a celebrity candidate with a big lead.

The first debate, on the radio on October 12, was largely a civil discussion of major policy issues, such as the war in Iraq, Illinois' infra-structure, trade, and prescription drugs. The candidates differed on tax policy, with Keyes favoring a national sales tax to replace the income tax and Obama arguing that it would mean higher taxes for most low-and middle-income Americans. Keyes was also more supportive of Bush administration policies in Iraq. Near the end, Keyes attacked Obama for not voting in favor of the "Born Alive Infants Protection Act, which required doctors to try to save the life of a fetus that survived an abor-tion.[90] Obama responded that existing Illinois law protected infants' right to life-saving treatment and that therefore the law was unneces-sary. By some accounts, Keyes "won" this debate, as Obama found it difficult to adjust to the fact that his opponent performed "as an almost normal candidate," rather than the "raving lunatic" he had expected to face.[91]

The second debate, a televised affair on October 21, was a more antagonistic clash over religion, morality, and which candidate was more authentically African American.[92] In response to Keyes's efforts to paint him as immoral, Obama presented an economically based vision of morality, arguing that taking away long-time workers' pensions and providing inadequate aid for college students was unjust. Keyes reiter-ated that he believed that Jesus would not vote for his opponent, to which Obama responded that he didn't like being lectured on religion by Keyes. "That's why I have a pastor. That's why I have a Bible. That's why I have my own prayer.... I'm not running to be minister of Illinois. I'm running to be its United States Senator."[93] Reacting to the debate, columnist Rich Miller noted, "Keyes, for his part, failed to disappoint his many detractors. His weird, herky-jerky hand gestures ... and his overly patronizing manner ... emphasized for spectators that the pom-pous river of moralizing invective flowing from his mouth wasn't even close to the Illinois mainstream."[94]

Also televised, the third debate took place on October 26. Like its predecessor, it featured clear disagreements between the candidates and was described as "sometimes testy," with the moderator struggling to keep control.[95] The contenders clashed on the role of government in solving poverty, with Obama arguing that it could help and Keyes responding, "the first mission of the United States wasn't government, it was self-government."[96] Gay rights was another area of conflict, with Obama accusing Keyes of gay-bashing and criticizing Keyes's claim that gay adoption led to incest, while struggling to explain his own opposi-tion to gay marriage. Keyes also criticized Obama for sending his children to private schools while opposing school choice.

The race ended on a sour note, as in a final fit of pique, Keyes refused to call Obama on election night to concede the contest. He blamed

"Republicans in name only" and the media for his defeat. In his own election night speech, Obama continued his pleas for political civility and called on his audience to "close the gap between the ideal of America and its reality."[97]

ANALYSIS OF RESULTS

In the end, Obama defeated Keyes 70 percent to 27 percent, the largest gap ever in an Illinois U.S. Senate race. He captured ninety-two of Illinois' 102 counties, limiting Keyes to a group of ten rural counties, primarily in southeastern Illinois. Obama had his best showing in Cook County, which cast nearly 40 percent of the statewide vote, winning with 81 percent of the vote, including 88 percent in the city of Chicago and 74 percent in the suburban part of the county.[98] Within the city, he won all fifty wards by at least 70 percent. He was most successful in black neighborhoods, exceeding 90 percent of the vote in each of the nineteen wards represented by an African American alderman and topping out at an amazing 97 percent in the Fifth, Eighth, and Thirty-fourth Wards. He generally received between 80 and 90 percent of the vote in Hispanic areas of the city. His worst showing was in the predominantly white Forty-first Ward on Chicago's far northwest side, where he got about 70 percent, but in more liberal white-dominated lakefront areas, he received over 80 percent of the vote.

He won more than 70 percent of the vote in four other counties: Fulton, Gallatin, Knox, and Rock Island. These jurisdictions generally fit the "rust belt" stereotype of struggling industrial areas coping with the loss of jobs and population. Knox County's largest city, Galesburg, for example, has received national attention as a symbol of industrial decline and the impact of the North American Free Trade Agreement. The 2004 election took place two months after a Maytag refrigerator factory that once employed 1,600 people closed and moved to Mexico, following on the heels of other major job losses. His strong showing here in such struggling industrial areas suggests that Obama did well among working class white voters concerned with economic issues. Exit poll results provide further evidence for this interpretation and showed Obama beating Keyes 79 percent to 20 percent among union members.[99] Obama also won the five Chicago suburban collar counties and every metropolitan area of the state with at least 60 percent of the vote.

Obama's weakest showing was in rural Illinois, although he still won 58 percent of the vote in the state's sixty-seven nonmetropolitan counties. He won fifty-seven of these counties and scored more than 60 percent of the vote in twenty-four. Obama tended to do better in more densely populated rural areas with more minorities, higher poverty, and lower incomes. Table 3-1 illustrates this contrast by comparing the

Table 3-1 Demographic Comparison of Rural Southern Illinois Counties that Obama Lost and Won with over 60 Percent of the Vote

	Population Density	Percent in Poverty	Per Capita Income	Percent White
Nine Counties Lost	42%	11%	$16,757.00	98%
Nine Counties Won over 60%	61%	16%	$15,846.00	87%

Source: Author calculations based on data obtained at www.census.gov.

demographic characteristics of the nine counties in southern Illinois (south of Springfield) that Obama lost with the nine counties in the same region that he won by over 60 percent.

Obama was able to capture nearly 40 percent of the Republican vote and one-third of self-identified conservatives. It was clear that many voters, especially conservatives from downstate, voted for Obama, even though they disagreed with him on many issues, because they couldn't abide the alternative and/or resented Keyes for having few connections to Illinois.[100] Obama's own issue-driven campaign style appeared to help him attract these voters, who might have sat out the contest if he had "gone negative."[101] Despite his race, Keyes failed to make in-roads with African Americans, as Obama won over 90 percent of their votes.[102] About the only major demographic group that Keyes won was conservative white protestants, who supported him overwhelmingly.[103]

Table 3-2 shows exit poll results comparing Obama and Keyes according to selected issues and qualities voters thought were most important. The results suggest that Obama's emphasis on issues like the economy, jobs, and health care resonated with voters concerned about those issues. By contrast, he did less well with voters concerned about moral values, terrorism, or taxes. Obama got high marks from voters who thought intelligence or the ability to bring about change were important qualities, but fared poorly among voters concerned about religious faith.

Statewide, Obama ran about fifteen percentage points ahead of Democratic presidential candidate John Kerry. His margin was even higher in suburban Chicago, especially outside Cook County. In the five collar counties, he got 65.4 percent, compared to Kerry's 45.5. In three rapidly growing counties—DeKalb, Grundy, and Kendall—on the western fringes of the suburbs, he got 62.9 percent of the vote, while Kerry got 43.2 percent. These results suggest that Obama appeals to suburban voters more than some Democrats do, which is significant because suburbs are becoming a political battleground where success is key to either party's chances.[104] Alternatively, suburbanites may have found Alan Keyes especially hard to stomach. Nevertheless, suburbanites were

Table 3-2 Exit Poll Results Comparing Obama and Keyes on Most Important Issue/Most Important Quality in Voters' Perceptions (Selected Issues/Qualities)

Most Important Issue	% Ranking #1	% for Obama	% for Keyes
Iraq	21	88	12
Economy/Jobs	20	93	4
Moral Values	18	38	61
Terrorism	18	51	40
Health Care	5	88	12
Taxes	5	59	41

Most Important Quality	% Ranking #1	% for Obama	% for Keyes
Will Bring Change	27	97	2
Strong Leader	20	52	43
Honest/Trustworthy	11	56	42
Intelligent	9	96	3
Religious Faith	8	26	74

Source: www.cnn.com/ELECTION/2004.

only slightly more likely than voters statewide to support minor party candidates. In the collar counties, the libertarian and independent candidates claimed 3.6 percent of the vote, compared to 3 percent statewide. This fact suggests that Obama was relatively appealing to suburban voters.

As in the primary, Obama ran a savvy campaign, but he was clearly lucky as well in facing Alan Keyes rather than Jack Ryan. Thus we raise a question similar to that in the last chapter—what if Jack Ryan's divorce files had remained sealed and he had stayed in the race? Although it is, of course, impossible to say, we believe that, although the race would have been closer, Obama would still have defeated Ryan, for at least four reasons. First, in Democratic-trending Illinois, Ryan's party was clearly at a disadvantage. The Democratic primary attracted nearly twice as many voters as the Republican contest, and Obama alone received more votes than the eight Republican candidates combined. Given Obama's strength in Cook County, Ryan would probably have had to win the suburban collar counties by at least 55 percent and downstate by 75 percent to have beaten Obama.[105] Because President Bush lost Illinois by twelve points in 2000, he did not plan to campaign much in the state, even before the divorce scandal, so Ryan was not in a position to benefit from his coattails.[106]

Second, polls taken before the divorce scandal broke showed Obama with a healthy lead. A *Chicago Tribune*/WGN poll from late May had Obama leading 52 percent to 30 percent.[107] The poll also showed two other advantages for Obama. He had a higher favorable/unfavorable ratio than Ryan, with Obama at 46 percent favorable and 9 percent unfavorable, compared to 29 percent favorable and 25 percent unfavorable for Ryan. Also, the poll revealed that Obama was actually less well known than Ryan, meaning that his voting base was less static than his one-time opponent's.

It is true that another poll taken in early June showed the race tightening.[108] Nevertheless, we still believe that Obama's speech at the Democratic National Convention and the other positives of his campaign are a third reason to believe that he would have defeated Ryan. Finally, Ryan was an inexperienced candidate and clearly had not worked out all the kinks in his campaign, even before the divorce scandal hit. Although the two candidates were arguably an even match in terms of charisma, Obama's loss to Bobby Rush in 2000 helped him perform better as a candidate. Also, his experience as a state senator gave him a superior understanding of politics and government, which prevented him from stumbling over basic facts, as well as providing vital campaign allies.

Understanding Obama's success in both the primary and general elections requires a closer look at two key elements of contemporary Senate campaigns: raising money and getting the candidate's message out through the media. The next two chapters examine these matters more closely. Chapter 4 looks at Obama's remarkable fundraising abilities and his efforts to compete with the wealthy, self-financed Blair Hull, and chapter 5 details his media strategy.

CHAPTER FOUR

"Money Is the Mother's Milk of Politics"—Raising Money and Spreading the Wealth[1]

P rior to running for the U.S. Senate, the most money Barack Obama had raised for one of his political campaigns was $500,000. In his U.S. Senate race, Obama would face multimillionaires willing to spend a fortune to get elected, and he would have to overcome opponents with more established political connections and with greater name recognition. Traditionally, Illinois politicians begin campaigning around Memorial Day the year before the spring primary, but the 2004 campaign season began nearly half a year earlier, in the summer of 2002. Candidates not only had to go after the money sooner; they knew they were going to have to dig deeper to compete against the wealthy big-spenders. One of the biggest questions for the Obama campaign was whether they could raise enough money to mount the kind of statewide organizing battle and advertising campaign needed to win. Television advertising is the most expensive aspect of political campaigns. Yet Obama proved himself an adept fundraiser with an astute media strategy.

Barack Obama, unlike many other candidates, did not mind raising money. Finance Director Claire Serdiuk noted, "He's great in making the ask and closing the deal."[2] He was remarkable at "cold-calling" potential donors and soliciting a contribution. Some weeks, Obama spent twenty to thirty hours on the phone asking for money. As he traveled the state, he would sit in the car and dial people. He was able to establish a rapport with people whom he had never met and make them feel "like buddies," which made people want to contribute.[3]

Because Blair Hull was self-financing, new campaign finance laws allowed his opponents to raise six times the normal $2,000 limit from individuals. This provision attempts to level the playing field between wealthy candidates who can rely on their own funds and those candidates who depend more on donations. The "millionaire's amendment" to the McCain-Feingold Bipartisan Campaign Reform Act requires wealthy candidates to file an estimate of how much personal wealth they plan on using when they declare their candidacy. Wealthy candidates have to notify opponents within twenty-four hours every time they contribute at least $10,000 of their own money. Opponents then are allowed to raise more money from donations, based on a complex formula derived from the voting-age population of the state. In Illinois, the ceiling is pierced when a candidate contributes just over a million dollars.

The law was just a few months old at the beginning of 2003. The main purpose of the act is to counter the influence of wide-open soft money contributions to political parties and to restrict third-party advocacy advertising in campaigns. The law was challenged in court because it allowed for different funding levels for campaigns for federal office and went against the Supreme Court's approval of strict fundraising caps. Other critics of the provision argue that it actually fuels the need for greater sums of money for campaigns, rather than reducing the cost of running for office. Larry Noble, executive director of the Center for Responsive Politics, thinks that less well-funded candidates will have to spend more time raising money outside their home states to hit up contributors who can give more under the millionaire's amendment. He thinks the law benefits incumbents who face a wealthy challenger, because incumbents have a wider circle of contacts and greater influence outside their states.[4]

Hull indicated that he was willing to personally contribute $40 million and notified his competition around Memorial Day that they could seek the higher donation level. By early February 2003, Hull had already transferred $1.3 million, which allowed others to seek individual donations of up to $6,000 for the primary. The donation limit reached the maximum of $12,000 before the primary race was over. Bettylu Saltzman, a veteran North Shore Chicago Democratic fundraiser and a member of Obama's finance committee, said, "I find it easy [to raise money for the campaign]. You say, 'You can give $12,000' and you might get $2,000, where otherwise you'd get $500."[5]

And Blair Hull spent the money—nearly $29 million of his own money. Hull made a fortune from playing blackjack and from trading securities and was estimated to be worth $400 million. Mr. Hull was not interested in raising money from individuals or political action committees (PACs). He limited individual contributions to $100 and collected only $120,000 from personal supporters. Hull also said he would not take any PAC money so that special interests would never have undue influence with him. Unlike some wealthy, self-funded candidates, Hull spent years making friends and networking. He was a board member of the National Abortion and Reproductive Rights Action League, and he received a national award for his support of Title IX, the federal program mandating funding for women's athletics. He also endowed a chair for women's studies at his alma mater in California.

Hull began spending money in Illinois elections a few years before he jumped into the Senate race. He donated nearly $1 million to other Illinois candidates from 2000 to 2003, in an attempt to quickly become a player in state politics. Hull also donated staff members on his payroll to other Democratic candidates to assist them, but also so that his people could learn the political ropes. Illinois Governor Rod Blagojevich accepted close to $260,000 from Hull for his 2002 gubernatorial reelection.[6] Mayor Daley of Chicago and the city's Democratic Party organizations also benefited from Hull's generosity. Hull even contributed to downstate candidates for city elections. Hull explained in an early debate, "I'm very proud of what I did in terms of supporting Rod Blagojevich [and] making sure we returned the Senate [to Democrats] here in Illinois. And I'm not expecting anything back from them. I'm not a special interest. I'm not a lobbyist."[7]

Hull used his vast personal wealth to construct one of the most sophisticated political operations in the country. He announced his candidacy at the end of June 2002 and began a $750,000 two-week television and radio advertising campaign detailing his economic and health care plans. Red, white, and blue billboards bearing his name were in every corner of the state. Advertisements ran on World Wide Web sites such as the *Washington Post* and Yahoo e-mail pages. By mid-July 2003, he had spent almost $24,000 on newspaper advertisements, $14,000 on yard signs, $3,000 on banners, and almost $1,000 on bumper stickers. A quarter of a million dollars had been spent with a dozen different political consulting firms, and another $85,500 went to computer consultants.[8] His campaign staff and payroll were larger than any of the Democratic presidential candidates. Hull chartered a jet for his longer trips, and he toured the state in a $40,000 recreational vehicle nicknamed "Hull on Wheels." His snappy staff dressed in Hull T-shirts and baseball hats with catchy slogans such as "Give 'em Hull." Journalist David Mendell explained, "All of this sometimes gives the campaign an artificial feel, sort of a 'Truman Show' meets 'The Candidate.'"[9]

He employed some of the savviest political consultants at the industry's highest salaries. For example, his campaign manager was paid $20,000 a month, and his policy director earned $15,000 a month. In the last quarter of 2003, Hull had twenty-eight consultants on his payroll and employed almost 150 people. There were no real volunteers, for even the people who installed yard signs were paid $75 a day. Most campaigns depend on an army of dedicated, passionate volunteers. Jason Erkes, Hull's spokesman, said, "We've put more people to work in Illinois than George Bush has in the last three months. So yes, we've had to pay some people. Blair is not a professional politician and doesn't have a built-in ward organization or patronage operation. That's why we have had to build this state-of-the-art campaign."[10] By mid-July 2003, Hull was spending nearly $20,000 a day, double what all other candidates, Democrats and Republicans, spent combined! At the end of 2003 alone, Hull had spent almost $12 million. By late February 2004, with the primary five weeks away, Hull had contributed $18.7 million to his campaign, setting an all-time spending record for a senate race in Illinois. At this point, he had spent nearly $4 million more than any other candidate in the state's history had spent running for the U.S. Senate in both the primary and general elections. This largesse propelled his campaign, but it also created a backlash. Forty percent of Democrats surveyed thought his financial advantage was unfair. About the same number thought it was fair, and 19 percent had no opinion. Susan Lagana, Hull's campaign spokesperson, explained, "As a first-time candidate, Blair is building his campaign from the ground up. But more importantly, this shows Blair is committed to giving Illinois a senator who will answer only to them."[11]

Blair Hull is one of a number of people who have spent their personal fortunes to seek elected office. The retiring Illinois senator, Peter Fitzgerald, spent $14 million of his wealth, but decided politics was not for him after just one term. Jon Corzine (D-NJ) spent $63 million successfully campaigning for a senate seat. Other big spenders, though, have often not been victorious. Rick Lazio, a Republican from New York, spent close to $41 million and lost his bid for the Senate. Big spending does not guarantee electoral success, but it provides a mechanism for being taken seriously.

When Obama publicly announced his campaign in January 2003, he had already raised close to $290,000. Gery Chico raised an impressive $1 million in 2002, but his fundraising prowess was short-lived. When Hynes entered the race in the spring of 2003, he raised more money than Chico every quarter thereafter. Chris Mather, a spokesman for Hynes, said, "I think too many candidates in this race want to make it a race about money. Organization and message are key components to winning campaigns."[12] Obama also overtook Chico in generating revenue by the summer of 2003. Obama indicated, "The first $250,000 that I raised was like pulling teeth. No major Democratic donors knew me, I had a funny name, they wouldn't take my phone calls. Then at a certain point we sort of clicked into the public consciousness and the buzz, and I benefited from a lot of small individual contributions that helped me get over the hump.... And then after winning, the notoriety that I received made raising money relatively simple, and so I don't have the same challenges that most candidates do now, and that's pure luck. It's one of the benefits of celebrity."[13]

Obama raised $878,359 between April and June 2003, which was about $69,000 less than that raised by frontrunner Hynes, but almost twice as much as Chico raised. However, Chico's early success allowed him to spend significant amounts of money throughout the campaign. Obama said, "We are going to have enough money to get on television and run a first-class campaign, we will not have the most money in the campaign. I'm confident that I have the track record behind me that doesn't exist for any of the other candidates. I'm the only guy who's ever passed a bill. I'm the only guy that's ever cast a vote."[14] See Table 4-1 for a summary of quarterly fundraising and expenditures for the Democratic primary candidates.

Obama's strong showing in the 2003 second-quarter campaign finance reports surprised some observers. Thomas Coffey, CEO of Haymarket Group, a political consulting firm that was not involved in the senate race, stated, "If you looked at this at the beginning, you'd say that [state] Senator Obama has a very small fundraising base. But if you look at the (second-quarter fundraisng) results, it shows a lot of people don't want to be left out."[15] Another unaffiliated political consultant, who did not want to be identified, remarked, "The buzz among Democrats has really changed from 'poor Barack' to 'this is a two or three man race.'"[16]

Some analysts thought he would have trouble raising money, but Obama explained, "I think a lot of people are surprised. It has exceeded my expectations and it's very heartening. I think we're going to be able to keep pace and be competitive with the other candidates."[17] Obama raised $1.4 million by July 2003, and at that point he had spent about $313,000. With a million dollars of cash-on-hand, he was not too far off from Hynes's $1.5 million and Chico's $1.3 million. In 1996, by contrast, Richard Durbin had $325,000 cash-on-hand in his three-way race for the Democratic nomination. Obama said, "We can't write a million-dollar check like a lot of candidates in this race. But they can't buy a record on the issues that matter to people across our state, like expanded health care, more job opportunities and tax relief for those who need it."[18] Summer is usually not the best time for fundraising, yet finance director Claire Serdiuk, a former fundraising consultant to Senator Durbin, said "$750,000 is what I'm shooting for" in the third quarter of 2003. She was right on target—the Obama campaign brought in $774,804 that quarter.

Table 4-1 Quarterly Revenue and Expenditures for Democratic Candidates (in millions of dollars)

2002 Total

	Total Revenue	Total Spending	Cash
Chico	1.012	0.201	0.758
Hull	0.923	0.871	0.521
Hynes			
Obama	0.290	0.065	0.226
Pappas			

1st Quarter: January–March 2003

	Revenue/Quarter	Spending/Quarter	Total Revenue	Total Spending	Cash
Chico	0.763	0.287	1.775	0.489	1.225
Hull	1.084	0.900	2.000	1.770	0.237
Hynes	0.897	0.096	0.897	0.096	0.801
Obama	0.232	0.101	0.522	0.166	0.356
Pappas					

2nd Quarter: April–June 2003

	Revenue/Quarter	Spending/Quarter	Total Revenue	Total Spending	Cash
Chico	0.471	0.357	2.251	0.845	1.344
Hull	4.000	1.740	6.000	3.510	2.502
Hynes	0.942	0.201	1.839	0.297	1.544
Obama	0.878	0.148	1.400	0.313	1.076
Pappas					

3rd Quarter: July–September 2003

	Revenue/Quarter	Spending/Quarter	Total Revenue	Total Spending	Cash
Chico	0.576	0.732	2.830	1.583	1.193
Hull	2.117	2.951	8.117	6.482	1.670
Hynes	0.915	0.363	2.754	0.659	2.100
Obama	0.775	0.373	2.175	0.686	1.479
Pappas					

4th Quarter: October–December 2003

	Revenue/Quarter	Spending/Quarter	Total Revenue	Total Spending	Cash
Chico	0.384	0.816	3.213	2.400	0.761
Hull	4.510	5.654	12.630	12.116	0.527
Hynes	0.708	0.987	3.461	1.646	1.827
Obama	0.828	0.519	3.002	1.205	1.790
Pappas	0.247	0.046	0.247	0.046	0.201

Primary Total

	Revenue/Quarter	Spending/Quarter	Total Revenue	Total Spending	Cash	$/Vote
Chico	0.675	1.319	3.888	3.753	0.140	$76.92
Hull	16.362	16.866	29.012	28.982	0.024	$223.59
Hynes	1.922	3.876	5.384	5.523	0.067	$18.86
Obama	2.947	4.496	5.950	5.701	0.241	$8.77
Pappas	0.846*	1.032	1.093	1.078	0.015	$14.44

*Pappas loaned her campaign $317,069 in the months before the election.

Vernon Jordan, the power broker who chaired President Clinton's transition team in 1992, held a fundraiser for Obama in his home in September 2003. This event introduced Obama to many of the power elite of Washington, D.C. Gregory Craig, an attorney with Williams & Connolly and a long-time Democratic operative, met Obama that night. He commented, "I liked his sense of humor and the confidence he had discussing national issues, especially as a state senator. You felt excited to be in his presence. He gets respect from his adversaries because of the way he treats them. He doesn't try to be all things to all people, but he has a way of taking positions you don't like without making you angry."[19] Mike Williams, vice president for legislative affairs at The Bond Market Association and a member of an African American lobbying association, commented, "He's a straight shooter. As a lobbyist, that's something you value. You don't need a yes every time, but you want to be able to count the votes. That's what we do."[20] The Bond Market Association held a fundraiser for Obama in June 2004.

By the fall of 2003, Obama was raising more money than the competition. He brought in $120,000 more than Hynes and almost half a million more than Chico, although Hull dropped in another $4.5 million from his bank account. But by November 2003, Hull had little to show for all the money he had spent. A *Chicago Tribune* poll showed him attracting only 6 percent of the vote. Pappas drew the most support among the candidates with 16 percent, although 45 percent were still undecided.[21]

During the two weeks at the end of February and the beginning of March 2004, nearly $500,000 in contributions allowed Obama to advertise in most downstate markets. Unlike the flagrant spending of Hull, Obama conserved his resources until early 2004. He spent almost $4.5 million from the beginning of the year until the primary; nearly 85 percent of the campaign budget was spent in these two and a half months. See Table 4-2 for a quarterly breakdown of Obama's campaign revenue and expenditures and Table 4-3 for a financial summary.

Obama spent $5.7 million to win the primary; only about $8.75 per vote. Republican Jack Ryan spent $4.9 million ($3.5 million of his own money), less than the second- and third-place Democrats. Ryan's per-vote cost was nearly $21. In second place in the Democratic field was Hynes, who spent $5.5 million at nearly $18.85 per vote. Hull spent almost $30 million, $223 per vote for the 134,173 ballots that put him in third place. Pappas spent a little over a million dollars, $14.45 per vote, and finished fourth. Chico spent just over $4 million, or $76.90 per vote, and placed fifth.[22]

Obama tapped into a growing number of young, affluent African American professionals, not only in Chicago, but in Boston, New York, and Washington, D.C. Fundraisers were held in all these cities in mid-2003. When the economy boomed in the 1990s, the black middle class

Table 4-2   Obama Financials by Quarter

Date	12/31/2002	3/31/2003	6/30/2003	9/30/2003	12/31/2003
Contributions/ Quarter	$290,010	$231,885	$ 878,359	$ 774,804	$ 827,809
Expenditures/ Quarter	$ 64,472	$101,025	$ 147,835	$ 372,479	$ 518,927
Cash on hand	$225,538	$356,353	$1,076,377*	$1,479,100	$1,789,877

Date	3/31/2004	6/30/2004	9/30/2004	10/13/2004	11/22/2004
Contributions/ Quarter	$1,672,503	$4,052,909	$4,098,811	$ 266,309	$ 696,570
Expenditures/ Quarter	$2,709,044	$ 987,918	$5,509,499	$ 177,847	$1,435,705
Cash on hand	$ 241,271**	$3,378,273	$1,767,125	$1,840,589	$ 951,985

*Campaign committee paid back $10,500 loan from candidate.

**Reconciling debt owed by and to the committee left cash-on-hand of $169,744.

Based on FEC filings. Numbers may not sum due to adjustments from one reporting period to another.

grew considerably. Valerie Jarrett, who chaired Obama's fifty-two per-son finance committee, agreed that "the pool is definitely larger."[23] business leaders stepped up to support the campaign. John Rogers, chairman and CEO of Chicago-based Ariel Capital Management (number one on the Black Enterprise Asset Managers list with $10.3 bil-lion in assets under management) contributed $9,000; Lou Holland, managing partner and chief investment officer of Chicago-based Holland Capital Management (number eleven on the Black Enterprise Asset Managers list with $1.3 billion in assets under management) gave the maximum allowed, $12,000.[24] Obama also picked up support from some of the heavy-hitter "lakefront liberals" such as Marjorie Benton, Irving Harris, Martin Koldyke, Daniel Levin, Abner Mikva, Newton Minow, Nicholas and Penny Pritzker, and John Schmidt. Obama's list of con-tributors included a roster of American popular culture: singers Barbra Streisand and Stevie Wonder; comedians Chris Rock and Chris Tucker; athlete Michael Jordan and Cubs manager Dusty Baker; and actresses Melanie Griffith and Jada Pinkett Smith. Obama also held a $350-per-person fundraiser in Chicago headlined by Wonder and comedian Robin Williams.[25]

Table 4-3   Obama Financials (Summary)

	Primary	General Election
Contributions	$5,950,000	$14,966,000
Expenditures	$5,701,000	$14,372,000
Cash on hand	$ 241,000	$ 803,000

Source: Author's analysis of FEC data.

More than two-thirds of Obama's three-thousand-plus donors gave less than $25. Twelve percent of his fundraising dollars in the primary came from contributions of $200 or less, totaling $740,000. Obama held a fundraiser for young professionals at a bar near Wrigley Field, spoke with potential voters at a hip-hop music concert and at a poetry slam, organized campus coordinators at various colleges, and worked with church youth groups. He said, "People feel like the cultural references they have and the issues that they face are ones that I'm familiar with, and I think that makes a difference."[26] Only 4 percent of his primary campaign income, $260,300, came from PACs.

In the three months after the primary, Obama brought in a record $4 million. George Soros raised money for him in New York, and Hillary Clinton had a fundraiser for him in Washington, D.C. When Jack Ryan dropped out of the race, business contributions also started flowing Obama's way. Many business PACs, sensing Obama's victory, now wanted to be associated with him. For example, PACs sponsored by Chicago's Exelon Corporation, LaSalle Bank, and the law firm of Piper Rudnick, LLP, each gave the maximum allowed, $10,000. Denis O'Toole, vice president of government relations for Household International, Inc., which contributed $2,000 to Obama, said, "You have to look at the reality of politics in Illinois. We aren't delusional he'll be a totally pro-business person, but he's not anti-business either."[27] Rodney Smith, PAC director for SBC Communication,which gave $5,000 after the primary, was even more honest: "We're contributing to Barack Obama because he's going to win. He doesn't always vote our way, but he's willing to listen, and sometimes finding someone to listen is the best you can do in this business."[28] Obama's much-lauded keynote speech at the Democratic National Convention in July spawned $150,000 in unsolicited donations, according to the campaign.

While enjoying a fifty-one point lead over Alan Keyes, Obama spent a good portion of his time campaigning for other Democrats. He was one of the hottest attractions for the Democratic Party. He traveled to more than a dozen states, including Wisconsin, Pennsylvania, Colorado, and Nevada. With $2 million in campaign funds in the bank, out of the $14 million he had raised, Obama was also generous, contributing nearly $300,000 to other candidates and committees.

Obama's popularity and generosity to other candidates put him in good standing with his future colleagues, but caused a little stir back in Illinois. Obama was criticized for not posting his out-of-state speaking engagements. He raised and contributed more than $750,000 to Democratic candidates and causes. In addition, people who had donated to his campaign were asked to give to other Senate candidates, generating $260,000. These direct contributions to candidates and state parties are in addition to the nearly $2 million Obama helped raise for others by

Table 4-4   Top Metro Areas for Campaign Contributions

Barack Obama		Alan Keyes	
Chicago	$7,380,043	Chicago	$182,607
New York	$ 864,220	Los Angeles	$ 17,874
Washington, DC	$ 500,050	Orange County	$ 12,450
Los Angeles	$ 410,809	Phoenix	$ 11,950
San Francisco	$ 263,725	Nassau-Suffolk	$ 11,600

Source: Center for Responsive Politics.

calling other donors or holding joint fundraisers. Senator Jon Corzine, chair of the Democratic Senatorial Campaign Committee, remarked, "It's unprecedented and historic to receive this level of support from someone who has yet to be elected to the Senate and it is a testament to Barack's sincere desire to elect a Democratic Senate Majority."[29]

Obama for Illinois raised just under $15 million and spent $14.3 million. The nearly $800,000 cash-on-hand formed the beginning of the war chest for future campaigns. PACs gave $1.2 million, or 8 percent of the campaign total. Business PACs outspent labor PACs almost two-to-one, $582,500 versus $274,000. Ideological or single-issue PACs contributed $259,657. Sixty-eight percent of contributions came from within the state of Illinois, whereas 67 percent of Keyes's funding was from outside the state. See Table 4-4 for a list of the top metropolitan areas for campaign contributions.

Obama's campaign funding is consistent with national trends. The Center for Responsive Politics reports:

> Historically, the financial sector has consistently been the biggest source of funds in U.S. elections. In 2002, financial interests gave $105 million to federal candidates. The sector includes banks, insurance companies, the real estate industry, accountants, and other financial professionals. Lawyers and lobbyists were second with $72 million, followed closely by ideological groups at $71.6 million. The catch-all "miscellaneous business" category gave $63.4 million. Labor unions kicked in $55.4 million, giving 89.4% to Democrats.[30]

Obama's largest category of donors is the financial, insurance, and real estate industry, with $2,315,177 in contributions. A close second are lawyers and lobbyists, with $2,238,436. As Table 4-5 shows, miscellaneous business, communications/electronics, and health concerns industries were generous donors to Obama. Liberal ideology and single issue concerns gave $526,385, and labor contributed just $287,375.

Among contributors to Keyes were Virginia McCaskey, matriarch of the family that owns the Chicago Bears; Denis Healy, the CEO of Turtle

Table 4-5   Campaign Contribution by Industry Sector

Barack Obama		Alan Keyes	
Finance/Ins./Real Estate	$2,315,177	Other	$525,751
Lawyers and Lobbyist	$2,238,436	Finance/Ins./Real Estate	$ 29,855
Other	$1,659,290	Misc. Business	$ 28,521
Misc. Business	$ 848,531	Health	$ 21,965
Communications/			
Electronics	$ 660,687	Ideology/Single-Issue	$ 13,519
Health	$ 566,702	Construction	$ 10,472
		Communications/	
Ideology/Single-Issue	$ 526,385	Electronics	$ 6,800
Labor	$ 287,375	Lawyers and Lobbyist	$ 6,750
Construction	$ 196,426	Agribusiness	$ 3,050
Energy/Natural Resources	$ 178,200	Transportation	$ 1,750
Agribusiness	$ 113,100	Energy/Natural Resource	$ 1,250
Transportation	$ 100,000		
Defense	$ 15,750		

Source: Center for Responsive Politics. This chart classifies all contributions into one of thirteen sectors: ten within the business community, one for labor, one for ideological/single issue groups, and one for other.

Wax Co.; Thomas Sowell, a conservative black economist at Stanford University's Hoover Institution; and Thomas Roeser, a conservative *Chicago Sun-Times* columnist. Keyes aides said more than twenty thousand donors had poured money into his campaign in the seven weeks after it began, most of it in small amounts that did not have to be itemized on reports to federal election officials.

Obama and Keyes had almost the same amount of cash on hand at the end of September, but the Obama campaign had already made its media buys for the fall. Julian Green, a campaign spokesman, said Obama had already paid $2 million for the television and radio commercials that would air in October. That came on top of the $1.2 million the Democrat had already spent on downstate advertisements in August and September.[31]

Other than advertisements, the largest expenditures for most campaigns are polling, staff salaries, and rent. In the Democratic primary, Hull spent $1 million on campaign staff alone. Keyes had few paid staff members, relying as much as possible on campaign volunteers, and could not afford much polling. Keyes took over the lease on Jack Ryan's campaign office in Chicago's West Loop, which cost about $3,000 a month in rent. In taking over office space and several staff members from Ryan, Keyes had to be careful not to take too many "in-kind" contributions from the Ryan campaign, as such contributions are strictly limited by law. After the big things like rent are taken care of, there are all the small things people who had donated to his campaign to add up,

Table 4-6   Campaign Contributions by Top Industries

Barack Obama		Alan Keyes	
Lawyers/Law Firms	$2,152,436	Retired	$520,551
Securities and Investments	$ 957,092	Health Professionals	$ 19,265
Retired	$ 801,994	Misc. Business	$ 18,250
Education	$ 489,574	Real Estate	$ 16,150
Real Estate	$ 481,225	Republican/Conservative	$ 11,019
Business Services	$ 372,216	Securities and Investment	$ 7,050
Misc. Finance	$ 350,998	Lawyers and Law Firms	$ 6,750
Health Professionals	$ 332,013	Construction Services	$ 5,922
TV/Movies/Music	$ 260,683	Education	$ 3,800
Commercial Banks	$ 252,203	Misc. Services	$ 3,521
Insurance	$ 169,232	Computers/Internet	$ 3,300
Printing and Publishing	$ 167,143	Accountants	$ 3,200
Misc. Business	$ 137,291	Special Trade Contractors	$ 2,800
Civil Servants	$ 133,219	Abortion/Pro-Life	$ 2,500
Non-Profit Institutions	$ 121,220	Printing and Publishing	$ 2,250
Hospitals/Nursing Homes	$ 118,550	Lodging/Tourism	$ 2,000
Computers/Internet	$ 98,535	Retail Sales	$ 2,000
Electric Utilities	$ 95,700	Hospitals/Nursing Homes	$ 1,700
Human Rights	$ 95,429	Crop Production	$ 1,650
Pro-Israel	$ 90,900	Business Services	$ 1,500

Source: Center for Responsible Politics. Industry totals are based on contributions from political action committees and from individual donors giving more than $200, as reported to the Federal Election Commission.

such as utilities, cell phones, pagers, and computers. In June 2004, Ryan's campaign paid almost $10,000 in cellular phone bills. Keyes relied less on trying to raise money for television advertisements and more on holding public events across the state to generate as much news coverage as possible.[32] His ostentatious style and sometimes outlandish rhetoric often kept him in the media.

Keyes raised and spent nearly $2.8 million. His campaign claimed to have raised $50,000 in donations on-line in the first thirty hours after he announced his candidacy on August 8, 2004. The Internet proved to be the greatest tool Keyes had for raising money.[33] PACs contributed slightly less than $51,000, about 2 percent of his total. Keyes's major donor base was consistent with that of Obama, and with national trends, with finance, insurance, and real estate interests first with almost $30,000 in contributions. Miscellaneous businesses, however, were the second most generous donors for Keyes with $28,500, followed by health concerns at nearly $22,000. See Table 4-6 for a breakdown by individual industry.

Keyes tried to tap into his national base of abortion opponents, gun rights supporters, and other conservative causes, but he did not garner the support he had hoped for. Despite Keyes's vehement opposition to abortion, the Republican National Coalition for Life was the only anti-abortion group that contributed, giving him $2,500. Two Republican groups in downstate Adams County donated a total of $1,000. Keyes was disappointed that he did not get greater financial support from the Republican Party and conservative interests. Keyes's slashing campaign rhetoric angered many Republicans, and prominent GOP groups did not chip in to help him with significant donations. His largest contribution came from the National Republican Senatorial Committee, which gave $35,000.

By spring 2006, Obama had raised another $2 million for his future war chest. He also created a leadership PAC, called the Hope Fund. Leadership PACs allow elected officials to donate to other campaigns. These PACs have fewer restrictions on raising and spending money than campaign accounts do. A person can give $30,000 to a leadership PAC, but only $4,200 to an individual's campaign. Leadership PAC money cannot be used for the candidate's own campaign, but it is often used to pay for travel, staff, polling, and other means of building name recognition and a national profile. As of February 2007, Hope Fund had raised $4.4 million and had contributed $3.8 million to other candidates.

With Obama's rock-star status, charisma, and mass appeal, he is well-positioned to raise staggering sums of money for his future campaigns. At just one event in Los Angeles in February 2007, he raised $1 million. In the first quarter of 2007, Obama raised an incredible amount of money for his presidential campaign: $25.7 million. This sum was only slightly less than Hillary Clinton, who has been on the national political scene since the early 1990s, eight times as long as Obama. Senator Clinton also had access to the donor lists from both her first senate campaign and Bill Clinton's two presidential races. Former Senator John Edwards raised the third most money, $14 million.[34] Obama did not accept money from federal lobbyists or PACs, and he had twice as many donors as Clinton. One hundred thousand people made contributions to Obama's campaign, and $7 million was generated over the Internet.

In the second quarter of 2007, Obama raised another $33 million, from 158,000 donors, and about a third of this amount was from small donations of less than $200. Senator Clinton, in comparison, raised an additional $27 million.[35] This fundraising prowess demonstrates that Obama is a viable candidate and that Hillary Clinton does not have the Democratic nomination sewn up.

The 2008 presidential race is expected to cost more than $1 billion! This will be the most expensive race in U.S. history, and it will effectively do away with the system of publicly funded presidential races. The fundraising for the 2008 presidential race started two years before the election, making it the earliest that candidates have ever started campaigning.

CHAPTER FIVE

Overcoming a Funny Last Name: Media and the Vote

B arack Obama, with his good looks, charm, and oratory skills, wowed both the voters and the media. Obama strategically conserved his resources for a media blitz in the last few weeks of the campaign. He was able to garner the public's attention in the beginning of 2004 and continued right up to the primary election. David Axelrod, chief strategist for the campaign, observed, "I think there was a tsunami out there for Barack Obama across the state and in the city of Chicago that completely overwhelmed any organization. I think people came out on their own because they wanted to vote for this attractive candidate they liked. And there was no organization that was going to stop them from doing it."[1] With the major impact the mass media has in "making or breaking" a candidate's image in the eyes of millions of voters, it is important to consider the role that mass media industries play in political campaigns. This chapter explores how the print and broadcast media covered the U.S. Senate race and how the candidates used the media to reach the voters.

TELEVISION

Television is certainly the most prevalent form of media today, and most Americans get their news from it. For political campaigns, television advertising is the most costly aspect of running for office. The Alliance for Better Campaigns estimated political advertisement spending in Illinois during 2004 at just $42 million.[2] This was low because the presidential nomination had been determined before Illinois' primary, President Bush did not compete for the state, recognizing that it would go to Kerry, and the U.S. Senate race was not competitive. In fact, most political television advertisements in Illinois were placed in February and March 2004, before the primary. By comparison, Florida was first in the country with $236 million spent. Even smaller states like New Jersey ($88 million), Delaware ($65 million), and Wisconsin ($54 million) had more spending than Illinois. Nationally, a record $1.6 billion was spent by parties, candidates, and independent groups on television advertising in 2004, more than double the amount spent in 2000.[3] In 2002, candidates spent $24.3 million on Chicago television advertising, and special interest groups spent almost another $20 million. In 2004, by contrast, candidates spent only $11.3 million (through August) and interest groups just under $400,000, just for the primary race.[4]

Thom Serafin, a Chicago political and public relations consultant, said that Jack Ryan and Barack Obama were not the only winners in the primary elections. "The winners are the TV stations," he suggested. While much less money was spent by candidates on television than in previous years, close to $44 million poured into the Chicago and downstate media markets, and "Illinois residents were subjected to an incessant barrage of ads that made household names out of unknowns."[5] For political neophytes in Illinois, expensive television advertisements are the only way to overcome entrenched field organizations. Serafin said, "Infrastructure takes a long time to build. Television gets you a short-term name identification, then you hope it filters into the neighborhoods. The old-timers used to build from the bottom up. Now, with the new guys, it's from the top down."[6] David Morrison, deputy director of the Illinois Campaign for Political Reform, a nonpartisan group that advocates for public funding of campaigns, for vouchers for television spots, and for campaign contribution limits, said, "We've seen plenty of millionaires run and lose. Our concern isn't about raising the ceiling, it's raising the floor. We've seen a number of folks raise around five million in the primary alone. If that's the new floor, that's going to discourage some credible candidates."[7] Trevor Jenson explained in an article for *Adweek*, "In a state that includes the expensive Chicago market, the race offered a two-tiered message: candidates do need significant money just to compete, but in the end, even the heaviest TV blitz does not always pay off at the polls."[8] Kevin Lampe, a principal with Chicago public relations and political consultants Kurth/Lampe, concluded, "Self-funded candidates win or lose with the same frequency as people that raise money from the general population."[9]

The primary candidates were not that different on policy positions, so a premium was put on old-fashioned politics, reaching the voters, and getting supporters out to vote. A month before the primary, 55 percent of likely Democratic voters said they had paid little or no attention to the race, so the final weeks of the campaign were key. Obama strategically conserved his resources for that time. Blair Hull, however, did not have financial constraints and flooded the airwaves as soon as he announced his candidacy.

Hull set a new record for Illinois by being the first candidate to run television advertisements for his campaign, in June 2003, ten months before the primary. Millionaire Peter Fitzgerald, who had won the seat in 1998 but was retiring, had previously held the record when he started advertising six months before the election. Millionaire candidates have begun to advertise far earlier than non-wealthy candidates simply because they could afford to incur the costs. For example, Jon Corzine, who spent $60 million in his New Jersey senate race, started running television advertisements three months before the primary in 2000, a very early start at that time. It is apparent that the first candidate to begin the television bombardment acts as a catalyst for other candidates to do the same, if they can afford it. Steve Brown, a spokesman and longtime political operative for Illinois House Speaker Michael Madigan said, "You hate to have one person [running commercials] while you're on the sidelines."[10]

In addition, such a media blitz may scare off the competition, or at least warn others that this is going to be an expensive campaign. "Clearly there is some muscle-flexing going on here," said Rick Reed, a Virginia-based advertising consultant who had worked on past Illinois campaigns. Reed was an advisor to Fitzgerald's successful campaign in 1998, which ran advertisements early in the year to tell voters about the relatively unknown candidate.[11] This downstate media advance may have influenced John Simmons, then a thirty-five-year-old millionaire trial lawyer from suburban St. Louis, who had considered entering the race but then backed down.

Hull began his media assault downstate, running television commercials emphasizing his liberal agenda and the need to reform the nation's health-care system. Hull's advertisements also highlighted his working-class background and his self-made, rags-to-riches story, including being the son of Depression-era parents, a union member, a food stamp recipient, a math teacher, and the father of four children. Hull stated, "In my case, I want to be able to connect to all the voters in the state. It takes some time to get to know the people."[12] Released as part of a multicity tour that included Springfield, the Quad Cities, Rockford, and Decatur, Hull's initial media campaign cost a total of $750,000, with $222,000 spent in the St. Louis market alone.

For months, Hull's television commercials were ubiquitous, as he emphasized his economic and health-care plans. Some of Hull's advertisements emphasized the creation of jobs, support for tax credits for working-class families, and investment in rural Illinois. Others blamed President Bush for the loss of jobs and for the healthcare crisis. Hull on three occasions bussed senior citizens to Windsor, Ontario, to buy prescription drugs at the cheaper Canadian prices. Even though candidates had been doing this since 2000, it still garnered Hull additional television and news coverage, and he developed an advertisement around the trips.[13] Hull's "media barrage" ultimately helped build his political name. Anecdotal evidence that his strategy had worked was provided by a woman in a McDonald's restaurant in Rockford, Illinois. "I know you—'I'm Blair Hull and I approved this ad,' " she recited the last line of a commercial to Hull himself.[14]

At the end of February 2004, just weeks before the election, half the Democrats polled had seen or heard Hull's advertising in the last three months, while only 26 percent had seen Hynes's advertisements, the next closest.[15] Polling also confirmed that Hull's commercials were reaching voters. His name recognition soared, with six of ten Democratic voters saying they had heard of him.[16] In late fall 2003, Obama was recognized by 32 percent of those surveyed, well behind Pappas, a Cook County board member or county treasurer since 1990, with 55 percent, or State Comptroller Dan Hynes with 54 percent. Chicago lawyer Gery Chico had a 38 percent recognition rate. Table 5-1, Democratic Primary Poll Standings, shows the trends of support for the candidates in the months before the primary election.

Shortly after Hull went on the air with commercials, other candidates, such as Hynes, Chico, and Republican Jack Ryan, followed suit in fall 2003. They all hoped to reach voters before the channels were cluttered with advertisements from other campaigns. In late September 2003, Gery Chico, who had been the first Democrat to declare his candidacy for the U.S. Senate, became the first candidate to advertise in the Chicago television market. Chico, the former president of the Chicago School Board, ran advertisements emphasizing his work in

Table 5-1 Democratic Primary Poll Standings

	Jan-04	Feb-04	Mar-04
Blair Hull	10%	24%	16%
Barack Obama	14%	15%	33%
Dan Hynes	14%	11%	19%
Maria Pappas	14%	9%	8%
Gery Chico	6%	5%	6%
Other	4%	2%	10%
Undecided	38%	34%	16%

Poll conducted by Market Shares Corp in Mt. Prospect.

education and his Chicago upbringing. "We believe being out there on television will help both fundraising and network building," Chico said.[17] However, this did not seem to be true in Chico's case.

The other candidates were focusing on introducing themselves to downstate voters, thinking that the Chicago electorate would be split into many factions based around remnants of the Democratic political machine, existing political bases, or ethnic rivalries. Jack Ryan commented, "One of the maxims in politics is to define yourself before others define you. We're trying to define me as a person. Once we establish that foundation, we can talk with credibility about how to solve the problems that face us now."[18]

Hull and Chico recognized that there were some disadvantages to overexposure. Hull even asked the question himself, around the time he started spending money on television advertisements: "Don't you think people kind of, you know, get sick of you after a while?"[19] Gery Chico had a stronger opinion. "I don't want to aggravate people. I think there is a point at which you over-saturate and people say, 'Oh no, not this guy again.'"[20]

While Hull's campaign imploded after revelations of spousal, drug, and alcohol problems, Hynes's strategy was cautious and deliberative. One commentator suggested that his theme was "bland is beautiful," and that Hynes was anticipating field support from labor and the traditional Chicago power base.[21] *Chicago Tribune* columnist Rick Pearson labeled the Democratic primary "lackluster" and commented, "Things were so bad that a recent press release from the campaign of deadpan-demeanor Dan Hynes, the state comptroller, declared that he had passion. Noting on his TV ads that his wife is a doctor may reassure voters who fear he often doesn't show signs of a pulse."[22]

Maria Pappas tried to distinguish herself from the male competition, running one advertisement that featured her against a background of suit-wearing mannequins. Rick Pearson observed that the spot was not effective downstate where she was not well known and that voters "conceivably could have thought she was promoting blazers and ties for Men's Wearhouse."[23]

Obama's earliest advertisements outlined his impressive resume in his attempt to distinguish himself from the competition. In early March, Obama began airing testimonial television advertisements with Congresswoman Janice Schakowsky, a liberal Chicago Democrat. Unfortunately, Ms. Schakowsky's husband, longtime social activist Robert Creamer, was indicted on federal charges of check kiting and tax evasion on the same day the commercials started running. Sheila Simon, the late U.S. Senator Paul Simon's daughter, appeared in one downstate commercial. Senator Simon was so well respected that this support gave him more credibility and helped him win voters downstate.

Despite the barrage of television commercials, many thought that free-spending Hull did not set himself apart from other, more modest contenders. Moreover, in the Democratic primary debate televised in early March 2004, Hull explained that his former wife's protection order was part of a legal tactic to extract a $3.4 million divorce settlement. He stated, "There are two kinds of divorce, one involves children and one involves money—this is the latter."[24] He abandoned the above-the-fray style of a front-runner and accused Obama and Hynes of taking large contributions from drug and insurance companies, which they denied. The controversy that surrounded Hull and the airing of it on television for all the news programs to cover only lessened his competitive edge, and it helped increase the popularity of the other candidates. Jim Cauley, Obama's campaign manager, recognized the advantages of Obama's television exposure when he remarked, "At the end of the day, if we can get Barack Obama in front of all the people of this state, they'll make a decision in his favor."[25] Ultimately, Obama's media strategy worked exceedingly well. Campaign advisor David Axelrod noted, "It was always our plan to finish hard, when people were paying attention. One of the great disciplines of the campaign was not to spend money early and waste those resources."[26]

After the primary, the general election race had hardly begun before Republican candidate Jack Ryan became embroiled in his own divorce record scandal. Ryan blamed the media for his campaign's collapse. By focusing on his divorce records, the media made it impossible to have "a rigorous debate on the issues." Ryan stated, "The media has gotten out of control. The fact that the *Chicago Tribune* sues for access to sealed custody documents and then takes unto itself the right to publish details of a custody dispute over the objections of two parents who agree that the re-airing of their arguments will hurt their ability to co-parent their child and will hurt their child is truly outrageous."[27]

With Jack Ryan stepping down, Obama modified his media strategy for the general election. He was originally going to start television advertisements in July, but instead waited until mid-August. At that time, a round of advertisements in downstate media markets began to tout his sponsorship of legislation in Springfield that would provide tax credits for low-wage workers, prohibit hospitals from charging the uninsured, and force insurance companies to provide coverage for mental illnesses and mammograms. The campaign also ran advertisements on NBC affiliates during the Olympics.[28] These spots promoted Obama's ability to work with both Democrats and Republicans in the state senate on tax relief and health-care issues, but made no mention of his new Republican opponent. Obama spokesman Robert Gibbs said, "We view this as a chance to introduce, to reintroduce Barack to places of the state that didn't necessarily get to see a lot of advertising during the primary."[29]

Julian Green, Obama's press secretary in the general election, said Keyes was getting media attention because "he said something outrageous everyday, and the press would call us for reaction. For us, it was about staying on the message."[30] Obama would not have been able to get his own message across if he kept responding to Keyes' public ranting.

Obama then relied on four commercials that ran in rotation until election day. He launched a $2 million television advertising campaign on October 19, 2004, in the Chicago area, the first commercials in this media market since the primary. The thirty-second spot did not ask for voters' support and did not indicate what office he was seeking. Rather, it showed part of Obama's keynote address at the Democratic National Convention. The convention delegates were shown waving blue and white "Obama" signs, and Obama was heard speaking one of the key lines from the speech: "There is not a liberal America, and a conservative America, there is the United States of America." In the final seconds, if viewers watched closely, they could see "Democrat for U.S. Senate" in the logo shown in the corner of the screen. David Axelrod, the campaign's media advisor, insisted that Obama was not being overconfident despite a 40 percent lead over Keyes. "If we were taking this for granted, you could run a rationale for not running any ad. But the act of running this ad says we are not taking any vote for granted."[31]

Keyes ran only two television commercials. The first hit the airwaves the last week of October 2004. Bill Pascoe, Keyes's campaign manager, explained, "We're waiting until we can see the whites of their eyes."[32] The silent spot featured a display of quotes from Ronald Reagan, Rush Limbaugh, Congressman Henry Hyde, former Chicago Bears coach Mike Ditka, and retiring senator Peter Fitzgerald, all praising Keyes. The advertisement was part of a $500,000 purchase of airtime across the state. The quote from Reagan read, "I've never known a more stout-hearted defender of a strong America," and then "Who are they talking about? Alan Keyes. U.S. Senate," flashed on the screen. The only spoken words were Keyes's, saying that he approved the advertisement. A Keyes aide explained, "We wanted to remind people in this state there are a lot of people who they respect who think an awful lot of Alan Keyes. If you like Ronald Reagan, you ought to like Alan Keyes. Ronald Reagan sure did."[33] Keyes explained his advertising strategy: "As I put it to my staff people, it's like leaves on a tree in autumn. You get to a certain point where the leaves are ready to fall. Our commercials are the breeze, and the leaves will fall."[34]

Despite Keyes's outlandish comments about Obama, his first television spot was low-key and positive. In fact, the Obama campaign had been prepared for Keyes to go negative. Robert Gibbs, Obama's spokesperson, stated, "I assume that he will take his negative campaign and put it on TV for a short time in Illinois. And I think voters will reject that as they have rejected Keyes' candidacy overall."[35] The Keyes aide stated, "Before you can go negative, you have to establish somebody's positives. Launching an attack in a campaign ... is like firing a Howitzer. A Howitzer is a big gun. It has lots of recoil. If you don't have that gun grounded firmly, the blowback hurts you as much as the other guy."[36]

However, Keyes's outlandish campaign was used against other Republicans downstate as Democratic candidates tied Keyes to their races. In the Twentieth District House seat in Chicago, two incumbents faced each other because of redistricting. A mailer from Democratic Representative Ralph Capparelli featured photos of his opponent Mike McAuliffe and Keyes with the statement, "Two Republicans, from the same party, running on the same ticket, with the same views."[37] In Peoria, a Democratic Party mailer showed Keyes with Republican challenger Aaron Schock, a twenty-three-year-old school board president, reminding voters that Keyes "was young once too" and pointing out that Keyes and Schock both opposed abortion for victims of rape and incest.[38]

Keyes's second advertisement hit the airwaves on Election Day. In this piece, Obama was rebuked for taking campaign money from trial lawyers and for voting to raise taxes. Keyes stated he would cap lawyers' fees, fight frivolous lawsuits, and "ease the tax burden on our working families."[39]

527 ADVERTISING

Interest groups also took to the airwaves in 2004 to express their views on the issues and to mobilize supporters. Two of these 527 groups shaped the presidential race: Swift Boat Veterans for Truth and Moveon .org. These 527 groups, named after the provision of the tax code that defines them, can raise unlimited amounts of money. They are not permitted to directly advocate for the election or the defeat of any candidate and, therefore, are not regulated by the Federal Election Commission. The organizations are not allowed to coordinate with a candidate's campaign, and the line between issue advocacy and campaigning for a candidate is often controversial, resulting in litigation.

The 2004 Illinois senate race was no exception. Empower Illinois Media Fund, a 527 committee run by an aide to Jack Ryan, sponsored an advertisement criticizing Obama's legislative record that began airing on the day of the first debate between Obama and Keyes. Jeff Davis of Aurora raised $100,000 from wealthy conservative Jack Roeser of Barrington, Illinois, to run the independent spot in the Springfield, Champaign, and Decatur markets. Davis produced the piece because he felt Obama had not been made to defend his liberal record before the voters. The thirty-second spot was brief and low-budget and showed Obama's face. There was no voice-over, only text which read, "Obama opposes tougher sentences for gangs who kill innocent children.... Obama wants schools to teach sex to kindergartners.... Obama supports aborting children even when they are born alive."[40] Empower Illinois ran $15,800 worth of anti-Obama advertisements on two Chicago television stations.

Robert Gibbs, Obama's spokesperson, responded that the advertisement by a "shadowy front group" distorted the state senator's record. Mr. Gibbs argued that the group was working with the Keyes campaign, and he stated, "It's like every typical attack ad and it's like every typical Keyes attack—it just doesn't tell you the whole story."[41] The claims in the advertisement were shown to be inaccurate and misleading.

Later, adding more fuel to the fire, the Citizens for Responsibility and Ethics in Washington, a left-leaning watchdog group, filed a complaint with the Federal Election Commission arguing that Empower Illinois was a political committee. Speaking in relation to the complaint, CREW's executive director, Melanie Sloan, stated,

> Empower Illinois, which was founded only this past August by the former treasurer for the Jack Ryan campaign committee, has made no secret that its goal is to defeat Barack Obama. It was created as a vehicle through which Jack Roeser could make an end run around campaign contribution limits. CREW called on the FEC to immediately investigate and stop Keyes, Roeser, and Empower Illinois from attempting to illegally influence the Illinois Senate campaign.[42]

Obama called attack advertisements "corrosive" and said that the "utter loss of civility" prevented problems from being constructively addressed. He went on to say, "You can lie about somebody. You can mischaracterize your position. You can go back on your word. You can spend all your time tearing somebody down instead of doing something positive. There is no other realm in our lives where that would be acceptable. It inhibits people from trying to introduce any complexity into the conversation, because as soon as they say something complex, it will end up in a television ad or in a mail piece that makes them look like they're crazy."[43]

RADIO

Radio, in the traditional, Internet, or satellite format, has transformed national and state politics with its transmittal of public debate to an increasingly growing audience.[44] About 99 percent of homes in the United States have radios, 95 percent of America's cars have radios, and more than 3,000 stations are webcasting on the Internet.[45] XM Satellite Radio Holdings Inc. and Sirius Satellite Radio, now a merged satellite radio giant, has fourteen million subscribers.[46] Because of the extensive audience, the radio is a media outlet that can have some influence in political campaigns, as well as much power in reaching potential voters. In addition, radio's utility applies in particular to state and local elections because radio stations are locally owned and directed enterprises and about 75 percent of advertising on the radio is local.[47] Advertising on radio is also significantly less expensive than on television. Conservative talk radio made the medium important again with its emphasis on news headlines, political coverage, and aim at reaching a broad audience during commuting hours in the morning and afternoon.[48] Several people point radio's revival to Rush Limbaugh's presence in keeping the medium in the lead of successful political consultants.[49] Radio has been a "secret weapon" in political campaigns. Al Salvi, the Illinois Republican candidate for U.S. Senate in 1996, was noted for his use of radio in the senate campaign. Salvi's radio campaign reached over nine million voters in three weeks at a price of less than $40,000.[50] Radio is used in political campaigns because of its ability to reach the people with quick turnaround time.[51] Candidates have taken advantage of radio by targeting more reliable voters by running ads in popular news programs. Radio advertising is significantly less expensive than television, and it allows the message to be focused to a more well-defined audience.

Blair Hull was the first in the Illinois Senate campaign to run radio advertising, and $30,000 of his money was put into a week-long radio campaign just two weeks after he signed Representative Bobby Rush as his campaign chairman. Although Obama had unsuccessfully challenged Rush for Congress in 2000, Rush claimed that his support for Hull was not a payback of any kind. One of the first clashes among the Democrats running for U.S. Senate was between Obama and Hull when Obama took "a swing" at millionaire investor Hull over these radio spots. Hull was trying to cut in on Obama's African American base by running commercials on stations popular with black listeners. The commercials featured Bobby Rush, who referred to Hull as "an independent voice who will make sure that we get our fair share."[52] In the sixty-second commercial, Rush also said, "Blair Hull, like me, comes from a working-class family and served in the Army. Blair Hull, like me, is committed to affordable health care, improving schools so our children can get a fair shake, and creating jobs to bring stability back into our communities."[53]

In response, Obama, one of two African Americans in the race, characterized Hull as a newcomer who was trying to buy support while he himself had a record of fighting for voters of all races. "The nice thing about actually having a track record of service in the community is that you don't have to pay for all of it," Obama said. "Whether the message is coming from Bobby Rush or anybody else, one would be hard-pressed to believe that an individual who has never worked on issues important to the African American community during the first sixty years of his life suddenly discovered these issues."[54] In reaction to Obama's statement, Hull called it "the proverbial glove slap in the face."[55] Hull's spokeswoman Susan Lagana defined Hull's commitment to black voters saying, "Blair Hull has committed early to reaching out to the African American community, and I guess it has touched a nerve. He is not going to concede any vote and not take anyone for granted."[56] Starting in October 2003, Obama launched advertisements on black radio stations.

Overall, political advertising on the radio, as in other media outlets, was less than it might have been because of the 2004 presidential race. Candidates George W. Bush and John Kerry both recognized that the state would vote Democratic in the presidential race, and, consequently, neither candidate put any time or money into media campaigns in Illinois.

The first Obama–Keyes debate was broadcast on radio, and Obama lacked the spark he had displayed at the Democratic National Convention. Obama was expecting Keyes to act outrageous, but instead he presented himself as a serious candidate. This evidently threw Obama off, and he stuttered and stumbled throughout the hour. Keyes had experience in the professional field of radio with his own radio show in the 1990s, which had made him an icon among social conservatives, including abortion opponents, during his 1996 and 2000 presidential campaigns.[57] Obama, in response to some of Keyes's claims, said, "Sometimes the statements made in this campaign are so outlandish, you've got to laugh. When I heard Jesus Christ wouldn't vote for me, I wanted to ask my opponent who his pollster was. I wanted to connect with him, because there are so many more important questions. Am I going up or going down? There's the eternal life thing. People recognize this is really helpful to us solving our problems."[58]

NEWSPAPERS

Although the number of newspapers produced has been decreasing, newspapers still undoubtedly reach a successful and educated readership.[59] A nationwide, bipartisan poll by the Newspaper Association of America in August 2004 showed that seven of ten registered voters regularly read a newspaper.[60] In the Information Age, national and local newspapers now have the capacity to reach even more readers through the promotion of on-line editions. Political campaigns are still using newspapers to reach voters, and candidate coverage in newspapers and newspaper endorsements prove to be quite useful in garnering support. On the whole, newspapers provide more detailed information than television, and the endorsements of editorial boards carry some weight in most communities. Candidates certainly publicize the number of newspapers that support them.

Considering the money, scandal, and background of the candidates, it is no surprise that the U.S. Senate race in 2004 captured the attention of a variety of newspapers. Newspapers act as society's watchdogs, investigating all aspects of a candidate. Along with the exciting headlines of any election, there is a strong focus on every aspect of candidates' lives—professional, political, and personal—that is brought out under the pressure of high competition.

Illinois' two largest newspapers, the *Chicago Tribune* and the *Chicago Sun-Times,* endorsed Obama in the primary and the general election. At least thirty-nine newspapers supported Obama in the primary election alone. Hynes was endorsed by Bloomington's *Pantagraph* and Joliet's *Herald-News*. Gery Chico was supported by Aurora's *Beacon News*, crediting as the basis of their endorsement Chico's "passion and problem-solving skills" and suggesting that, as Chico rebuilt a disastrous Chicago public school system in 1995, he would apply a similar plan to education, health care, and economic reforms.[61] The *Beacon News* also added a warning to its readers: do not be fooled by "electronic media hype": if a candidate "of substance" was what one desired, look to Gery Chico.[62]

In the months leading up to the general election, on top of newspaper endorsements, the national media provided extra support for Obama through their glowing pieces written about him after his 2004 Democratic National Convention speech. Traditionally, the position of keynote speaker is reserved for eminent figures or rising superstars. The success of his speech began to pave Obama's way in national politics. "One of the things I'm planning to do is to give voice to all the families in Illinois I'm meeting who are struggling to make ends meet," he said of his new visibility.[63] According to the Kerry campaign, Obama was an asset, especially in mitigating disapproval of Kerry's campaign officials' neglect of African American voters. After meeting Obama for the first time and listening to him speak at a fundraiser in Chicago in April 2004, Kerry began to consider Obama for the keynote speech at the convention.[64] An aide to Kerry said that he was taken aback by Obama's "passion, eloquence, and charisma."[65]

The Springfield *State Journal-Register* was the last large newspaper to endorse Obama in the general election, conferring an additional advantage in Obama's race to gain voters' support. The newspaper wrote, "If Illinois voters were being asked to elect an ayatollah November 2, Alan Keyes would be the obvious choice. But on Tuesday, we will elect a U.S. Senator and for that office we support Barack Obama."[66] Despite the fact that all of the foremost Illinois newspapers endorsed

Obama, however, most newspapers across the state expressed regret that it was not a competitive race. In addition, the more conservative editorial boards offered only lukewarm endorsements, indicating that they did not agree with Obama on several issues but praising him for his commitment to improve education and health care. For example, the Freeport *Journal-Standard* wrote, "Though his potent brand of liberalism is extreme, we believe that given the choice between Barack Obama and Alan Keyes, Obama is the best man to represent our state."[67] Obama, unlike Keyes, had a comprehensive knowledge of Illinois. Obama remarked, "It feels good that newspapers across the state feel like I'm going to represent their communities well."[68]

Republican candidate Alan Keyes stated that he thought media coverage, including the newspapers, had been unfair. "I have not been impressed with the standard of journalism in the State of Illinois. I think it's a disgrace to the people of this state that you all don't do your jobs very well. You've got work to do because you're not up to snuff."[69] Obama's media endorsements were exceptionally transparent, and his opponent felt inclined to comment: "I think I've made it pretty clear the media in this state have sort of had their preferred candidate all along. The corrupt elites have been promoting him with an extremism that is wrong," Keyes said.[70] Keyes indicated that the people who supported him did not rely on "biased newspapers" for information. Keyes also added that the campaign was a "fight between good and evil," and that Obama's positions on moral issues were "wicked and wrong."[71] In response to Keyes's attack, Obama said that Keyes's argument about a media conspiracy "defies logic," pointing out that many state newspapers historically support Republicans and that many endorsed George W. Bush.[72] Throughout the history of Illinois political campaigns, local newspapers did by and large endorse Republican candidates, especially in the twentieth century.[73]

INTERNET

The newest electronic information source and media industry is the Internet, and it is growing so fast we can hardly keep up. The number of consumers on-line increased 40 percent between 2000 and 2005, and the money spent on Internet advertising increased 25 percent—from $8 billion in 2000 to $10 billion in 2005. With the constant growth of profit-centered Internet businesses, the amount of political news available is immense: outlines of news stories, on-line editions of newspapers and magazines, political rumors, and an overload of gossip and commentary through the blogosphere.[74] Furthermore, the Internet plays an important role in building grass-roots support, raising money, and putting together campaign infrastructure. The Internet can therefore be very useful to political campaigns both for advertising purposes and for building support.

Consequently, the Internet had become a powerful political tool by 2004. The Pew Internet and American Life Project reported that in the 2004 campaign, sixty-three million people used the Internet to obtain political information, forty-three million people discussed politics through e-mail, and thirteen million made on-line political contributions or volunteered to work with a campaign. In total, seventy-five million people participated in at least one of these activities. The Internet has shifted the focus from checkbook activism to credit card participation through websites. With the click of a button, supporters can send tens, hundreds, and thousands of dollars. Not everyone can attend a $250-a-plate dinner, but thousands of people can send a hundred dollars electronically. The accessibility and convenience of the World Wide Web for making campaign donations helped Barack Obama, who had to rely more on donations and fundraising opportunities on the Internet, as opposed to candidates like Blair Hull who spent money out-of-pocket. The ability of the Internet to transform politics is staggering. Consider this point: "The on-line political news consumer population grew dramatically from previous election years (up from 18% of the U.S. population in 2000 to 29% in 2004), and there was an increase of more than 50% between 2000 and 2004 in the numbers of registered voters who cited the Internet as one of their *primary* sources of news about the presidential campaign."[75] In the 2004 Illinois Senate campaign, it is quite obvious that the Internet was yet another media outlet that was broadly utilized. While the first major campaigns used candidate websites in 1996, "the 2004 elections saw the most significant employment of the Internet in campaigns to date in terms of both depth and scope."[76]

In June 2003, Obama's detailed website focused on his extensive legislative experience and political history. Obama's official campaign website also included an array of photographs showing the smiling, young-looking Ivy League graduate in a number of settings with his family and political supporters. The site, obamaforillinois.com, rolled over into the site for obama2010.com and then to his presidential campaign website, obamaforamerica.com. Keeping these URLs current and rolling one into the other is another sign of the Obama campaign's technological savvy and helped boost his name recognition.

Gery Chico also needed to increase his name recognition. On top of every page of his website was a large red, white, and blue banner with his name and "U.S. Senate." Blair Hull's site spelled out his name in bright, bold letters across every page. There was also a section in Spanish, clearly aimed at Illinois' large Hispanic community. Also jumping on the Internet campaign bandwagon were Illinois comptroller Dan Hynes and

Cook County treasurer Maria Pappas. Hynes used his website to remind voters that he held the statewide elected position of comptroller and had helped erase the state's large budget deficit. Pappas' official website provided only basic biographical information and a description of her official duties.[77]

Moreover, Alan Keyes, the Republican contender, relied heavily on Internet campaigning. On his official campaign website, "Alan Keyes for Senate 2004," Keyes featured a section titled "About Alan," which highlighted his opinions on issues such as abortion and affirmative action, and utilized streaming media and pictures. Other links on the website included "Help Alan," "Calendar," and "Media." Under the media section, he included recent articles, press releases, archives, a media kit, press photos, and radio, television, and Internet advertisements.

The World Wide Web was and is used for informing voters, mobilizing supporters, raising money, and communicating messages. With the Internet, candidates could promote their issues and define their images. During the senate race Obama said, "I'm not interested in becoming a symbol. I'm interested in becoming a good senator for Illinois voters. To the extent that the attention gives me more of a bully pulpit to talk about issues that I care about, or to the extent that my status ... as potentially the only African American U.S. senator serves to inspire other young people to get involved in public service or gives people who've historically felt locked out a greater sense of hope, then I'm happy to serve that role."[78]

In the 2004 Illinois Senate race, the media focused on who was spending the most money and who was more popular and concentrated less on the issues. The amount of money spent captured the attention of the public more than a comparison of the candidates' views, which were not that different in the primary races. Three candidates thought the media had inappropriately invaded their personal lives. The role of the media as an overseer of the public interest was once again pitted against a candidate's privacy. The moral character of those seeking public office has been considered a relevant campaign issue since Bill Clinton ran for the presidency in 1992. Exposing a candidate's past mistakes, errors of judgment, character defects, and hypocritical positions is considered newsworthy, often times at the expense of social concerns and their remedies.

Barack Obama had some youthful indiscretions, but otherwise he has been a role model as a citizen and public servant. Obama benefited in the primary from the media's probing of other candidates, and he became the media's darling during the general election. Obama's face was on the cover of *Time* and *Newsweek* before he was even sworn into office. He was mentioned on television sit-coms like *Will and Grace*. Grace, one of the main characters, dreamed she was in the shower with

Obama, who was "ba-rocking my world." Very few other candidates have gained this type of national popularity as quickly as he has done. Obama also used the media with political savvy, buying television advertisement close to the election to shore up his support after stumping through all parts of the state. The campaign's use of the Internet was advanced for its time and was a precursor for the expanded role media and technology would play in a presidential race.

CHAPTER SIX

Barack Obama and Post-racial Politics

My view has always been that I'm African American. African American by definition, we're a hybrid people. One of the things I loved about my mother was not only did she not feel rejected by me defining myself as an African American, but she recognized that I was a black man in the United States and my experiences were going to be different than hers. My daughters will grow up with a cousin who looks entirely Asian but who carries my blood in him. It's pretty hard not to claim that larger community.[1]

—Barack Obama

Barack Obama is just the fifth African American to serve in the U.S. Senate and only the third since the Reconstruction era. During Reconstruction, two African Americans were appointed from Mississippi to serve in the U.S. Senate. Hiram Rhodes Revels served only two years, 1870–1871, and Blanche Kelso Bruce served from 1875 to 1898. Edward Brooke was elected in 1966 as a Republican from Massachusetts for two terms. Interestingly, the state of Illinois sent the two most recent blacks to the Senate: Obama in 2004 and Democrat Carol Moseley-Braun in 1992. Furthermore, in 2004, for the first time in American history, African Americans were the U.S. Senate candidates from both the Democratic and Republican parties.

Racial issues continue to be an important aspect of American politics. The Obama campaign illustrates the progress people of color have made in winning public office, and it allows us to explore the role race plays in politics today. The candidacy of Barack Obama permits an examination of the changing climate and political culture for minority politicians. This chapter will explore the constraints that black candidates have faced in the past and how Obama's racial background was perceived on the campaign trail. The factors that distinguished this campaign from previous attempts by people of color to win statewide office will also be considered. In a perhaps ironic twist, one campaign theme questioned whether Obama was black enough! We begin the discussion with an overview of the experiences of other recent black candidates for statewide office.

BLACK CANDIDATES IN STATEWIDE ELECTIONS

Black candidates have usually taken one of two campaign strategies: reach out to a coalition of black and liberal voters or downplay race and attempt to attract those in the middle of the road politically. Carol Moseley-Braun, the last African American U.S. Senator before Obama, targeted blacks and the liberal Lakeshore voters of Chicago, especially in her primary campaign. She also received significant support from white suburban women, however, as discussed in chapter 2. The primary race was extremely divisive. While her opponents destroyed each other, Braun garnered a paltry 38 percent of the vote to win the nomination. She then rode Bill Clinton's coattails to win against an underfunded right-wing Republican opponent.

Harvey Gantt, the black, charismatic, pro-business, former mayor of Charlotte, North Carolina, lost twice in races for the U.S. Senate to Jesse Helms, who encouraged white resentment of affirmative action. New York state comptroller Carl McCall lost by sixteen points to Republican George Pataki in the 2002 gubernatorial campaign, even though New York has two million more registered Democrats than Republicans. Missouri Representative Alan Wheat lost his 1994 race for the U.S. Senate against former governor John Ashcroft because black voter turnout was low. Wheat had spent too much time courting the white vote, which alienated his presumed African American base.

On the other hand, Douglas Wilder was successful taking the middle-of-the-road approach in his bid to be Virginia's governor. He deemphasized race so much that he would sometimes not even appear in his own campaign commercials. His record in the military and in the state senate was touted. Wilder won by less than 1 percent, and the support of pro-choice Republican women was an important factor.

The number, variety, and quality of black statewide candidates significantly increased in elections after 2000. Although some black candidates were not successful in the primary race, many were serious contenders. Also of significance was that both the Democratic and Republican Parties were fielding serious black candidates.

In 2004, Democratic Congresswoman Denise Majette abandoned her campaign for reelection to pursue the Senate seat from Georgia being vacated by Zell Miller, while another African American, Herman Cain, former CEO of Godfather's Pizza, failed to win the Republican nomination. He was thought to be the most conservative candidate in the race. Although Majette won the Democratic nomination, she was soundly defeated in the general election.

In 2006, Massachusetts, Maryland, Ohio, Pennsylvania, and Tennessee had high-level political races with black candidates. Democrat Deval Patrick was elected governor of Massachusetts, becoming only the second African American to win a state chief executive post by popular vote. Kweisi Mfume, former congressman and NAACP leader, vied unsuccessfully for the Democratic nomination for the U.S. Senate in Maryland, losing to Benjamin Cardin, 43.7 percent to 40.5 percent. Lieutenant Governor Michael Steele, the first black to win statewide office in Maryland, won the Republican nomination but lost to Cardin. In Tennessee, Congressman Harold Ford, Jr., lost his bid for the U.S. Senate by less than three percentage points.

Two African Americans won the Republican nomination for governor in 2006, but lost handily in the general election. Lynn Swann, the former Pittsburgh Steeler, ran in Pennsylvania. Kenneth Blackwell, who had been elected Ohio's Secretary of State, was also unable to take the governor's mansion. He was considered the most conservative Republican candidate.

INSTITUTIONAL CONSTRAINTS ON BLACK CANDIDATES

Historically, African Americans have not done well outside of predominantly black communities. Black politicians like Jesse Jackson, Sr., originally had their base in the civil rights movement, when gaining representation for minorities was itself the objective. However, this institutional development also focused these candidates on policy issues that were of greatest concern to the inner-city poor. Racially gerrymandered congressional districts created after the post-1990 Census redistricting and supported by the Supreme Court for a while intensified this focus. In any event, to win at the district level requires candidates to emphasize issues of great significance to black communities, such as affirmative action, leading them to appear to be soft on crime and as favoring big government programs. These stances often limit their appeal to whites such as soccer moms or rural voters. Noam Scheiber explains, "The reason for the poor showing is that African American candidates for statewide office nearly always end up in a catch-22. Attempts to motivate their African American base usually alienate white moderates. And, when black candidates try to tailor their message to white moderates, they dampen enthusiasm among African Americans and liberals."[2] Obama has had to balance these warring viewpoints. As his former Illinois state senate colleague Kirk Dillard noted, "I feel sorry for this guy, because he's got to justify himself to blacks and whites alike."[3]

Clearly the Obama campaign was aware of the need for biracial appeals. As Barack Obama himself said, "We have a certain script in our politics, and one of the scripts for black politicians is that for them to be authentically black they have to somehow offend white people. To use a street term, we flipped the script."[4] As suggested above, however, black politicians like Obama have to prove that they are not abandoning the African American community when multiracial coalitions are assembled, while no longer concerning themselves with just racial grievances and civil rights. The comments of prominent African American scholar Cornel West, an Obama critic turned supporter, are one illustration of the complex racial environment in which Obama operates. West said, "I don't care what color you are ... you can't take black people for granted just 'cause you're black.'"[5]

Another institutional impediment to black statewide electoral success is that African Americans were historically concentrated in southern states with white populations less likely to be open to minority candidates. In 1910, 90 percent of blacks lived in the south, and 54 percent still do today.[6] Garance Franke-Ruta noted, "In an era in which ethnic and racial diversity are heralded as the result of liberal values, it's also important to recall that the presence of large numbers of African Americans in some regions of the United States and not others is, in fact, a legacy of America's most illiberal chapter. When it comes to black elected officials, geography has for too long been destiny."[7] The majority of African Americans are found in just twenty-two states. Only two northern states—Michigan and Illinois—are in the top ten for the highest number of elected black officials. Franke-Ruta explained, "This demography has created unique challenges for African American politicians with national or statewide ambitions. Mississippi, Alabama, and Louisiana may lead the way in the election of black officials, but they are also places where white voters are less likely to vote across racial lines."[8] In other words, African American politicians may be elected in majority-minority districts, but they still struggle to win in statewide contests.

DISCRIMINATION AND BLACK CANDIDATES

Racial discrimination is another factor in the difficulty of electing African Americans to statewide offices. The impact of racial bigotry is hard to measure, but the research of political science professor Philip Klinkner estimates it at 5 percent of the vote.[9] In preelection surveys, black candidates are sometimes ahead by as much as ten percentage points, but come election time, black candidates may lose or win by a very narrow margin. This was Virginia Governor Wilder's experience in 1989. Whites would not publicly admit to being racist, but when the curtain was closed to vote, the racial baggage that has plagued this country made them question black political power and leadership.

Many white Americans have negative perceptions of black Americans, yet hold positive images of newly arrived African or West Indian immigrants. Native blacks are viewed as more prone to crime and less responsible, while new black immigrants are seen as hard-working and pursuing the American dream.[10,11] Obama's exotic last name did not sound like a traditionally American black name, and he consequently did not have to overcome some of the bigotry that other African American candidates experience. When Obama was associated with other black public officials, like Jesse Jackson, Jr., however, his standing with white suburban and exurban voters diminished. Nevertheless, with Chicago's deep Irish roots, one commentator suggested Obama would do better with the last name of O'Bama.

Barack Obama represents a new age of African American public officials. The background of black politicians has changed dramatically, and Obama is the face of the next generation. Older black politicians tended to be from segregated communities and local political cultures. Because of the civil rights movement, younger black politicians experienced a more integrated world, though hardly one without discrimination. Many younger black officials attended elite, predominantly white educational institutions. Recently elected black officials, such as Newark Mayor Cory Booker, Massachusetts Governor Deval Patrick, Washington, D.C. Mayor Adrian Fenty, and Maryland Lieutenant Governor Anthony Brown try to appeal to all races in their campaigns, but dismiss the term "post-racial" as a media construct.[12] They feel this term negates the benefits they have received from African American politicians of the past. "Though still rooted in and nurtured by predominantly black political districts, the new generation's comfort in a highly competitive, integrated world may well allow its members to reach out across the racial lines they have been bridging their whole lives and gain support in white districts as well," stated Franke-Ruta.[13] Among black elected officials over the age of sixty-five, 76 percent attended segregated high schools, while only 34 percent of those under the age of forty did.[14] Nearly 70 percent of those over sixty-five years old attended historically black colleges, compared to 37 percent of those under forty. David Bositis, senior scholar at the Joint Center for Political and Economic Studies, remarked, "It gives them advantages that older generations of African Americans did not have."[15] Obama stated, "The African American community is not divorced from larger trends in the country. It's harder to obtain leadership positions in a modern highly technological society without some familiarity with the institutions of leadership."[16]

BLACKS IN ILLINOIS POLITICS

Whatever disadvantages (or advantages) Obama's racial background creates, running in Illinois undoubtedly helped his Senate candidacy. As noted earlier, Illinois has a history of electing black officials to state-wide office, and the state has probably elected more black statewide officials than any state in the country. The state is unique as it has a fairly middle-of-the road voting public and, unlike other liberal northern states such as Minnesota, has a fairly large African American constituency comprising about 15 percent of the population.[17]

The most successful African American politicians in Illinois were Roland Burris, who won statewide office four times, and Jesse White, who has done so three times. Burris made history by becoming the first African American to hold statewide office in Illinois. He was elected three times as state comptroller (1978, 1982, and 1986) and once as attorney general in 1990. Burris lost to Paul Simon in the 1984 U.S. Senate primary. He unsuccessfully sought the Democratic nomination for governor in 1998 and in 2002. Burris had excellent qualifications, experience, and name recognition, but, in contrast to Obama, he was seen as unexciting and an establishment candidate. In previous elections, Burris had carried up to 90 percent of the black community's vote.[18] In the 2002 gubernatorial election, however, the majority of black leaders supported a white candidate with a background in education, Paul Vallas.

White was elected secretary of state in 1998, and was reelected in 2002 and 2006. Carol Moseley-Braun was elected to the U.S. Senate in 1992, but lost her bid for reelection in 1998. Two other black candidates won Democratic primaries, but lost in the general election. Cecil Partee, the first black candidate for statewide office in Illinois, lost his bid for attorney general in 1976, and Earlean Collins was defeated for comptroller in 1994.

There is little doubt that the success of black candidates in the past helped Obama's cause. Not only did they show that African Americans could win, but they provided a blueprint for doing so, especially in the case of Carol Moseley-Braun's senate campaign. Like Obama, the most successful black candidates had "crossover appeal." Before his unsuccessful gubernatorial bid in 1998, Burris was known as a politician who had "made a career of not running as a black candidate."[19] He was so unthreatening that he was deemed "a tanner version of Al Gore, smart but stiff, politically astute, but pretty starchy."[20] Carol Moseley-Braun appealed to white suburban women in winning her 1992 senate campaign. Before winning election as Cook County recorder of deeds, Secretary of State Jesse White had represented a state legislative district in which blacks were the minority.[21]

Nevertheless, it is also clear that Obama differs from previous African American politicians. To begin with, most previous black candidates have depended on the Chicago Democratic machine to help them succeed. For years the machine had depended on black votes, despite often providing little in return other than limited housing choices and poor public schools. By the 1970s, black voters and politicians had grown restless with this state of affairs, threatening Mayor Richard J. Daley's political future, forcing him to put black politicians in higher level positions. In 1976, state senate president Cecil Partee was slated for the statewide office of attorney general in an effort to reach out to black voters. The move was perhaps somewhat cynical, as Partee was given little chance against incumbent Republican William Scott, and some saw the nomination as a ploy to clear the way for the mayor's son, Richard M. Daley, to become state senate president.[22] Nevertheless, the decision set a precedent for a black candidate to be slated for statewide office in future elections, even after Mayor Daley's death in December 1976.

Candidates who were more successful than Partee also had machine ties. Roland Burris began his career as an independent Democrat. He ran unsuccessfully for comptroller in 1976, losing by over 500,000 votes and losing Chicago by over 250,000. In 1978, running with the machine's support, he won Chicago by nearly 170,000 votes, which accounted for most of his statewide plurality. Jesse White's mentor was a prominent machine figure, former Cook County Democratic Party chair and Cook County Board President George Dunne. White's biographer describes Dunne as akin to the "grease that lubricates the engine" of the machine.[23]

A second contrast with Obama is that most previous black statewide candidates have struggled to raise money, perhaps explaining why they have been more successful in winning the "down ballot" offices like comptroller and secretary of state. For example, Roland Burris's gubernatorial campaigns were underfunded compared to his Democratic rivals in 1998 and 2002.[24] Burris explained, "It's a concrete ceiling. You have to overcome the lack of resources and overcome those who believe a black man can't win the top job in the state and even black people who believe a person of color can't be governor."[25] Obama, on the other hand, more than held his own in fundraising.

Finally, Obama was able to generate much more support outside Chicago than other black candidates, who largely depended on the city as an electoral base. Because Obama ran against another African American in the general election, perhaps the best way to illustrate this is to compare his success in the Democratic primary to that of other African Americans. Table 6-1 shows the plurality vote in Chicago and statewide

Table 6-1 Plurality Vote for Nonincumbent Black Democratic Primary Winners in Chicago, Statewide, and Downstate

Candidate—Office (Year)	Plurality over 2nd Place Candidate: Chicago	Plurality over 2nd Place Candidate: Statewide	Support outside Chicago (State–Chicago)
Partee—Attorney General ('76)	296,061	308,065	12,004
Burris—Comptroller ('78)	169,162	183,543	14,381
Moseley-Braun—Senate ('92)	123,029	53,617	−69,412
Collins—Comptroller ('94)	105,520	9,630	−95,890
White—Secretary of State ('98)	150,428	100,195	−50,233
Obama—Senate ('04)	231,184	361,206	130,022

Source: Author calculations based on Illinois State Board of Elections data.

for nonincumbent black Democratic primary winners for statewide office. The table shows how dependent black candidates are on a strong Chicago vote. The third column shows that, other than Obama, black candidates gain very few votes in the rest of the state. In fact, three of the six lost outside Chicago, as the negative numbers show, and the other two had very small pluralities.

Table 6-2 shows vote patterns for every black statewide general election candidate in Illinois through 2004. The first numeric column shows the plurality over the candidate's Republican opponent in Chicago, and the second column shows the difference in statewide vote. A negative number in the second column indicates that the black candidate lost the election. The level of support outside the city is shown in the last column, which is the difference between the statewide vote and Chicago vote. A positive number means that the black candidate won more votes outside Chicago than his or her opponent, whereas a negative number means that he or she did not. An examination of the downstate and suburban vote in the third column shows that no candidate other than Obama would have won the election without the Chicago plurality the first time he/she ran for office. Roland Burris and Jesse White were able to win a positive vote outside Chicago when running for reelection. Neither, however, was able to come near Obama's vote total outside Chicago.

OBAMA FOR ILLINOIS

In this section we examine how Obama handled racial issues in his Senate race. On the campaign trail, Barack Obama used his racial background in a way that would appeal to voters of all races, mentioning that his father was from Kenya and his mother was from Kansas. As discussed earlier, he used his unusual surname to help him avoid some of

Table 6-2 Vote for Black General Election Candidates Compared to Republican Opponent in Chicago and Statewide

Candidate—Office (Year)	Plurality over Republican Candidate: Chicago	Vote Difference from Republican Candidate Statewide	Vote Difference in Suburbs and Downstate
Partee—Attorney General ('76)	221,399	−1,116,213	−1,337,612
Burris—Comptroller ('78)	411,540	153,934	−257,606
Burris—Comptroller ('82)	968,509	1,117,312	148,803
Burris—Comptroller ('86)	457,563	805,490	347,927
Burris—Attorney General ('90)	308,102	95,214	−212,888
Moseley-Braun—Senate ('92)	558,218	504,346	−53,872
Collins—Comptroller ('94)	250,658	−406,994	−657,652
White—Secretary of State ('98)	472,698	437,206	−35,492
Moseley-Braun—Senate ('98)	515,197	−98,615	−613,812
White—Secretary of State ('02)	519,327	1,338,509	819,182
Obama—Senate ('04)	796,460	2,206,766	1,410,306

Source: Author calculations based on Illinois State Board of Elections data.

the discrimination other black candidates have faced. His life was framed as part of the great American narrative of rising above challenges, even though Obama benefited from many upper middle-class institutions, such as private schools. In his first television advertisement, the telegenic candidate looked directly into the camera and stated, "They said an African American had never led the *Harvard Law Review*—until I changed that. Now they say we can't change Washington, D.C.... I approved this message to say, 'Yes, we can.'"[26] David Axelrod, a media consultant to Obama, remarked, "It worked on two levels. For those for whom the knocking down of barriers is important, it was very important. For others, *Harvard Law Review* was a big credential."[27]

One issue in the primary was whether Obama could mobilize the black community. Obama actively campaigned in black churches in Chicago and on the city's south side for months before the primary, giving sermon-like stump speeches in the vein of Martin Luther King, Jr. He echoed a message of inclusion and the need to lift everyone up. The call-and-response speech technique resonated with these listeners and seemed natural for Obama. Fifteen hundred people attended a speech given at the Liberty Baptist Church.[28]

In early March 2003, polls showed about 38 percent of blacks behind him. Obama aired a television spot in early March invoking the memory of Harold Washington, Chicago's first black mayor and a beloved figure in African American communities.[29] Congressman Danny Davis stated, "He has built a solid feeling among African Americans, renewed their hope, re-energized the base, and there is more energy than I've seen since Harold Washington."[30] The advertisement also featured the daughter of the late U.S. Senator Paul Simon, which called out to white liberals. Television advertisements highlighting his legislative record gave him greater name recognition by the end of the month, by which time he had the support of 62 percent of African Americans. Obama's support among blacks increased as his chances of winning the primary improved, after Blair Hull's divorce records became public. Obama told a group of black professionals, "I've got brothers saying 'I've been with you all along,' but you know they haven't been."[31]

Obama's appeal in the primary was widespread. Many black voters indicated that they did not vote for him just because of the color of his skin. A construction worker commented, "It's what he's about that matters. It's not color, skin, or race. It's the words he speaks."[32] Black voters said much of his appeal came from his outreach in the neighborhoods and in the churches. An election judge in Chicago remarked, "For a lack of a better word, it's like he's multicolored. He's everyone's candidate."[33] For the most part, blacks voted in the Democratic primary rather than the Republican one. In the city of Chicago's twenty majority-black wards, Jack Ryan, the Republican primary winner, received 1,443 votes, compared to Obama's 193,477 votes.

Obama did well in the white-collar counties surrounding Chicago. Although finishing third downstate in the primary, he had a respectable showing in the region, performing better than Carol Moseley-Braun had twelve years earlier. He was able to achieve this success without undermining his base of support in black Chicago and with liberal whites. Obama's victory signaled a new era in racial politics. Obama was received like a rock star in small, downstate Illinois towns. In mostly white Danville, Illinois, population forty thousand, 650 people came out for a rally, the largest turnout in decades. Obama took the question of racial difference head-on, remarking, "We have shared values, values that aren't black or white or Hispanic; values that are American and Democratic."[34]

Lowell Jacobs, a retired plumber in Rock Falls, Illinois, was one of only two Democratic County chairmen outside of the Chicago region to endorse Obama in the primary. He commented, "Obama tells you the hard truths, and other politicians, particularly from Chicago, they tend to tell you what they think you want to hear. Barack's got something different. He makes you feel like he's not a politician, but a leader."[35] Columnist David Moberg noted, "Obama demonstrates how a progressive politician can redefine mainstream political symbols to expand support for liberal policies and politicians rather than engage in creeping capitulation to the right."[36]

White candidates emphasized that they cared about the plight of blacks. Jack Ryan compared himself to Bill Clinton in his level of concern about black issues. Ryan said, "If you look at my life history, you'll see that I care a lot, too. The same people who were drawn to Bill Clinton will be drawn to me."[37] Obama remarked, "Unfortunately, I don't see anything in Mr. Ryan's embrace of George Bush's agenda that will appeal to African American voters who are disproportionally working people more likely to lack health insurance, need jobs or need more funding for their schools."[38]

In August 2003, Congressman Bobby Rush produced a radio advertisement for Blair Hull that aired on stations popular with black listeners. In it Rush said that Hull was "an independent voice who will make sure that we get our fair share.... Blair Hull, like me, comes from a working-class family and served in the Army. Blair Hull, like me, is committed to affordable health care, improving schools, making sure we can get a fair shake, and creating jobs to bring stability back into our communities." Obama dismissed the claim by pointing to his own record of service to the black community and questioning Hull's new-found interest in these issues.[39]

Black leaders endorsing Obama included the Reverend Jesse Jackson, Congressman Jesse Jackson, Jr., and Illinois senate president Emil Jones. Congressman Bobby Rush, whom Obama unsuccessfully challenged in the 2000 Democratic Primary, supported Blair Hull, while Cook County board president John Stroger backed Hynes. Stroger is a longtime friend of Dan Hynes's father, Chicago's Nineteenth Ward committeeman. Despite this, Obama received more than 90 percent of the vote in Stroger's ward. In Hynes's own predominantly white northside ward, Obama garnered a majority of the vote. In the southwestside ward of Hynes's father, Obama netted 40 percent of the vote.

His campaign in the general election was the first time in U.S. Senate history that two African Americans were pitted against each other. The selection of Alan Keyes as the Republican candidate after Jack Ryan withdrew, though, was not without much controversy. Many people felt that the selection of Keyes was based more on race than anything else. Salim Muwakkil, a columnist for *In These Times*, wrote, "Tellingly, the same GOP leaders who selected Keyes never before managed to slate a black candidate to run for a major office in Illinois. Their choice of outsider Keyes was not just a cynical racial ploy: It was a slap in the face of the state's Republican electorate. It stinks of rank political opportunism and deep hypocrisy."[40] *The Economist* also ridiculed the decision to slate Keyes:

Mr. Keyes's Senate run will produce nothing but disaster—humiliation for Mr. Keyes, more pie on the face of the already pie-covered Illinois Republican Party, and yet another setback for Republican efforts to woo minority voters. The Keyes candidacy also smacks of tokenism. The candidate routinely denounces affirmative action as a form of racial discrimination. But what other than racial discrimination can explain the Illinois Republican Party's decision to shortlist two blacks for the Illinois slot—and eventually to choose Mr. Keyes? He brings no powerful backers or deep pockets and was thrashed in his two runs for the Senate in Maryland. The Illinois Republicans are not just guilty of tokenism. They are guilty of last-minute scraping-the-bottom-of-the-barrel tokenism.[41]

The race issue was transformed into a question of who was "black enough." Congressman Davis stated, "He [Obama] understands that the black community is extremely diverse and wooing the black vote is far more complicated than rousing a crowd. The question of whether someone is black enough implies that there is a system of weights and measures that just doesn't exist. It also implies a construct that allows for one type, or one standard of blackness. And that's just plain silly."[42]

Alan Keyes questioned whether Mr. Obama should claim an African American identity. Keyes remarked, "Barack Obama and I have the same race—that is, physical characteristics. We are not from the same heritage.... My ancestors toiled in slavery in this country. My consciousness, who I am as a person, has been shaped by my struggle, deeply emotional and deeply painful, with the reality of that heritage."[43] Not surprisingly, Obama held a different view of whether the term African American should refer only to the descendents of slaves and not to recent immigrants who do not share the history of discrimination. "For me the term African-American really does fit. I'm African, I trace half my heritage to Africa directly, and I'm American." In keeping with Obama's style of emphasizing commonalities rather than differences, he says black descendents of slaves and black immigrants have a great deal in common, such as fighting poverty and colonialism. Obama's grandfather worked as a servant in Kenya and was described as a "house boy" by whites even when he was a middle-aged man. Obama said he belonged to the "community of humanity" and that his struggle to define his community included not only race but also geography and class, having friends who were rice-paddy farmers and dignitaries. Obama has a half-sister who is half Indonesian and is married to a Chinese Canadian. Obama said, "I am not running a race-based campaign. I'm rooted in the African American community, but I'm not limited by it."[44]

Obama's ascent to prominence occurred at a time of evolving definitions of race, due in part to immigration. The Census Bureau in 2000 allowed people to identify themselves as "African American" as a subset of the racial category "black." A 2003 survey reported that 48 percent of blacks preferred the term African American, 35 percent identified with black, and 17 percent liked both terms.[45] During the decade of the

1990s, the number of blacks with recent roots in sub-Saharan Africa nearly tripled, and the number of blacks from the Caribbean grew by more than 60 percent. By 2000, foreign-born blacks constituted 30 percent of the blacks in New York City and 28 percent of the blacks in Boston.[46] The demographic shifts, which gained strength in the 1960s after changes in federal immigration law led to increased migration from Africa and Latin America, have been accompanied in some places by fears that newcomers might eclipse native-born blacks. And they have "touched off delicate musings about ethnic labels, identity, and the often unspoken differences among people who share the same skin color," noted Rachel Swarns.[47]

Obama and Keyes appealed to different themes that traditionally resonate in African American communities. Obama emphasized chronic policy concerns like jobs, education, and health care. He approached the issues of race by putting them in context of broader themes. He balanced the responsibilities of society at large with the responsibilities of individuals for overcoming racism. Obama thinks education is the most important racial issue facing the country today, providing the foundation to succeed in a global economy. He has derided the anti-intellectual culture that is sometimes heralded in rap music or black families. He has challenged black men to take responsibility for themselves and their families. Obama commented, "I also think that people take pride in my academic accomplishments because they know that there are a lot of cultural trends pushing against us. It's interesting how frequently I have parents come up to me just to say 'We're so pleased just to have a black man on TV who's not a sports star or a rapper.' And that, by itself, communicates a sense of hope."[48] Obama can speak to the black community in ways that whites cannot.

Keyes stressed the conservative social morals preached in black churches for generations: traditional family values are the cornerstone of society, and abortion and gay marriage are wrong. He thought the Republicans' views on these issues could lure blacks away from the Democratic Party. Alvin Williams, president and CEO of Black America's Political Action Committee, founded by Keyes to promote conservative candidates, explained, "This campaign ... will help bury this monolithic stereotype that all African Americans think alike."[49] The *Peoria Journal Star* echoed this theme in an editorial: "Whoever is elected, this race should shatter the assumption that you can look at a person's skin color and assume what he believes. Stereotypes are always worth breaking, and no more so than when race is their source."[50] Keyes's bombastic style and extreme stand on positions led him to make some outlandish comments, however. As discussed in chapter 3, for example, Keyes called Obama's pro-choice votes the "slaveholder's position," for denying unborn children

Table 6-3   Top 5 Voter Concerns by Race

Black Population	2004	2002	2000
Employment/Economy	34%	23%	14%
War in Iraq	22%	6%	—
Prescription Drugs/			
Health Care	29%	5%	18%
Terrorism	10%	17%	1%
Education	7%	14%	26%
White Population	**2004**	**2002**	**2000**
War in Iraq	25%	4%	—
Employment/Economy	21%	18%	4%
Prescription Drugs/			
Health Care	17%	7%	18%
Terrorism	16%	27%	3%
Education	3%	10%	24%

Source: Joint Center for Political and Economic Studies, 2004 National Opinion Poll. David C. Ruffin, "State of the New Black Power," *Black Enterprise*, January 2005, 22.

equal rights. The top concerns of black and white voters in elections from 2000 to 2004 are outlined in Table 6-3.

Salim Muwakkil noted that Obama has "mastered the cultural jargon of the Ivy League" and is "the literal embodiment of our cultural hybridity."[51] Everyone can relate to Obama, or at least a part of him. Bamani Obadele, chairman of the African American Political Organization and a deputy director of the Illinois Department of Children and Family Services, remarked, "To black people, he's black. To some whites, they don't see him as a black man. They see him almost as one of them. Barack Obama is whatever you want him to be."[52]

Obama is a racially complex person, which allows him to transcend some cultural constraints. Some pundits argue that this prevents him from being completely at home in any community, but Obama disagrees, claiming to feel comfortable in them all. William Finnegan reported, "Obama's ease in front of predominantly white crowds—or, for that matter, all-white crowds—is a source of wonderment in Illinois. I've seen it, and it looks so effortless that it doesn't seem remarkable. The sight of big white corn farmers proudly wearing big blue "Obama" buttons and lining up to shake his hand is, I must say, slightly more striking."[53] Obama offered an explanation of his ability to connect with white rural and small-town voters to Mr. Finnegan: "I know those people. Those are my grandparents. The food they serve is the food my grandparents served when I was growing up. Their manners, their sensibility, their sense of right and wrong—it's totally familiar to me."[54]

Salim Muwakkil, observing the mix of people in a crowd of Obama supporters, noted, "It wasn't diversity cobbled together by good intentions. This was people coming together with shared concerns and hopes—a genuine coalition. Illinois residents of all ethnicities seem to trust that Obama will speak to their specific issues without bias."[55] In an interview with National Public Radio, Obama was asked if he might have a different policy agenda if he were white. He responded:

> There are certain instincts that I have that may be stronger because of my experiences as an African American. I don't think they're exclusive to African Americans but I think I maybe feel them more acutely. I think I would be very interested in having a civil rights division that is serious about enforcing civil rights. I think that when it comes to an issue like education for example, I feel great pain knowing that there are children in a lot of schools in America who are not getting anything close to the kind of education that will allow them to compete. And I think a lot of candidates, Republicans and Democrats, feel concern for that. But when I know that a lot of those kids look just like my daughters, maybe it's harder for me to separate myself from their reality. Every time I see those kids, they feel like a part of me.[56]

Barack Obama is a "post-racial" candidate, even though he rejects the concept as representing a "shortcut to racial reconciliation" that ignores the "long legacy of Jim Crow and slavery."[57] Still, he clearly has been successful in appealing to many white voters as well as to blacks. Obama remarked, "I don't have a lot of patience with identity politics, whether it's coming from the right or the left." This impatience includes claims of "colorblindness as a means to deny the structural inequalities" in society and those self-appointed arbiters of African American culture who declare who is and who isn't black enough.[58] Obama argues that his ability to attract widespread support is not due to his race but rather to his ability to make people feel comfortable and to feel that he cares. "That level of empathy is not a consequence of my DNA. It's a consequence of my experience," Obama explained.[59]

CONCLUSION

Today, a number of public officials are part of the Tiger Woods phenomenon. Tiger Woods is a multiracial golf champion, and his background gives him enhanced publicity at country clubs across America. Colin Powell, whose parents were Jamaican immigrants, is also part of this trend. While General Powell is black, he is not a descendent of American slaves. Benjamin Wallace-Wills observed:

> Yet there are a few black politicians for whom their race isn't a ball-and-chain, but a jet engine—the feature that launches them into stardom. For

this small group of black politicians, race has been an advantage because whites see in them confirmation that America, finally, is working. Consequently, all give off the sense that they have transcended traditional racial categories, by signaling in their speech and demeanor, their personal narratives and career achievements, that they fully share in the culture and values of mainstream America; they are able to transcend race through the simple fact of class. Just as importantly, they also transcend ideology by declaring with their rhetoric and policy positions a self-conscious independence from the conventional politics of their parties.[60]

People who fit this description tend to be either products of the military, such as Douglas Wilder and Powell, or were educated at elite universities, such as Harold Ford and Obama. Dealing with the complex intersections of race and ideology is difficult, but Obama shows that it is possible. As Congressman Bobby Rush, a former political rival turned supporter of Obama's presidential bid, mused in an interview with *Newsweek* magazine, "You know, Moses could not have been effective had he not been raised the son of Pharaoh's daughter. Moses had a relationship inside the palace, he knew the ways and wherefores of the palace.... Barack has that capacity to move in and out of privilege and power."[61]

As he entered the Senate, Obama reflected on the exclusive club to which he now belongs, "When you think of the history of the Senate, what is striking is the degree to which this institution has single-handedly blocked the progress of African Americans for much of our history. That's a sad testament to our institution. It's a stain on the institution. I don't perceive now that the battles that are going on in the Senate revolve around race as much as they revolve around economics."[62] During his first two years in the Senate, Obama did not generally emphasize racial issues, with the possible exception of his statements in the aftermath of Hurricane Katrina, discussed in the next chapter. He also has not played a leading role in the Congressional Black Caucus. It appears that he does not want to be seen as the leader of black America. When he spoke at a Congressional Black Caucus reception recently, the senator graciously thanked several caucus leaders by name and then concluded with a short but telling statement: "I'm looking forward to working with you on behalf of all Americans."[63]

CHAPTER SEVEN

Mr. Obama Goes to Washington

Despite his high-profile campaign and celebrity acclaim, Barack Obama arrived in Washington ranked ninety-ninth out of one hundred senators.[1] All eyes were upon him—some expecting brilliance and innovation, others waiting for a blunder to mar his enviable image. As Jeff Zeleny of the *Chicago Tribune* observed, "He will not have the luxury of learning in obscurity."[2] Obama himself commented, "Given all the hype surrounding my election, I hope people have gotten a sense that I am here to do work and not just chase cameras. The collateral benefit is that people really like me. I'm not some prima donna."[3]

Obama's first year was considered low-key by most political observers. He seemed to have taken a page from Senator Hillary Rodham Clinton's book and kept a low, more deferential profile than his fame deemed necessary. He stressed that he was there to learn and quickly made alliances with more senior senators on a variety of issues. Nevertheless, other Democratic senators were quick to capitalize on Obama's fame, using him to raise money and visibility for less well-known candidates, although he admitted to feeling like he was being "used as a prop" at these rallies and news conferences.[4] In addition, his position as the Senate's only African American member and his presidential ambitions may have shaped his agenda. Like any senator, Obama's first tasks were to show he understood the concerns of his state.

ILLINOIS ISSUES

Obama, despite speculation about his presidential ambitions, was always clear about his desire to be a good senator and to represent the people of Illinois. He explained, "I don't think humility is contradictory with ambition. I feel very humble about what I don't know. But I'm plain ambitious in terms of wanting to actually deliver some benefit for the people of Illinois."[5]

He was assigned to three committees: Environment and Public Works, Veterans Affairs, and Foreign Relations. His membership on the first two committees provided a venue for promoting home state concerns. Obama lobbied for a $2.5 billion locks and dams project for Illinois rivers. In another drive for his home state, Obama blocked Environmental Protection Agency nominees until they took a stronger stance on lead paint regulations, which is a prevalent issue in Chicago homes.[6]

He also pushed administration officials for more pay for veterans in Illinois.[7] Obama was appalled to learn that Illinois' disabled veterans received some of the lowest benefits in the country.[8] He and Dick Durbin, the senior senator from Illinois, worked to increase veterans' benefits and were not afraid to speak out against uncooperative Veteran Administration officials. This increased the respect both veterans and other Illinois residents had for Obama.

Overall, his activism for his state has translated into powerful support from Illinois citizens. In a *Tribune*/WGN-TV poll taken during his first year, Obama scored high approval ratings. Obama had a 72 percent approval rating nine months into his term, with Republican respondents giving him a 57 percent approval rating. In May 2005, Obama's approval rating was still high, at 59 percent overall, while 42 percent of Republicans supported his performance as a senator.[9] Obama boasted, "Illinois is serving notice to the rest of the country that Democrats can do well."[10] In 2005, Obama was the most popular senator in the country based on job approval rating by constituents.[11]

Energy costs are always an important issue to voters. Ethanol is a hot issue in Illinois, as the state is a giant producer of corn in this country. Senator Obama proposed legislation to give a tax break to build E85 ethanol fueling stations around the nation.[12] It would be a 30 percent tax credit, providing $30,000 to install E85 pumps. At the time this legislation was proposed, Illinois had six ethanol plants and another one in progress. In 2004, Illinois produced 875 million gallons of E85 using 325 million bushels of corn.[13] Obama promised to keep Illinois issues on his agenda, and this legislation proved he was keeping his word to his constituents. Obama stated, "We've talked too long about energy independence in this country. E85 gives us an opportunity to actually get something done about it."[14]

E85 is made from 85 percent corn-based ethanol and 15 percent gasoline. The war in Iraq made many Americans much more serious about alternative fuel sources. As Obama stated, "If you turn on the news you can see that our dependence on foreign oil is keeping us tied to one of the most dangerous and unstable regions in the world. We need to develop a comprehensive plan to make America energy-independent."[15] Many Americans also see using alternative fuels as a smart way to start competing in the global economy. E85 fuel could be a smart move financially for this country. Obama supported this position, stating, "Now is the opportunity to get this done; not only for the future of our farmers, the future of our economy and the future of our environment, but to make our country a place that is independent and innovative enough to control its own energy future."[16]

The state of Illinois is seen by many political observers as having particularly strong representation. As Senator Ted Kennedy (D-MA) quipped, "Illinois is blessed and the rest of the country is envious. They have the one-two punch in the United States Senate."[17] That "one-two punch" is Senator Dick Durbin, the number two Democrat in the Senate, and Barack Obama. Obama fashioned himself as Durbin's student. Durbin has been a member of the U.S. Senate representing Illinois since 1997. More than half of Illinois voters have a good opinion of him, and he is well respected by other members of Congress.[18] Durbin and Obama meet weekly for "coffee and constituents" meetings while Congress is in session.[19] Working as a team, Durbin and Obama recommended a federal judge to Speaker Dennis Hastert (R-IL). An opening on the Chicago bench created an opportunity for the three Illinois congressmen to act bipartisanly to fill the vacancy.[20]

Obama was a hot ticket on the speakers circuit, with hundreds of requests daily for appearances from him.[21] Obama, keeping Illinois at the forefront, would speak at commencement ceremonies only in his own state during his first year in the Senate. He chose to speak at Knox College in Galesburg, the University of Chicago School of Medicine, and an elementary school on the southwest side of Chicago. Obama's press secretary Julian Green stated simply, "We wanted to make sure that we went to the various parts of Illinois, not just Chicago; including the southern half."[22] Obviously, Obama has since increased his national visibility, giving speeches all across the country as he runs for president.

Obama and Durbin also requested $47.6 million from the Bush administration for low-income families unable to pay their high energy bills during the scorching summer temperatures of 2005.[23] Farmers also received some relief from the heat, as Durbin and Obama requested and obtained federal disaster relief for them.[24] Obama said, "After a summer of extreme heat and drought conditions, I am pleased that the president has granted our request to give hard-working Illinois farmers some much-deserved relief."[25] Obama even attended the Farm Aid concert given to aid Gulf Coast farmers after Hurricane Katrina.[26] Illinois roads were also attended to, with $286.4 billion passing both houses of Congress in the five-year plan of the Transportation Enhancement Act. Of his friend Obama, Dick Durbin has crowed, "Hang on tight, they ain't seen nothing yet."[27]

DOMESTIC ISSUES

Barack Obama's racial identity puts him in a position to be a spokesman on issues related to race and social justice. He continues to emphasize issues he has cared about since his years as a state senator, such as education. More prominently, he has emerged as a leading spokesman on issues of social injustice, such as voting rights and the government's handling of Hurricane Katrina. Obama was an outspoken critic of the federal government's response to Hurricane Katrina. The U.S. Senate is not known for its socioeconomic diversity, and Obama is only the third African American senator since Reconstruction. He was quick to squelch cries of racism as the reason for the slow and inept governmental response to the hurricane's aftermath.[28] Obama blamed "bureaucratic blindness," not racism for the fiasco.[29]

More vocal in his second year, Obama spoke out against the $236 million deal with Carnival Cruise Lines to house displaced victims.[30] Along with Senator Tom Coburn (R-OK), one of the most conservative members of the Senate, Obama publicly asked why this exorbitant amount was given to Carnival when the country of Greece had offered ships as free aid to American victims.[31] The Federal Emergency Management Agency said the deal was signed with Carnival the day before the Greek ships were offered. At the time, these cruise ships sat mostly empty. When they were used, it was to house government workers more than actual evacuees. The last thing these hurricane survivors wanted was a home floating in open water. Obama stated that this "is merely the latest example of poor decision-making from FEMA."[32]

Obama and Coburn proposed legislation to appoint a federal watchdog to oversee reconstruction spending in the wake of Hurricane Katrina. Congress pledged up to $200 billion for this purpose.[33] Of these reconstruction efforts by the Bush administration, Obama stated, "In the immediate aftermath of the hurricane, I think it's important that we don't just assume that George Bush is lying when he says he's finally been awakened to the fact that there is poverty and racism in our midst. It's tempting to do so, especially when he decides to put Karl Rove in charge of reconstruction."[34] Obama, however, did not hold Republicans solely responsible for the incompetence after Hurricane Katrina. He said both parties had an obligation to hold the White House accountable. He shared the blame, confessing, "I share the anger and I share the outrage. But what I also want to do is accept some responsibility.... We've been a little complacent."[35] This accountability included an admission that New Orleans had faced problems for years, and no one had done anything to prevent this tragedy from occurring. Obama said, "I hope we realize that the people of New Orleans weren't just abandoned during the hurricane. They were abandoned long ago to murder and mayhem in the streets, to substandard schools, to dilapidated housing, and inadequate health care, to a pervasive sense of hopelessness."[36]

Obama feels strongly about the importance of education in this country. The first bill he introduced in the Senate was legislation that would increase the maximum dollar amount a recipient of the Pell Grant could receive to $5,100 a year, up from $4,050. He felt that this raise would help low-income students better afford college tuitions.[37] Obama looks at education as a civil rights challenge. This issue is deeply tied to his racial identity, because most of the worst schools are heavily populated with minority students. Outsourcing and globalization are adding to the economic competition for our young people.

American students face new challenges on the home front as well. Television and video games have replaced the pleasure of a good book. As Obama put it, "Our kids aren't just seeing these temptations at home, they're seeing them everywhere. Whether it's their friends' house or the people they see on television or a general culture that glorifies anti-intellectualism, so that we have a president that brags about getting Cs. It trickles down, that attitude."[38] Obama campaigned on improving education as a part of his platform, and upon winning the election, he said, "It's a promise I intend to keep in Washington."[39]

The issue of voters' rights is extremely important to Barack Obama. As an African American, he understands the hardships people for generations have endured to secure the right to vote in the United States. He supported the extension of the Voting Rights Act. He felt that discrimination still exists, and the government must have the proper laws to counteract it. Both Democrats and Republicans supported this extension. Many lawmakers, including Obama, were adamant that federal supervision was still a necessary protection for voting minorities, especially in the southern states.[40] Obama charged that, "Despite the progress these states have made in upholding the right to vote, it is clear the problems still exist."[41]

The importance of voting rights was underscored by another position taken by Senator Obama. The issue was the proposed legislation to require photo identification in order to vote. He opposed this requirement, pointing out that it would adversely affect minorities, the poor, the disabled, and the elderly.[42] Minorities disproportionately lack the funds needed to obtain state identification cards, as do the poorer segments of all races. The elderly and disabled often have difficulty maintaining their identification documents because of lack of transportation. These are people who are likely to vote for the Democratic Party, and this mandatory regulation would adversely affect turnout and obstruct the democratic process.

Obama voted against the "Clear Skies" proposal advanced by the Bush administration. He stated it "would roll back key environmental protections and create new loopholes that could make pollution worse."[43] Obama's vote was one of several key "no" votes against the bill. The bill proposed industry caps on mercury, sulfur dioxide, and nitrogen oxide emissions, but neglected to cap carbon dioxide emissions, the main cause of global warming.[44] Obama asserted that these measures were inadequate and would not protect citizens from air pollution. Senator Lincoln Chaffee (R-RI) lamented, "It's a shame that the United States Congress is the last bastion of denial on climate change."[45]

While most environmental groups are exceedingly pleased with Obama's performance as a senator, some greens are skeptical of his support of liquefied coal as an energy source. Southern Illinois is a major producer of the nation's coal, and many environmentalists believe that it is that, and not the coal itself, that makes this energy source so attractive to the senator. As pointed out previously in this chapter, he is very prone to promoting Illinois' economic interests. Obama stated that liquefied coal is another energy source that can aid in U.S. energy independence. Environmentalists reply that it is still coal, which is a fossil fuel and not a clean-burning energy source.[46]

Along with Senator Jim Bunning (R-KY), Obama endorsed the Coal-to-Liquid Fuel Promotion Act of 2007. This bill supports new research and facilities that would allow coal to be converted to a diesel fuel that has the same emissions rating as gasoline.[47] Some environmentalists see this as a contradiction that they cannot abide. They do not agree that the economic growth this fuel could provide counteracts the environmental damage it would cause. Obama saw his stance as a pragmatic one. Using energy sources from our own country will provide enough economic growth to fund research into cleaner, alternative fuel sources. This position again highlights Obama's willingness to work with both sides of an issue for a satisfactory outcome.

Part of this bipartisan effort included working on ethics reform with Senator John McCain (R-AZ). Obama was assigned this contentious issue by then Senate Minority Leader Harry Reid (D-NV). Reid chose him specifically because of his lack of experience. As an outsider, Obama would have a clearer view of what direction the reformation needed to take. His lack of entrenchment was seen as his greatest asset.[48] The idea of ethics reform was nothing new to Obama. As a state senator, he was instrumental in implementing the first ethics reform measures in the state of Illinois in over twenty-five years.[49] Obama took this cause seriously, and along with Senator Durbin, vowed to no longer accept gifts, meals, or travel from any lobbyists.

Some gifts are acceptable under the current congressional rules, but Obama, in almost biblical fashion, wants to stay away from even the appearance of impropriety.[50] McCain and Obama worked closely together on this issue, and their relationship had its ups and downs. McCain became incensed at Obama for not backing the bipartisan ethics model they had spoken about, but Obama preferred the model his own party endorsed. McCain sent him a letter sharply criticizing this decision and called him "disingenuous."[51] McCain was the first senator to openly criticize Obama, and this did not enhance his own popularity. McCain was seen as unyielding and "grumpy," while Obama was respected for standing up for his beliefs and for treating McCain with respect.[52] "People see John McCain as a prima donna. I think of him as a role model,"[53] said Obama. McCain and Obama quickly reconciled and promised to deliver a plan that was best for America. They jokingly called themselves "pen pals" and continued to support bipartisan reform efforts.[54] Soon, however, they became rivals for the U.S. presidency, as each is vying for his respective party's backing. While he wants to work with Republicans to come up with viable bipartisan solutions, Obama is not afraid to speak his mind when he is in disagreement. "Look, I am a Democrat," he said, "and I believe in the values of the Democratic Party. There are aspects of the Republican agenda that I strongly disagree with, and I won't be afraid to say so."[55]

The great number of Americans without health insurance coverage is a problem Obama sees as devastating for the entire country. He stated, "Today, the greatest single threat to the health of our nation is not a scarcity of genius or a failure of discovery; it is our inability, after years of talk and gridlock, to finally do something about the crushing cost of health care.[56] As an African American, Obama is particularly concerned with the disparities in health between the races. Obama said that people should be discussing "how we are going to close the health disparities gap that exists, and make sure that African American life expectancy is as long as the rest of the nation."[57]

Senator Obama also supported putting health-care records into on-line databases that physicians and other medical personnel can access immediately. No matter where patients are being treated, their entire medical histories can be at their attending doctors' fingertips. Because medical errors cause up to ninety-eight thousand deaths a year in the United States, this type of technology could save countless lives.[58] Experts estimate that this would also save $140 billion per year, which in turn could lower health-care costs.[59] This could go a long way in closing the gap in health-care quality in this country, and Obama believes this to be an essential part of the solution.

Barack Obama teamed up with Senator Richard Lugar (R-IN) and promoted the importance of greater preparation for a possible avian flu outbreak. The U.S. Department of Agriculture was criticized by a bipartisan group of senators for its "failure to develop a comprehensive program to monitor for bird flu."[60] Bird flu is actually common in poultry flocks in the United States. It is the virulent Asian strain that is responsible for the avian flu deaths in human beings. The Asian strain has not been found in the United States, but it is only a matter of time before a disease such as this is able to mutate and spread globally.[61]

Another concern is the insufficient supply of vaccine for the avian flu. Many states are adequately prepared, but several are vulnerable to an outbreak of epic proportions. Officials warned that a bird flu outbreak "could rival or even surpass the 1918 Spanish Flu outbreak that killed 50 million people, including 550,000 in the United States."[62] Senators banded together to recommend that the Bush administration work with the health industry, pharmaceutical companies, and the international community to establish a plan to stem the spread of avian flu and other infectious diseases that affect the entire world population.[63] Obama is unique as a senator due to the fact that he has lived outside of the United States and is the son of an African. He has a global view that sets him apart and shapes his decision-making. He understands that problems that affect other countries can have consequences in the United States.

The most controversial vote Obama cast may be his support of the Class Action Fairness Act of 2005. This bill was heavily endorsed by President George W. Bush and the Republicans. Many pundits were surprised when Obama was one of eighteen Democrats to vote in favor of the legislation.[64] This bill was strongly lobbied for by financial firms, and much of Obama's campaign funding comes from these types of groups. Also, as an attorney, Obama has first-hand knowledge of such suits and their costs. Ken Silverstein said of this vote in the November 2006 issue of *Harper's*:

> He is really not a political warrior by temperament. He is not even, as the word is commonly understood, a liberal. He is in many respects a civic republican—a believer in civic good faith. These concepts are consonant with liberalism in many respects, but since the rise in the 1960s of a more aggressive, rights-based liberalism, which sometimes places particular claims for social justice ahead of a larger universal good, the two versions have existed in some tension.[65]

Obama is able to look past narrow party line voting if he feels it is important.

INTERNATIONAL ISSUES

Obama made headlines with his trip to Africa in August 2006. The trip was designed to highlight U.S. interests in the war-torn, AIDS-crippled continent. Obama said simply, "I'm going because Africa is important."[66] On Obama's agenda were discussions on ending tribal divisions, promoting women's rights, increasing the quality of education, providing more efficient government services, and ending pervasive government corruption.[67] Obama arrived in Africa as a celebrity coming home to his family and to his people. He hoped to use his new-found fame to influence Africans on these issues, but most importantly, to promote AIDS awareness.

AIDS is pervasive in sub-Saharan Africa. Five million people are infected with the HIV virus in South Africa alone. That translates to one in five people, with nine hundred South Africans dying each day from AIDS-related illnesses. The government is exacerbating the problem with its archaic and completely unscientific views on how to deal with the AIDS epidemic. For example, South African president Thabo Mbeki does not believe that HIV leads to AIDS, despite all of the scientific evidence to the contrary. The health minister Manto Tshabalal-Msimang told citizens not to take antiretroviral drugs and instead promoted his own home remedy of "olive oil, beets, lemon, and African potato." Obama, appalled by this lack of knowledge, stated, "The information being provided by the ministry of health is not accurate. It's not scientifically correct."[68]

Not only is the science of AIDS transmission and treatment questioned in South Africa, but testing for the virus is feared and is sometimes thought to actually infect a person with the HIV virus. The stigma carried by those who are infected with HIV is great, and many Africans would rather die than diagnose and treat their illness. To counteract this stigma, Obama and his wife Michelle both received public HIV tests to show that it was nothing to be ashamed of and nothing to fear. Obama sees AIDS as a huge threat to global security. He said, "Now, more than ever, we must care about each other's problems. Not just when there's a missile pointed at us or a dictator on the march, but wherever conditions exist that could give rise to human suffering on a massive scale."[69]

Also on the agenda in Africa were foreign relations with Sudan. As a permanent member of the United Nations Security Council, China was extremely reluctant to sanction the Sudanese government for its laxness in stopping the mass genocide in their country. China is the primary funding source of the Sudanese oil industry, and therefore has a vested interest in keeping in good standing with the Sudanese government.[70] Obama blasted, "Unfortunately, our foreign policy seems to be focused on yesterday's rather than anticipating the crises of the future. Africa is not perceived as a direct threat to U.S. security at the moment, so the foreign policy apparatus tends to believe that it can be safely neglected. I think that's a mistake."[71]

Obama teamed with Senator Richard Lugar, then the chairman of the Foreign Relations Committee, to create legislation that would add conventional weapons, such as shoulder-fired missiles and abandoned land mines, to the Cooperative Threat Reduction Program.[72] This program is over ten years old, and with Lugar at the helm it has worked to eliminate nuclear weapons in Russia. Obama and Lugar were very concerned that these easily transferred conventional weapons were not included in the program. Obama stated, "We've all seen how it could take far less time for these weapons to leak out and travel around the world, fueling insurgencies and violent conflicts from Africa to Afghanistan. By destroying these inventories, this is one place we would be making more of a difference."[73]

Obama and Lugar traveled to Russia in August 2005 to inspect nuclear weapons sites. The security at these sites is lax, and this is a very unsafe situation. Nuclear, chemical, and biological weapons are poorly guarded, so Russia allowed three U.S. inspections. The goal of these inspections was to promote more specialized training, encourage closer oversight, and increase awareness of the actual contents of these sites.[74] This trip to Russia constituted Obama's first foreign trip as a senator. Traveling with Lugar, who has visited Russia many times, proved to be a learning experience for the junior senator. He stated, "I very much feel like the novice and pupil. I'm spending most of my time listening as opposed to trying to interject myself into the process."[75]

The tours of the nuclear sites were eye-opening for Obama. Seeing dangerous weapons so improperly guarded reinforced that this was an issue that needed to be in the forefront. He mused, "People can sort of put it off, and it's not confronting you day-to-day in an immediate sort of way. The consequence of inaction can be enormous, but I think it's one of those issues where until it's too late, you don't see a problem."[76] The tour of Russia was not all doomsday predictions, however. When touring Lenin's tomb and learning that many of the women buried near the tomb were the dictator's lovers, Obama quipped, "I didn't know Lenin was a player."[77]

Leaving Russia proved to be a challenge for the U.S. delegation. Lugar and Obama, along with twelve other Americans, were detained at the airport by Russian border officials. International law as well as a non-search agreement between the United States and Russia states that official aircraft do not need to be searched. The border officials insisted on a search anyway, which was vehemently opposed by U.S. military pilots. Airport officials confiscated the Americans' passports and papers.

A standoff ensued, and both Washington and Moscow became involved in the incident. Three hours passed, time that Lugar and Obama utilized for a nap, and the issue was finally resolved. Passports and official documents were returned. One Russian guard even apologized. The media had a field day with the incident, but Obama wanted the reason for the visit to stay at the forefront. "It's one thing to be able to describe what I've seen. You realize as a senator there are so many issues out there tugging on people, you've got to make things vivid for them in order to capture people's attention."[78]

VOTING RECORD

As discussed elsewhere, Obama had a liberal reputation as an Illinois state senator, which he tried to moderate somewhat during the general election campaign. Tables 7-1 and 7-2 lay out his voting record for his first Senate term. Table 7-1 shows his ranking from selected interest groups, and Table 7-2 shows his *National Journal* composite rankings, as well as his score on economic, foreign, and social policy. The tables clearly show that Obama has compiled a liberal voting record as a

Table 7-1 Obama Voting Record Rating

Interest Group	Year of Rating	Percentage Rating or Grade
National Right to Life Committee	2005–2006	0
National Federation of Independent Business	2005–2006	12
U.S. Chamber of Commerce	2005	39
American Civil Liberties Union	2005–2006	83
National Association for the Advancement of Colored People	2005	100
National Education Association	2005	100
League of Conservation Voters	2005	95
U.S. Public Interest Research Group	2006	86
National Rifle Association	2004	F
Service Employees International Union	2006	94
United Auto Workers	2005	93
American Federation of State, County, and Municipal Employees	2005	100
Americans for Democratic Action	2005	100
NETWORK, A National Catholic Social Justice Lobby	2005	100
Disabled American Veterans	2006	80

Source: Project Vote Smart. http://votesmart.org/issue_rating_category.php?can_id=BS030017. March 5, 2007.

Table 7-2   Obama *National Journal* Rankings for 2005

Composite Liberal Score	More Liberal than 83% of Senators
Liberal on Social Policy	More Liberal than 77% of Senators
Liberal on Economic Policy	More Liberal than 87% of Senators
Liberal on Foreign Policy	More Liberal than 76% of Senators
Composite Conservative Score	More Conservative than 18% of Senators
Conservative on Social Policy	More Conservative than 18% of Senators
Conservative on Economic Policy	More Conservative than 12% of Senators
Conservative on Foreign Policy	More Conservative than 15% of Senators

Source: Project Vote Smart. http://votesmart.org/issue_rating_category.php?can_id= BS030017. March 5, 2007.

senator. He receives low ratings from traditionally Republican sectors such as right-to-life groups, business interests, and gun rights lobbyists. In turn, Obama receives high marks from the more liberal sectors such as pro-choice groups, minority interest groups, education interests, and conservationists. The *National Journal* numbers clearly show that Obama is in the most liberal quintile of senators.

Senator Obama has shown himself to be a dedicated representative of the people who elected him. Upon entering office, he repeatedly claimed that he would serve his full senate term and would not be a presidential candidate in 2008. This turned out to be false, when on February 10, 2007, in Springfield, Illinois, Obama announced his candidacy to thousands of freezing, but jubilant, fans. While there is no particular reason to suspect that these promises were not sincere at the time, it is evident that from the beginning of his senate term he positioned himself for a presidential run at some point. He remarked, "There's a large gap between the power that I'll wield in Washington and the enormous needs that I see in Illinois, such as health care, lack of well-paying jobs, and need for educational reform. What I do expect to be able to accomplish is where there are issues that everyone agrees need to be worked on, I'll be able to insinuate myself into the debate and see that voices that otherwise would be left behind are introduced into those negotiations."[79] He has established strong credentials on foreign affairs, especially with respect to nuclear disarmament. He also emphasized two other issues: health care, which is likely to be among the most important domestic policy concerns in the 2008 election, and the environment, which is particularly important to Democratic presidential primary voters.

CHAPTER EIGHT

"There Is No Red or Blue America": Obama's Message

D espite a distrust of rhetoric and a preference for action over words in American culture, political speech and writing have had a profound influence on American history. For example, Lincoln's Gettysburg Address helped redefine the country from a plural collection of states to a singular nation and elevated the importance of equality in the national consciousness.[1] Franklin Roosevelt's first two inaugural addresses set a domestic policy agenda that would endure for at least fifty years, while his second two greatly influenced U.S. foreign policy after World War II.[2] Parts of William Jennings Bryan's famous 1896 "Cross of Gold" speech, which inspired Democratic National Convention delegates with its oratory on behalf of populist farmers, were recycled nearly one hundred years later by an actor at the first Farm Aid concert.[3] Undoubtedly it is premature to lump Obama with the major historical figures above, but his emerging reputation as an orator justifies an examination of his rhetoric. The ecstatic reaction to his 2004 Democratic National Convention address, where his impact on political speeches was compared to Marlon Brando's on acting after "A Streetcar Named Desire," suggests that some day he may deserve to be on the list above.[4]

This chapter examines Obama's message, primarily through his speeches, but also in a few cases through his writings. Three important themes will be examined: his view of the American Dream, his calls for political reform and uplifting the tone of political debate, and his post-partisan stance. In each case, we will show how he has developed his ideas in speeches and writing and consider whether his message will resonate with voters in the future, including his 2008 presidential bid.

OBAMA'S VIEW OF THE AMERICAN DREAM

Some of the most memorable and powerful political rhetoric in American history relates to defining and interpreting the "American Dream." This concept refers to the idea that the United States is a "Land of Opportunity," where success depends on hard work, not one's place in a rigid class system. In 1993, President Clinton explained it as the idea that "if you work hard and play by the rules, you should be given the chance to go as far as your God-given ability will take you."[5] As such, it rests on beliefs in individualism and free enterprise. Republicans and Democrats differ somewhat in their basic interpretations of the American Dream, with the former emphasizing the frontier and cowboy metaphors and the latter the immigrant experience in teeming cities.[6] President Reagan was particularly adept at communicating the GOP version, which stresses the role of individual initiative and limited government in promoting economic growth, but also touches on communitarian themes such as volunteerism. He encapsulated the individualistic and materialistic perspective on the American Dream in a 1983 press conference, where he said, "what I want to see above all is that this country remains a country where someone can always get rich."[7]

Directly challenging the ideas of classlessness and meritocracy that underpin the belief in the American Dream is usually political dynamite. Thus, few politicians take this dare, absent a national crisis such as the Great Depression. A notable exception is 1984 Democratic National Convention keynote speaker Mario Cuomo, who attacked President Reagan's vision. He argued that the president's emphasis on individualism and materialism led to policies that favored the rich and strong, leaving many unable to attain the American Dream.[8] Without overstating the role of convention rhetoric on elections, Reagan's landslide victory in 1984 suggests that his vision of the American Dream trumped Cuomo's critique. In 1990, Paul Wellstone won a U.S. Senate seat in Minnesota challenging the "fable" of a classless society where individual merit determined one's station in society.[9] Clearly, his success while pushing this message is exceptional, however.

Allusions to the American Dream pervade Obama's speeches, including, of course, his 2004 Democratic National Convention keynote address. The phrase even appears in the subtitle of his 2006 book *The Audacity of Hope*. Obama does not attack the idea's mainstream, individualistic interpretation head-on. Instead, he pays homage to this view, while trying to persuade people that a commitment to the values of community and equality underlie the American Dream. In his convention speech, he noted how his father's "hard work and perseverance" allowed him to study in a "magical place, America, that shone as a beacon of freedom and opportunity to so many who had come before."[10]

Elsewhere, he has said that "if you're willing to work hard in this country of American dreamers, the sky is the limit on what you can achieve."[11] He sometimes uses himself as an example, citing his journey from obscurity and near penury to fame between the Democratic National Conventions of 2000 and 2004. At the former, he had just lost to Bobby Rush in his bid for Congress and had his credit card initially rejected when trying to rent a car at the Los Angeles airport. At the 2004 convention, of course, he had achieved a much more exalted status. In a commencement speech at the University of Massachusetts at Boston, he concluded this tale by saying, "But of course, America is an unlikely place—a country built on defiance of the odds; on a belief in the impossible. And I remind you of this, because as you set out to live your own stories of success and achievement, it's now your turn to help keep it this way."[12]

As the quote above suggests, Obama's vision of the American Dream transcends individualism and economic success, implying that each of us has an obligation to keep the dream alive for everyone. In his many commencement addresses, he almost always calls on graduates to look beyond wealth as a measure of the success of their lives. For example, in his 2005 address to the graduating class of Knox College, he told them, "You can take your diploma, walk off this stage, and go chasing after a big house, and the nice suits, and all the other things that our money culture says you can buy. But I hope you don't. Focusing your life on making a buck shows a poverty of ambition. It asks too little of yourself."[13]

Although he acknowledges the importance of individual initiative and capitalism in America's success, he also argues that they are meaningless without a sense of mutual responsibility and guarantees of equal opportunity.[14] He contends that an excessive commitment to individualism as a public philosophy undermines the ability of some to achieve the American Dream. One of his strongest statements on the limits of individualism and self-reliance as a world view came after the Hurricane Katrina disaster in 2005, when he argued that this perspective doomed New Orleans' poor to unnecessary suffering. "Whoever was in charge of planning and preparing for the worst-case scenario appeared to assume that every American has the capacity to load up their family in an SUV, fill it up with $100 worth of gasoline, stick some bottled water in the trunk, and use a credit card to check into a hotel."[15]

More broadly, he rejects President Bush's notion of the "ownership society" as excessively individualistic. In his speech to Knox College graduates, he criticized the president and other conservatives for over-emphasizing the roles of individual initiative and personal freedom in nurturing the American Dream. He argued that, without its other foundations, community and equality, Americans are likely to struggle to meet the challenges of the global economy. Speaking of the threat to American living standards, he charged:

> There are those who believe that there isn't much we can do about this as a nation. That the best idea is to give everyone one big refund on their government—divvy it up into individual portions, hand it out, and encourage everyone to use their share to buy their own health care, their own individual retirement plan, their own child care, education, and so forth. In Washington they call this the Ownership Society. But in our past there has been another term for it—Social Darwinism, every man and woman for him or herself. It's a tempting idea, because it doesn't require much thought or ingenuity. It allows us to say to those whose health care or tuition may rise faster than they can afford—tough luck. It allows us to say to the Maytag workers who have lost their job—life isn't fair. It lets us say to the child born into poverty—pull yourself up by your bootstraps.... But there's a problem. It won't work. It ignores our history. It ignores the fact that it has been government research and investment that made the railways and the internet possible. It has been the creation of a massive middle class, through decent wages and benefits and public schools that has allowed us to prosper. Our economic dominance has depended on individual initiative and belief in the free market; but it has also depended on our sense of mutual regard for each other, the idea that everybody has a stake in the country, that we're all in it together, and everybody's got a shot at opportunity—that has produced our unrivaled political stability.[16]

The passage above shows how Obama connects the ideas of community and equality to the American Dream. Communitarian values provide a foundation and egalitarian beliefs insure that all can attain it. Thus, Obama sees individualism, community, and equality as woven together in the fabric of the American Dream. Because the latter concepts have been less prominent in recent political rhetoric, however, it is worthwhile considering how Obama views them individually.

The communitarian tradition in American life competes with, and sometimes complements, the more obvious individualistic strains.[17] Communitarianism rejects the idea of people as atomistic individuals, viewing us instead as social beings who need a sense of belonging and a shared moral framework that we find in political activity.[18] Often nongovernmental institutions such as churches or civic clubs are viewed as particularly important to fostering healthy communities. Participation in public life and deliberation about common problems help individuals mature into citizens who become aware of the mutual obligation between society and its members. Part of this awareness involves understanding the balance between rights and responsibilities and realizing that the former are rarely absolute if their exercise harms society as a whole. Admittedly there is a more negative strain of communitarianism in American life, which Obama does not stress, that promotes "the repressive side of American ethnocentrism."[19]

Obama's own communitarian ideals stem, at least in part, from his work as a community organizer. Initially somewhat standoffish, as he developed deeper relationships within the communities he was trying to organize, he learned that people's self-narrative, originating in the struggles they or their loved ones had faced in their lives, shaped their political perspectives as much as narrow self-interest.[20] Close calls with illness or watching a family member struggle with their problems led people to community involvement more than the desire for an immediate political payoff.

Reflecting communitarian sentiments, he often speaks of how Americans should view and treat each other, particularly emphasizing the importance of empathy. In a commencement address at Xavier University in New Orleans, he discussed the idea of caring for others in the community. "You know, there's a lot of talk in this country about the federal deficit. But I think we should talk more about our empathy deficit—the ability to put ourselves in someone else's shoes, to see the world through the eyes of those who are different from us—the child who's hungry, the steelworker who's been laid-off, the family who lost the entire life they built together when the storm came to town."[21]

His communitarian bent sometimes leads him to advocate positions at odds with traditional liberal policy approaches. For example, his experience working with churches as a community organizer led him to conclude that faith-based approaches to solving social problems are often more effective than government initiatives, because they reflect a deeper understanding of human experience. In a widely covered speech on the relationship between religion and politics, he argued that although gun control laws are necessary, "when a gang-banger shoots indiscriminately into a crowd because he feels somebody has disrespected him, we've got a moral problem. There's a hole in that young man's heart—a hole that government alone cannot fix."[22] He made a similar argument regarding AIDS prevention in a speech to southern California evangelicals. While emphasizing that condoms played a key role in fighting the disease, he also stressed the "spiritual component to prevention" and the idea that "the relationship between men and women, between sexuality and spirituality has broken down and needs to be repaired."[23] He notes that historically black churches are especially able to foster social change, because of their deep roots in the experiences of a particular community. "Because of its past, the black church understands in an intimate way the Biblical call to feed the hungry and clothe the naked and challenge powers and principalities."[24]

Like others on the so-called "religious left," he has challenged other Democrats to take religion's role in the public sphere more seriously, rather than hiding behind concerns about separation of church and state. He points to leaders of the past, including Frederick Douglass,

Abraham Lincoln, Martin Luther King, Dorothy Day, and Williams Jennings Bryan, who were motivated by faith and used religious language to argue for change. At the same time, he warns that public policy cannot be justified solely on religious grounds, but must be subject to argument and reason. He argues that opponents of abortion, for example, must "explain why abortion violates some principle that is accessible to people of all faiths, including those with no faith at all."[25]

When promoting the communitarian idea of balancing rights and responsibilities, Obama once again acknowledges the individualistic component of the American Dream, while pointing out its limits. For example, he argues that while society has an obligation to make the American Dream attainable, individuals must make the most of their opportunities. In speaking about the challenges facing the country in a global economy, he posed the following questions to his audience. "Can we honestly say our kids are working twice as hard as the kids in India and China who are graduating ahead of us, with better test scores and the tools they need to kick our butts on the job market? Can we honestly say our teachers are working twice as hard, or our parents?"[26] In a somewhat different vein, Obama stresses the limits of individualism when he criticizes the irresponsible use of the right of freedom of expression. He argues that "a mass media culture that saturates our airwaves with a steady stream of sex, violence, and materialism" threatens American culture.[27] This support of a balance between rights and responsibilities allows Obama to challenge traditional liberalism in a politically effective fashion, reminiscent of Bill Clinton's "third way" approaches.

In addition to his message of community, Obama also emphasizes that the American Dream involves a commitment to equality. Although less central to the American ethos than individualism, and often violated historically, the egalitarian ideal has been an element in the American creed since the Declaration of Independence. This value has been central to Obama's message since his primary campaign, where his rhetoric promoted the idea that Americans regardless of race, ethnicity, faith, and income are bound by a common human decency.[28] In his primary election night victory speech, he linked the belief in equality to the mission of the Democratic party: "At its best, the idea of this party has been that we are going to expand opportunity and include people that have not been included, that we are going to give a voice to the voiceless, and power to the powerless, and embrace people from the outside and bring them inside, and give them a piece of the American dream."[29] He argues that when luck and accidents of birth determine life outcomes, it undermines the American Dream. Instead, he contends that Americans must "build a community where, at the very least, everyone has the chance to work hard, get ahead, and reach their dreams."[30]

To translate this belief into practice, he has advocated more egalitarian public policies in areas ranging from health care to bankruptcy reform. On the latter, he argued on the Senate floor for treating rich and poor equally. "If we're going to crack down on bankruptcy abuse, we should make it clear that we intend to hold the wealthy and powerful accountable, too.... What kind of message does it send when we tell hardworking, middle-class Americans, 'You have to be more responsible with your finances, but the corporations you work for can be as irresponsible as they want with theirs?'"[31] In a similar vein, he has at times argued for European-style social policies, such as paid leave for women after they have babies.[32] He has criticized the repeal of the estate tax for disconnecting the economic fates of people in different social classes, arguing, "once your drapes cost more than the average American's yearly salary, then you can afford to pay a bit more in taxes."[33]

He often speaks of equality in connection with the role that public education plays in supporting the American Dream. He notes that the government has promoted equality of opportunity through the system of free public high schools and the GI Bill. He quotes approvingly Thomas Jefferson's declaration that "talent and virtue needed in a free society, should be educated regardless of wealth, birth or other accidental condition."[34] Current inequalities in education stemming from funding differences undermine this ideal, Obama contends. In a speech on education he claimed that "in too many places, kids are going to school in trailers where rats are more numerous than computers."[35] In the same speech, he cites reports of a Los Angeles high school that offers students two levels of hairstyling courses, but does little to prepare them for college.[36] His emphasis on the role of education in promoting equality reflects a canny understanding of its more fundamental relationship to the American Dream. In contrast to its history of being a laggard in creating most social programs, the United States has been a policy and spending leader on public education. This commitment reflects the American view that it is the government's responsibility to provide opportunity for citizens to achieve an appropriate standard of living, rather than to guarantee a livelihood for all, a view more prevalent in Europe.[37]

Obama's themes of the importance of equality and community come together as he discusses the global economy's challenges to the American Dream. He contends that while globalization threatens to create economic stagnation that undermines the American Dream, it also presents the opportunity to revitalize it. In his speeches he often points out that the competition and mobility that the global economy creates increases the importance of skills in determining individual success. He notes that workers in Illinois are competing with those in China and India, while those countries are upgrading their educational systems, especially in math, science, and technical areas.[38] This leads him to conclude that collective action and not just individual competitiveness is necessary to keep the American Dream alive. Therefore, he believes that government must step in to make the United States more competitive, through upgrading education, making college more affordable, increasing funding for job retraining for laid-off workers, and making scientific research a top priority. He also calls for a safety net to protect against the rough edges of the global economy by guaranteeing health insurance and pensions.[39] Promoting this agenda, he argues, will lead the Democratic party to become the party of opportunity and the American Dream.[40]

We now turn to the question of whether Obama's vision of the American Dream will resonate with the public. At some level, this message has been successful, helping him win his senate seat and putting him in great demand as a speaker. Concerns about the future of the American Dream are also particularly relevant as Americans struggle to adapt to the global economy. A poll taken by Opinion Research in October 2006 revealed that a slight majority (54 percent) thought that the American Dream had become impossible for most people to achieve.[41] These results contrast with surveys taken in the 1950s and 1980s showing that 70 percent or more of the public thought the American Dream was attainable.[42]

Still, the egalitarian and communitarian values that Obama advocates may not mesh with the centrality of individualism and freedom in the American belief system.[43] It's not that equality and community have no significance for Americans. The commitment to equality motivated the Progressive Movement of a century ago, which saw government power as a way to address the inequities of capitalism, not to mention Jacksonian Democracy, the New Deal, and the Civil Rights movement.[44] The belief in community shaped America's founding, as well as paving the way for post–World War II prosperity.[45] Nevertheless, it is hard to dispute that economic individualism has been a dominant value since at least the 1980s. Contemporary polls show that Americans are much more attached to political equality than its economic component, especially compared to citizens in other advanced democracies.[46] Furthermore, Americans generally tend to be optimistic, even unrealistically so, about their own economic prospects. Thus, they are not inclined to accept appeals to redistribute income.[47] Moreover, Obama's calls for government action to solve problems, especially those related to inequality in areas like health care, conflict with widespread antigovernment beliefs that prevail in the United States.[48]

Obama seems to have recognized that there are limits to how much public sector activity the public will accept. Thus, he stresses his openness to nongovernmental means to solving social problems, including market- and faith-based approaches.[49] He also tries to root his appeals to equality and community in U.S. history, perhaps to make them more palatable, thus providing his listeners with a narrative that connects current policy conundrums with past efforts to resolve them. In a speech to the American Federation of State, County, and Municipal Employees national convention, he noted that today's workers wonder whether their children will have a better future, be able to afford college and retirement, and avoid losing their jobs. He placed these concerns in historical context, comparing them to the problems facing sanitation workers in Memphis in the 1960s who acted collectively and successfully, despite arrests, police brutality, and, ultimately the assassination of Martin Luther King.[50] In another speech, he described how the efforts of meatpackers to organize in the 1930s also promoted visions of community and equality.

> Imagine—these people would slave away in these plants all day long, freezing in the winter and sweltering in the summer, watching coworkers get their bones crushed in machines and friends get fired for even uttering the word "union"—and yet after they punched their card at the end of the day they organized. They went to meetings and they passed out leaflets. They put aside decades of ethnic and racial tension and elected women, African Americans, and immigrants to leadership positions so that they could speak with one voice.[51]

He notes that he shares the belief in government action with revered historical figures such as Abraham Lincoln, who promoted government-sponsored scientific research, infrastructure spending, and higher education to nurture the American Dream.[52]

In addition to grounding them historically, he packages the egalitarian elements of his message in a way that makes them more appealing. For example, as noted above, he emphasizes equality in the context of education, an issue that has an intimate connection to the American Dream. He also advocates policies that achieve egalitarian ends by serving all social classes, such as parental leave or universal health care, rather than advocating explicit income redistribution or programs targeted to the poor. He qualifies his support for affirmative action by noting, "an emphasis on universal, as opposed to race-specific, programs isn't just good policy; it's also good politics."[53] The widespread public acceptance of broadly targeted programs in the past, such as social security, in contrast to, say, Aid for Dependent Children, suggests that this emphasis is politically astute. In a more politically risky vein, perhaps, he defends immigration in the context of the American Dream, arguing that immigrants reflect the classic American story of "ambition and adaptation, hard work and education, assimilation and upward mobility."[54]

In sum, Obama's rhetoric challenges assumptions about individualism and the role of government that have been fairly prevalent since the tax revolt of the late 1970s. Nevertheless, he packages his message carefully and does not offer the kind of head-on challenge that, say, the late Senator Paul Wellstone did when he called more forcefully for policies that would redistribute income. In fact, his current rhetoric contrasts somewhat with his record as a state senator, when he pushed for more explicitly redistributive programs. Still, given the fact that egalitarian sentiments appeal to Americans more during times of relative crisis, his caution is probably astute.

POLITICAL REFORM AND IMPROVING THE QUALITY OF POLITICAL DEBATE

Since his days in the Illinois state senate, Obama has positioned himself as a political reformer. He has continued in this role in his first term as a U.S. Senator, becoming the point man for Democrats on ethics reform. As part of this effort, he has criticized the role of money and connections in politics. He has called the necessity of fundraising the "original sin" of everyone who's run for political office, leading politicians to spend an inordinate amount of time with lobbyists and the wealthy, while ignoring the concerns of the less affluent, such as Americans without health insurance.[55] Along somewhat similar lines, he has criticized the Bush administration for giving billions of dollars tax breaks to oil companies with powerful lobbyists, while underfunding alternative energy proposals.[56]

His reformist bent is not limited to institutional reform, however, as he has advocated broader efforts to improve the tone and quality of political discourse. As discussed in chapter 3, he often emphasized this theme in his general election campaign, when he criticized Alan Keyes for negative campaigning, misleading rhetoric, and ignoring bread-and-butter issues that were fundamental to voters.[57] Damning negative campaigning is, of course, politically advantageous for a candidate with a forty-point lead in the polls. When Obama was less well known, his rhetoric sometimes had a harder edge. For example, in a 2002 anti–Iraq War speech that fueled his support among liberals, he called presidential adviser Karl Rove a "political hack" and dismissed other prominent administration figures as "armchair warriors."[58] His 2000 congressional opponent Bobby Rush also accused Obama of running misleading radio ads that lied about his opponent's record.[59]

In fairness, his few forays into negativity pale in comparison to the tone of much contemporary, or even historical, campaign rhetoric. Furthermore, Obama rarely used negative attacks, even when he was far behind in the primary race. In any event, his Democratic National Convention speech pointedly criticized campaign consultants who foster divisions among Americans. More recently, he has argued that a divided public plays into the hands of antigovernment conservatives, because "a polarized electorate that is turned off to politics and easily dismisses both parties because of the nasty tone of the debate works perfectly well for those who seek to chip away at the very idea of government, because, in the end, a cynical electorate is a selfish electorate."[60]

In Washington, he has, quoting his predecessor Senator Paul Simon, called for politicians to "disagree without being disagreeable," arguing that "the American people sent us here to be their voice. They understand that those voices can at times become loud and argumentative, but ... they expect both parties to work together and get the people's business done."[61] As such, he has often tried to separate personal and policy disagreements. For example, in a speech criticizing President Bush's plans to privatize programs such as social security and the public schools, he gave the president at least a back-handed compliment. "I don't think George Bush is a bad man. I think he loves his country. I don't think this administration is full of stupid people—I think there are a lot of smart folks in there. The problem isn't that their philosophy isn't working the way it's supposed to—it's that it is."[62] Similarly, in criticizing the Bush administration's efforts to enhance the president's power to fight terrorism, he said that he disagrees with the president's interpretation of the Constitution, without "doubting his sincerity."[63]

Connecting institutional and rhetorical reforms, he has denounced the "game" of politics as it is currently played in Washington. He contends that the obsession with how a party's or individual's political standing is helped or hurt by a particular event or decision undermines the ability to have a serious debate on issues like climate change or health care. In a speech on the latter issue, he noted, "we just spent three weeks arguing over the filibuster, but I can count on one hand the number of times we've talked about health care since I was sworn in last January. Yet, when I come back here and talk to families in Illinois, that's all they tell me about."[64] This same dynamic, in Obama's view, leads to an inordinate focus on issues that have political traction with a portion of the electorate, such as the constitutional amendment banning gay marriage. His most pointed criticisms in this realm have come on the Iraq issue. In a speech to the Chicago Council on Foreign Relations, he chastised the Bush administration for conducting a "political war—a war of talking points and Sunday news shows and spin" that detracts from "a pragmatic solution to the real war we're facing in Iraq."[65] In the same speech, he criticized the administration for trivializing the debate about the war by forcing it into two over-simplified options: "stay the course" or "cut and run."

To improve the tone of political debate, he calls for self-examination, doubt, and awareness of one's own fallibility. A notable aspect of his

July 2006 speech on the role of religion in politics is his emphasis on his own mistakes. He expressed regret for not adequately defending his own faith in the face of Alan Keyes's charge that Jesus wouldn't vote for Obama and for not speaking of abortion in "fair-minded words."[66] In an interview after the speech, he elaborated the idea of reconsidering and questioning one's premises. "I think the advantage that progressives and Democrats have is that we have the facts on our side ... and if we are willing to tolerate ambiguity and dissent in our own camp, and if we're willing to look critically at ourselves, and reflect and remain open-minded to other points of view, over time that's where the American people are."[67]

Somewhat paradoxically, he calls for a bolder and more visionary politics, citing political leaders of the past, such as Abraham Lincoln, Theodore Roosevelt, Martin Luther King, and Robert Kennedy. "It's the timidity of our politics that's holding us back right now—the politics of can't-do and oh-well. An energy crisis that jeopardizes our security and our economy? No magic wand to fix it, we're told. Thousands of jobs vanishing overseas? It's actually healthier for the economy that way. Three days late to the worst natural disaster in American history? Brownie, you're doing a heck of a job."[68] Ultimately, he sees the failure of politics to address the concerns of ordinary Americans as a threat to the American Dream. In a speech at the Emily's List Annual Luncheon, he said, "Americans ... still believe in an America where anything's possible— they just don't think their leaders do. These are Americans who still dream big dreams—they just sense their leaders have forgotten how."[69]

Once again, we turn to the question of whether this message will resonate. It is hard to go wrong criticizing politicians and Washington, given widespread beliefs that the U.S. political system is broken. Criticism alone can be a bad move for progressive politicians, however, as it can delegitimize the very institutions they need to accomplish anything. Thus, Obama must walk a fine line when pushing for reforms because the critiques that justify the improvements may make voters more cynical. Hence, as discussed above, while criticizing contemporary politics, he also criticizes the critics who would only tear down existing institutions. While in some respects he resembles the leaders of the Progressive Movement of a century ago, he seems to recognize that the procedural reforms of that era, such as direct democracy through the initiative, have a mixed legacy. In fact, this may be why Obama himself spends more time talking about improving the "tone" of politics than about procedural reforms. In his book *The Audacity of Hope*, he writes approvingly of reforms like public financing of campaigns or changing archaic Senate rules. Nevertheless, he notes that real improvements in the current state of politics require political courage more than procedural tinkering.[70]

Obama's efforts to refocus political debate on bread-and-butter issues is likely to appeal to many centrist voters who are tired of narrow political appeals to a small base of voters and who don't consider morality issues a top concern. The question is whether the public will really pay attention. Americans have gotten used to emotional appeals that dramatize politics and politicians who "appeal to their vanity rather than speak to their needs."[71] In his Senate campaign, Obama called for a more engaged citizenry, and people seemed to respond, but it is not clear whether the public can break its addiction to political junk food.

Obama's emphasis on fallibility and doubt, while appealing as a human quality, may be too complex in the contemporary political environment and may tarnish his image as a leader. The nuances of his rhetoric and his willingness to accept different points of view may make it seem as if he is not resolute enough to be an effective leader, at least as that has been defined in the public mind in the post-9/11 era. Some pundits have noted the negative connotations of his reputation for thoughtfulness. For example, in analyzing Obama's 2006 book *The Audacity of Hope, Time* magazine writer Joe Klein complained, "I counted no fewer than 50 instances of excruciatingly judicious on-the-one-hand-on-the-other-handedness...."[72] On the other hand (pun intended), this style may be a welcome change from the inflexibility of the Bush administration.

POST-PARTISAN POLITICAL THINKING

During his time as a state senator, although known as open-minded, Obama had the reputation as a "darling of the Democratic Party's liberal wing."[73] In his primary campaign, Obama promised to "act like a Democrat" if he were elected, and early in the general election race he fended off attacks from Republicans that he was too liberal. While he was in the race, Republican candidate Jack Ryan's campaign disseminated widely a comment by Republican State Senator Steve Rauschenberger that Obama was "to the left of Mao Tse-Tung.[74]

Later, he adopted a more nonideological vision, arguing that the political debates of the 1960s, which shape Republican and Democratic thinking even today, present false "either/or" choices when applied to contemporary policy issues.[75] In his Democratic National Convention speech, he famously stressed that "there is not a liberal America and a conservative America—there is a United States of America."[76] In the Senate, he has often advocated (and practiced) bipartisanship, working with Republicans on issues like immigration reform, improving government contracting practices, and energy policy. With respect to the latter, he has called for market-based solutions involving tax credits, often favored by Republicans, rather than the more traditional Democratic approach involving regulation.[77] In a similar light, he has expressed skepticism that new programs or new bureaucracies alone will solve the country's problems.

In an interview with the *American Prospect* magazine, he was asked to define himself as a liberal, progressive, or centrist. His answer was that "I like to think that I'm above it. Only in the sense that I don't like how the categories are set up." He later added, "I share all the aims of Paul Wellstone or Ted Kennedy when it comes to the end result. But I'm much more agnostic, much more flexible on how we achieve those ends."[78] In a sense, he rejects the very concept of ideology, arguing that it leads people to ignore facts that contradict their theoretical assumptions.[79] He has cited Robert Kennedy as a political role model for combining moralism and pragmatism in politics in a way that was both "hard-headed and big-hearted."[80]

While criticizing the Bush administration for politicizing issues like Iraq and gay marriage to promote political ends over good policy, he has taken his own party to task for being blinded by ideology as well. For instance, he has charged that left-wing Democrats are becoming too intolerant of any deviation from the party line, such as supporting John Roberts to be Chief Justice of the Supreme Court. He argues that most of the country views the world in a "nonideological lens," and that Americans "don't think that George Bush is mean-spirited or prejudiced, but have become aware that his administration is irresponsible and often incompetent."[81] "To the degree that we brook no dissent within the Democratic Party, and demand fealty to the one 'true' progressive vision for the country, we risk the very thoughtfulness and openness to new ideas that are required to move the country forward."[82] Still, he has warned against a centrism that simply seeks middle-of-the-road approaches or compromise for its own sake.[83] Although he sees conventional political ideologies as a restraint, simply splitting the difference does little to promote better policies.

This message is likely to resonate with ordinary voters, who appear to be tired of excessive partisanship. Clearly, it is less likely to appeal to partisan Democrats, who are angry over the Iraq War and the Bush administration in general. Critics on the left have questioned Obama's support for Connecticut Senator Joe Lieberman, rather than his 2006 anti–Iraq War Democratic primary opponent Ned Lamont. Similarly, his vote for the reauthorization of the USA Patriot Act, and his support for centrist Democratic Senators through contributions from his political action committee have upset many in the liberal "base." One of his most vociferous critics on the left, Alexander Cockburn of the *Nation* magazine, wrote, "What a slimy fellow Obama is, as befits a man symbolizing everything that will continue to be wrong with the Democratic party for the next twenty years."[84] His more sophisticated critics on the left, while critical of Obama's apparent move to the center, realize that, given the cost of contemporary campaigns, it is impossible to both win elections and promote dissenting views in the Senate.[85]

More generally, the connection that many people feel with Obama leads to the danger (for him) that they will be disappointed if his record does not meet their expectation.[86] Finally, he must avoid appearing excessively technocratic. Criticizing the Bush administration's incompetence is likely to appeal to many, especially Democrats, but presidential nominee Michael Dukakis famously lost the 1988 election with the message that competence was more important than ideology.

CONCLUSION

As discussed above, the ideas of incorporating equality and community into the American Dream, reforming politics and political debate, and post-partisan political approaches are central themes in Barack Obama's rhetoric. The first is probably the most politically delicate, a fact that the nuance and even caution in his rhetoric on the subject appears to recognize. Reform and post-partisanship are likely to appeal widely to voters, but realizing these ideals may be more complicated than it appears on the surface. Clearly the three concepts are connected in Obama's rhetoric, as he argues that excessive partisanship and the corruption of honest political argument subvert policies that would promote the American Dream.

Past research in political science suggests that successful politicians cultivate personal images that emphasize traits such as competence, leadership, integrity, and empathy.[87] Obama clearly stresses these themes in his rhetoric. When he ties his own journey toward success to the American Dream, it subtly reinforces an image of competence and achievement. As discussed above, he often emphasizes the importance of empathy in his speeches. His focus on ethical government, such as trying to stop no-bid contracts or criticizing the role of money in politics reinforces the message of integrity. In his widely covered trip to Kenya in August 2006, he emphasized how government corruption undermined the nation's economic progress. Leadership is a less prominent theme in his rhetoric. When he does talk about the concept, it is sometimes in the context of the Democratic Party, not himself as an individual, however.[88] Moreover, the relative complexity of his rhetoric may undercut his image as a leader.

Obviously, a politician's image depends not only on what he says, but how he says it. Richard Fenno argues that politicians are like actors, who use both a verbal script and, often more importantly, nonverbal cues to build an effective relationship with the public.[89] Clearly, Obama has developed a "presentation of self" that further reinforces his positive qualities in the audience's mind. To cite just one example, he often speaks with his fingertips slightly entwined, which is a sign of intelligence, an obvious element of competence.[90] More broadly, his speaking style unites the disparate elements of his life story in a way that supports his larger message. When asked to describe what influences his rhetorical approach, he cited the black church, his experience as a law professor, and "a smattering of Hawaii, Indonesia, and maybe Kansas."[91] The fusing of different styles supports his basic message that many different kinds of people can live successfully in one nation.

CHAPTER NINE

Conclusion

T he previous chapters have examined Obama's political career so far, tracing his rise from obscurity to fame. We conclude the book by looking back at the lessons that Obama's experience teaches us about American politics. We also consider his presidential prospects, both as a candidate and as a potential chief executive.

LESSONS

Obama's political career illustrates several lessons. First, it shows that progressive candidates can compete in the contemporary money-driven political environment, but not necessarily without making some compromises. As discussed in chapter 4, Obama has more than held his own in the financial side of politics and has become one of the Democratic party's star fundraisers.

In the first six months of 2007, Obama raised nearly $59 million from over a quarter-of-a-million people, thousands of whom contributed more than once to the campaign. The Obama campaign spent $22.6 millions during this time period. Barack Obama remarked, "Together, we have built the largest grass-roots campaign in history for this stage of a presidential race."[1] Obama's use of the Internet to reach contributors and voters is also groundbreaking. Hillary Clinton raised a total of $63 million from January to June 2007 and spent $17.8 million. These figures do not tell the whole story, however. In the second quarter, Obama raised $10 million more than Clinton in contributions that can be used in the primary race. Many of Clinton's supporters have already given the maximum amount allowed by law for both the primary and general elections.

Ironically, given his opposition to the current campaign financing system, his very success backs up the claims of those opposed to regulating political money. Specifically, these opponents argue that only weak candidates need public subsidies, and Obama's ability to raise great deals of money supports this point.[2] Like mainstream voters, important Democratic fundraisers have found his intelligence, charisma, and diplomatic skills compelling.[3]

However, Obama enjoys a popularity rarely seen among candidates, and the impact of money in campaigns cannot be discounted. In the 2004 elections, 96 percent of House races and 91 percent of Senate races were won by the candidate spending the most money. Top spenders won 95 percent of House races and 76 percent of Senate races in 2002.[4]

On the larger question of whether money buys influence over legislators, Obama's experience reflects the base realities of national politics. Critics charge that he has changed his position on issues like energy policy and financial services regulation to satisfy large contributors.[5] For example, in contrast to his efforts to stop predatory lending practices in the Illinois senate, he voted against a U.S. Senate provision that would have capped credit card interest rates at 30 percent.[6] In his book *The Audacity of Hope,* he acknowledges that the necessity of raising money can undermine progressive concerns by isolating him from the poor. "I know that as a consequence of my fundraising, I became more like the wealthy donors I met.... I spent more and more of my time above the fray, outside the world of immediate hunger, disappointment, fear, irrationality, and frequent hardship of ... the people that I'd entered public life to serve."[7] Obama's voting record, though, demonstrates a commitment to the less fortunate and to clean government.

A second lesson is that Obama shows that a candidate can be effective without adopting scorched-earth political tactics. As discussed in earlier chapters, Obama has been successful while largely eschewing negative campaigning. The conventional wisdom suggests that negative campaigning is pervasive because it works better than positive appeals, although scholarly research casts some doubt on that conclusion.[8] The impact on the American political system is not completely benign, as harsh and fact-challenged attack advertisements tend to discourage voting, especially among citizens with low levels of interest in and knowledge about politics.[9] It is possible that Obama's experience will change conventional ideas about the effectiveness of negative advertisements.

Third, in a somewhat similar vein, Obama's rhetoric shows that messages targeted to the concerns of the majority of voters, rather than a narrower, if more passionate, "base" can succeed. Like Obama himself, a number of commentators have noted that American politics has gotten stuck in a "culture war" politics rooted in the 1960s that ignores issues more important to most voters, such as health care, the economy, effective schools, and the like.[10] While subjects like abortion and gay marriage mobilize a passionate few, they tend to turn off more centrist voters. Thus, political elites, including candidates, have become more polarizing than voters appear to want them to be.[11] As discussed in chapters 3 and 8, Obama has tried to refocus attention towards more "bread-and-butter" issues and has explicitly argued for moving past the political categories of the Vietnam War era. So far, at least, citizens appear to be responding.

Fourth, Obama's experience suggests that the "glass ceiling" for minority candidates may be lifting. In the early 1990s, commentator Neal Peirce argued that it was difficult for black candidates to win in a constituency that is less than 65 percent black.[12] The exceptional ones succeeded at winning lower-level offices, but rarely ticket-topping positions like governor or U.S. Senator. While Obama is certainly an extraordinary politician, his victory, along with that of Deval Patrick as governor of Massachusetts in 2006, suggest that the United States may be entering a new era for black candidates. The number of black candidates for statewide office from both major political parties continues to increase, and there are a greater number of African Americans that hold public office than ever before, providing the steppingstones to higher office. In 2004, the number of black elected officials nationwide was at a historical high of 9,101.[13] While the elections over the next decade will indicate whether this trend continues, it is clear that African American candidates are becoming more competitive for top political positions.

Finally, Obama's 2004 Illinois Senate campaign suggests that primary election voters deserve more credit for picking good candidates than they sometimes get. Some political scientists contend that party leaders would do a better job selecting nominees.[14] It is a mistake to put too much stock in one U.S. Senate race to prove a more general point, but most observers agree that Obama and Jack Ryan were the best candidates in large fields. Moreover, Ryan was, by almost any standard, a better candidate than Alan Keyes, the choice of party leaders.

PRESIDENTIAL PROSPECTS

Speculation about Obama's presidential ambitions swirled around him since his 2004 Democratic National Convention speech. During his October 2006 tour to promote his book *The Audacity of Hope*, Obama was encouraged by figures as diverse as talk show host Oprah Winfrey and conservative *New York Times* columnist David Brooks to run for president. On the October 22, 2006 edition of NBC's *Meet the Press*, he acknowledged he was considering a run, which he formally announced in February 2007. This section analyzes the plusses and minuses of an Obama candidacy, as well as a few "wild cards."

On the plus side, Obama may be well positioned to put together a winning coalition of voters, especially in the general election. John Judis and Ruy Teixeira predict that, in the future, a coalition of highly skilled professionals working in post-industrial occupations, minorities, women, and the white working class will form the basis of a resurgent Democratic party majority.[15] Obama seems likely to succeed with at least the first three of these groups, as discussed in the analysis from chapters 2 and 3. He ran particularly well in affluent suburbs and areas of the state where highly skilled service jobs are more common, as well as in black and Hispanic areas of Chicago. Exit polls taken after the 2004 general election showed he ran about six points higher among women than men.[16] His appeal to the white working class is less certain. As noted in chapter 3, he did very well in some relatively rural, declining industrial areas of Illinois in the 2004 general election and among voters concerned about the economy. In the Democratic primary the same year, however, he lost many of these same areas to Dan Hynes, who had much more support among industrial unions.

Applying this logic to the 2008 Democratic nomination contest, he should do well in the critical New Hampshire primary, given the state's growing number of affluent, highly skilled professionals. He should also be able to count on the support of black voters in southern state primaries where they make up a large percentage of the Democratic electorate, although, given previous questions about whether he is "authentically black," this may not be a sure thing. A *Washington Post/ABC News* poll taken in January 2007 showed that, in a head-to-head match-up with Hillary Clinton, Obama trailed by twenty-six points among black voters, which was greater than his deficit among whites.[17] Iowa, home of the nation's first delegate-selection contest and a state where unions are a major force in the Democratic party, is less certain, as is Nevada, which will have a coveted early position for its caucuses in 2008. South Carolina will go to the polls in late January, and February 5, 2008 will be the political equivalent to football's Super Bowl Sunday. On this day, dozens of states all across the country will hold their primary elections. Large states like Florida, California, and New York wanted to increase their role in the nominating process, and they all shifted their polling dates as early as possible. Naturally, this truncates the selection process and requires a different campaign strategy. It will be almost impossible for anyone but the frontrunners to be viable after the first week of February.

He also has some issues working in his favor. In contrast to one of his anticipated rivals, Senator Hillary Rodham Clinton, he can point to long-standing opposition to the Iraq War, which should serve him well in Democratic primaries and caucuses and is unlikely to hurt him in the general election. His emphasis on economic issues should appeal to an electorate anxious about the effects of the global economy. In an effort to neutralize any negative political fallout from his liberal stances on "culture war" issues like abortion, he is reaching out to Evangelical Christians, a key Republican constituency in the past, on issues like fighting AIDS. As such, he is trying to court one of the few constituencies with which he fared poorly in his U.S. Senate race. Although he is unlikely to get a majority of their votes, he may win some converts. At the very least, he can neutralize efforts to paint him as hostile to religion.

It appears that voters will be in the mood for stylistic and substantive change in 2008. If this prediction pans out, Obama should benefit. His policy emphases and bipartisan approach to governing would be a marked change from the Bush administration's approach. Stylistic differences are also likely. Bill Clinton has sometimes been called the "first black president," and columnist Maureen Dowd suggests that Obama could, after a similar fashion, be the "first woman president." "His approach seems downright feminine compared to the Bushies. He languidly poses in fashion magazines, shares feelings with Oprah, and dishes with the ladies on *The View*. After six years of chest-puffing, Obama seems very soothing."[18]

Pundits and pollsters have been trying to gauge the public's perception of the candidates for over a year now. National polls of whom the Democrats or Republicans favor for their party's nomination are not of much value because the race will be decided state by state. However, it is fair to say that Obama has gained name recognition and is generally seen as positive, while Hillary Clinton is seen somewhat less favorably. A nationwide *USA Today*/Gallop Poll taken in early August 2007 showed 48 percent of respondents had a favorable opinion, of Obama, 34 percent had not heard of him, and 9 percent were unsure. Senator Clinton, on the other hand, had a 47 percent favorable opinion, 49 percent unfavorable, no one indicated that they had not heard of her, and 3 percent were unsure. In most hypothetical races pitting Democratic and Republican candidates against each other in a presidential race, the Democratic candidate defeats the Republican candidate. Interestingly, though, Senator Clinton is victorious by a few more percentage points.[19]

To have more influence in the presidential selection process, states have rushed to move their primaries earlier in 2008, and nearly half the states will have had their elections by February 5, the so-called "National Primary." As of August 2007, polls in Iowa did not show any clear frontrunner, but Clinton and Edwards were at the top of the pack, with Obama closing in. In New Hampshire, Obama seems to be catching up to Clinton, with a July 28, 2007, American Research Group poll showing Clinton and Obama both favored by 31 percent, and Edwards at 14 percent. This trend seems evident in South Carolina as well. In Florida and California, however, Clinton has continued to have a 15- to 20-percent lead over Obama. In Illinois, Obama had a slight lead over Clinton, but she seemed invincible in New York, with close to half of those surveyed supporting her.[20]

While these polls are interesting, they do not reflect the grass-roots support for a candidate or the ability of a campaign to get out the vote. Both Obama and Clinton have strong organizations and the funding to endure the entire primary season. If no candidate receives a majority of delegates, which for the most part are awarded on the basis of the proportional vote a candidate receives in a given state and on the number of delegates from that state, there many be a need for a brokered convention. This last occurred in the Republican's 1976 convention when President Ford did not have a majority of delegates and was challenged by Ronald Reagan for the nomination. Ford went on to receive the nomination on the first ballot, but the internal battle may have been a factor in his losing the general election.

Another factor in Obama's presidential campaign is his lack of experience on the national stage. Despite the power of his rhetoric, he still may need to fine-tune his message to appeal to voters in a presidential contest. For example, his September 2006 speech during his visit to the Tom Harkin steak fry, a mecca for presidential aspirants, got a lukewarm reception by some in the crowd, as many found it overly cerebral and academic.[21] As discussed in chapter 8, his rhetoric is sometimes so nuanced as to appear equivocal. Although a visit to New Hampshire in late 2006 met with adoring crowds, it is not clear that this worship resulted from his message.

In addition, he has never dealt with the pressure of a high-profile campaign. Due to his safe state senate district and the idiosyncratic nature of his 2004 general election race, he has never had to face full-on Republican attacks. His most favorable coverage from the national media is almost certainly behind him. As *Washington Post* media critic Howard Kurtz observed, "Reporters have a way of discovering the dark side of even the most admirable public figures. And if Obama takes his pristine image into the muddy arena of presidential politics, even the warm embrace of Oprah won't protect him."[22]

In fact, by 2006, he was already experiencing something of a local media backlash in Illinois. First, he was criticized for supporting "anti-reform" candidates in local races. He took heat for refusing to endorse political reformer Forrest Claypool in the 2006 Democratic primary for Cook County Board President. Critics charged that he sacrificed his moral authority as a reformer to protect his own political prospects.[23]

In the general election race for the same office, newspaper columnists hectored Obama for an endorsement letter that allegedly misrepresented the Republican candidate's position on abortion and for tarnishing his reform credentials by supporting a "machine hack."[24] In the 2006 primary election, he also appeared in campaign commercials for victorious state treasurer candidate Alexi Giannoulias, a financial backer of his 2004 Senate campaign, who generated controversy with bank loans to a reputed mobster. Most recently, his involvement in a real estate deal with indicted political fundraiser Tony Rezko, which resulted in Obama's purchase of a house at a very favorable price, created further media headaches.

In his 2004 Senate campaign, Obama's charisma helped him connect with ordinary voters. A campaign staffer noted that when voters met Obama they "fell in love with him."[25] Presidential campaigns have different dynamics, however. After the intimacy of the first few primaries and caucuses, there is little chance for person-to-person politics, "retail" politics. Although Obama is obviously very effective at giving speeches to large crowds, he will also need to learn to deal with the "freak show" of bloggers, talk radio hosts, and cable TV commentators described by Mark Halperin and John F. Harris in their book *The Way to Win*.[26] A positive for Obama is his willingness to engage the denizens of this realm. He communicates with bloggers by airing his views on Daily Kos, a popular liberal blog, and elsewhere.

More than any other candidate, Obama has utilized the Internet. In April 2007, Obama had nearly 1,543,000 "friends" on MySpace.com, the social-networking website. Hillary Clinton only had 41,500 people in her network. In fact, Obama has 50 percent more MySpace friends than all the other Democrats combined. Similarly, at this time, close to 2.8 million people watched Obama on his YouTube channel, the free-access, web-based media outlet. This is two million more viewers than the rest of the entire Democratic field.[27]

He has appeared on cable television shows ranging from the *Daily Show* to *Countdown with Keith Olbermann*. He and his staff are very quick to respond to negative media attacks. For example, when *Harper's* magazine printed an article criticizing his fundraising practices, he fired back quickly with a response on his website, calling the article "misleading" and offering a point-by-point rebuttal.[28]

One wild card question is whether he can appear "presidential" enough. His relative youth and limited high-level government experience are obvious lines of attack against him, especially in the post-9/11 environment. Obama has already tried to downplay the experience factor, arguing that "Dick Cheney and Donald Rumsfeld have an awful lot of experience, and yet have engineered what I think is one of the biggest foreign policy failures in our recent history."[29] He has also tried to draw parallels between his own career and Abraham Lincoln's, implicitly sending the message that someone with limited time in Washington can be a strong president. For example, his decision to announce his presidential candidacy at the Old State Capitol in Springfield implicitly draws this parallel.[30] As discussed earlier, leadership may be the Achilles heel of his image. His Democratic primary opponents in 2004 saw this quality as a potential weakness, and the exit polls in Table 3-2 showed that he did not score particularly well on this trait among voters in his senate race. Similarly, his sometimes self-deprecating manner may appear unpresidential to some. Critics writing at the end of 2006 note that he has offered very little policy rationale for his candidacy, appealing to voters instead on his celebrity and biography.[31]

Interestingly, Obama seems to be willing to challenge conventional wisdom about what affects electability in presidential races. For example, he does not apologize for his teenage drug use or seem to fall into the trap that "a single miscalculation or misstatement is fatal to American political careers."[32] Although voters often say they want "authenticity" in a candidate, it's probably worth remembering that John McCain's famed "Straight Talk Express" in the 2000 Republican presidential primaries took him straight back to the Senate.

Race is another wild card. None of the five previous black candidates for president—Shirley Chisholm, Jesse Jackson, Carol Moseley-Braun, Al Sharpton, and Alan Keyes—have come close to getting nominated. Public opinion surveys suggest that a large majority of Americans are willing to vote for a black candidate.[33] In practice, however, the racial dynamics of political campaigns work on more subconscious levels as voters react to a candidate's race in ways in which they may not be fully aware. The clever use of subtle racial cues in commercials, for example, can tap latent racism.[34] As discussed earlier in the book, Obama's unique background inoculates him from some of the negative stereotypes that whites have about black candidates. Nevertheless, he may not be able to overcome the fact that black contenders face a more complicated task in marketing themselves than whites do. African American candidates must persuade black voters that the political system and white officials can be trusted and white voters that race relations are good, a more complicated task than white candidates face.[35]

WOULD HE BE A GOOD PRESIDENT?

Political scientists have identified several qualities that effective presidents possess, including aptitude for public communication, organizational capacity, political skill, vision, intellectual ability, and emotional intelligence.[36] Often it is hard to judge a president on these criteria until he has left office, so what follows is somewhat speculative. Still, it is clear that Obama possesses exceptional intellectual gifts. In addition, former colleagues praise his emotional intelligence and maturity.[37] Long before he had even entered public life, one of his law professors noted Obama's unique combination of intellectual and emotional intelligence. "He's very unusual, in the sense that other students who might have something approximating his degree of insight are very intimidating to other students, or inconsiderate and thoughtless. He's able to build upon what other students say and see what's valuable in their comments without belittling them."[38]

How he will fare on the other qualities listed above is harder to judge. He has clearly mastered many of the skills of public communication. As discussed in chapters 2 and 3, his rhetorical style persuades many who are inclined to disagree with him, and he uses effectively the nonverbal tools that appeal to audiences. The discussion in chapter 8, however, raises the question of whether his rhetoric is sometimes too cerebral and nuanced to reach the average voter.

Political skill requires the ability to overcome the stalemates inherent in the separation of powers system, as well as a reputation for effectiveness among other political elites.[39] Before assessing Obama's prospects on the first of these criteria, it is worth noting that the challenges the next president will face are likely to be particularly daunting. He or she will have to operate in a challenging fiscal environment, as the retirement wave of the baby boomers begins and the bill for the Iraq War comes due. The trust in government that grew after 9/11, and can help ease institutional gridlock, has largely dissipated.[40] Complicating Obama's task in overcoming stalemate, if he were to be elected, is the fact that his celebrity may have raised expectations so high that whatever he actually accomplishes will be a disappointment. This frustration may be especially bitter because voters often forget that the U.S. political system is designed to frustrate, not facilitate, action. In fact, he is already beginning to stress the point that American institutions limit action, in response to critiques on the left that he is not progressive enough.[41] Although it has also engendered criticism on the left, Obama's ability to raise money from Washington lobbyists and power brokers implies that he is accepted by the Capital's elite "players."[42] Obama's track record in the Illinois state senate also bodes well, but that is obviously a much smaller stage.

The biggest questions surrounding the likely success or failure of an Obama presidency may hinge on organizational capacity and vision. His lack of high-level executive experience raises questions about his organizational capacity, which includes ensuring that aides speak honestly, promoting teamwork, and creating effective institutions.[43] A campaign aide, however, noted that he is very receptive to feedback from staffers and is willing to change his mind on the basis of their input. In talking to him, the staffer commented, "it doesn't feel like it's going in one ear and out the other."[44] His success in building the size and budget of the Developing Communities Project in Chicago and his ability to organize civic projects like voter registration drives are impressive, but their scale does not compare to the presidency. If the organization of his presidential campaign is any indication of his ability to manage and lead large organizations, he seems to have the necessary skills and the ability to bring in strong, high-quality people. On vision, Obama has been praised for his ability to conceptualize problems, but he may be less effective at translating his broad ideas into specific policies in a creative way.[45]

He will probably have a great deal of appeal internationally. His boyhood experience in Indonesia is likely to be viewed favorably in developing nations. However, his international experience as a youth may cause some to misjudge him, intentionally or unintentionally. Obama was accused of attending a radical, Muslim "madrassa" school in Indonesia when he was a boy. This story was originated by *Insight Magazine*, which is owned by the same company as the conservative newspaper, *The Washington Times*, and it was repeated on *Fox News*. The story was not accurate, and an Obama aide called the *Fox* broadcast "appallingly irresponsible."[46] Obama would be a president "who can speak directly to the world" and who would restore and promote strong alliances across the world.[47] As president, he would expand and modernize the military as well as increasing foreign aid.

Barack Obama has the potential to make significant contributions on both the domestic and international political scene. After decades of bitter partisanship, he offers pragmatic policy considerations. After too many cycles of negative campaigning, he demonstrates that it is better to stand for something in politics than to besmirch others. Barack Obama represents a new face in American politics, and he is inspiring many other people to care about the challenges and opportunities that face the next generation.

Appendix A

A BRIGHTER DAY, BY BARACK OBAMA

Delivered to the Democratic National Convention

Boston, Massachusetts
July 27, 2004

On behalf of the great state of Illinois, crossroads of a nation, land of Lincoln, let me express my deep gratitude for the privilege of addressing this convention. Tonight is a particular honor for me because, let's face it, my presence on this stage is pretty unlikely. My father was a foreign student, born and raised in a small village in Kenya. He grew up herding goats, went to school in a tin-roof shack. His father, my grandfather, was a cook, a domestic servant.

But my grandfather had larger dreams for his son. Through hard work and perseverance my father got a scholarship to study in a magical place: America, which stood as a beacon of freedom and opportunity to so many who had come before. While studying here, my father met my mother. She was born in a town on the other side of the world, in Kansas. Her father worked on oil rigs and farms through most of the Depression. The day after Pearl Harbor he signed up for duty, joined Patton's army and marched across Europe. Back home, my grandmother raised their baby and went to work on a bomber assembly line. After the war, they studied on the GI Bill, bought a house through FHA, and moved west in search of opportunity.

And they, too, had big dreams for their daughter, a common dream, born of two continents. My parents shared not only an improbable love;

they shared an abiding faith in the possibilities of this nation. They would give me an African name, Barack, or "blessed," believing that in a tolerant America your name is no barrier to success. They imagined me going to the best schools in the land, even though they weren't rich, because in a generous America you don't have to be rich to achieve your potential. They are both passed away now. Yet, I know that, on this night, they look down on me with pride.

I stand here today, grateful for the diversity of my heritage, aware that my parents' dreams live on in my precious daughters. I stand here knowing that my story is part of the larger American story, that I owe a debt to all of those who came before me, and that, in no other country on earth, is my story even possible. Tonight, we gather to affirm the greatness of our nation, not because of the height of our skyscrapers, or the power of our military, or the size of our economy. Our pride is based on a very simple premise, summed up in a declaration made over two hundred years ago, "We hold these truths to be self-evident, that all men are created equal. That they are endowed by their Creator with certain inalienable rights. That among these are life, liberty and the pursuit of happiness."

That is the true genius of America, a faith in the simple dreams of its people, the insistence on small miracles. That we can tuck in our children at night and know they are fed and clothed and safe from harm. That we can say what we think, write what we think, without hearing a sudden knock on the door. That we can have an idea and start our own business without paying a bribe or hiring somebody's son. That we can participate in the political process without fear of retribution, and that our votes will be counted—or at least, most of the time.

This year, in this election, we are called to reaffirm our values and commitments, to hold them against a hard reality and see how we are measuring up, to the legacy of our forbearers, and the promise of future generations. And fellow Americans—Democrats, Republicans, Independents—I say to you tonight: we have more work to do. More to do for the workers I met in Galesburg, Illinois, who are losing their union jobs at the Maytag plant that's moving to Mexico, and now are having to compete with their own children for jobs that pay seven bucks an hour. More to do for the father I met who was losing his job and choking back tears, wondering how he would pay $4,500 a month for the drugs his son needs without the health benefits he counted on. More to do for the young woman in East St. Louis, and thousands more like her, who has the grades, has the drive, has the will, but doesn't have the money to go to college.

Don't get me wrong. The people I meet in small towns and big cities, in diners and office parks, they don't expect government to solve all their problems. They know they have to work hard to get ahead and they want to. Go into the collar counties around Chicago, and people will tell you they don't want their tax money wasted by a welfare agency or the Pentagon. Go into any inner city neighborhood, and folks will tell you that government alone can't teach kids to learn. They know that parents have to parent, that children can't achieve unless we raise their expectations and turn off the television sets and eradicate the slander that says a black youth with a book is acting white. No, people don't expect government to solve all their problems. But they sense, deep in their bones, that with just a change in priorities, we can make sure that every child in America has a decent shot at life, and that the doors of opportunity remain open to all. They know we can do better. And they want that choice.

In this election, we offer that choice. Our party has chosen a man to lead us who embodies the best this country has to offer. That man is John Kerry. John Kerry understands the ideals of community, faith, and sacrifice, because they've defined his life. From his heroic service in Vietnam to his years as prosecutor and lieutenant governor, through two decades in the United States Senate, he has devoted himself to this country. Again and again, we've seen him make tough choices when easier ones were available. His values and his record affirm what is best in us.

John Kerry believes in an America where hard work is rewarded. So instead of offering tax breaks to companies shipping jobs overseas, he'll offer them to companies creating jobs here at home. John Kerry believes in an America where all Americans can afford the same health coverage our politicians in Washington have for themselves. John Kerry believes in energy independence, so we aren't held hostage to the profits of oil companies or the sabotage of foreign oil fields. John Kerry believes in the constitutional freedoms that have made our country the envy of the world, and he will never sacrifice our basic liberties nor use faith as a wedge to divide us. And John Kerry believes that in a dangerous world, war must be an option, but it should never be the first option.

A while back, I met a young man named Shamus at the VFW Hall in East Moline, Illinois. He was a good-looking kid, six-two or six-three, clear-eyed, with an easy smile. He told me he'd joined the Marines and was heading to Iraq the following week. As I listened to him explain why he'd enlisted, his absolute faith in our country and its leaders, his devotion to duty and service, I thought this young man was all any of us might hope for in a child. But then I asked myself: Are we serving Shamus as well as he was serving us? I thought of more than 900 service men and women, sons and daughters, husbands and wives, friends and neighbors, who will not be returning to their hometowns. I thought of families I had met who were struggling to get by without a loved one's full income, or whose loved ones had returned with a limb missing or with nerves shattered, but who still lacked long-term health benefits because they were reservists. When we send our young men and women into harm's way, we have a solemn obligation not to fudge the numbers or shade the truth about why they're going, to care for their families while they're gone, to tend to the soldiers upon their return, and to never ever go to war without enough troops to win the war, secure the peace, and earn the respect of the world.

Now let me be clear. We have real enemies in the world. These enemies must be found. They must be pursued and they must be defeated. John Kerry knows this. And just as Lieutenant Kerry did not hesitate to risk his life to protect the men who served with him in Vietnam, President Kerry will not hesitate one moment to use our military might to keep America safe and secure. John Kerry believes in America. And he knows it's not enough for just some of us to prosper. For alongside our famous individualism, there's another ingredient in the American saga.

A belief that we are connected as one people. If there's a child on the south side of Chicago who can't read, that matters to me, even if it's not my child. If there's a senior citizen somewhere who can't pay for her prescription and has to choose between medicine and the rent, that makes my life poorer, even if it's not my grandmother. If there's an Arab American family being rounded up without benefit of an attorney or due process, that threatens my civil liberties. It's that fundamental belief—I am my brother's keeper, I am my sister's keeper—that makes this country work. It's what allows us to pursue our individual dreams, yet still come together as a single American family. "*E pluribus unum.*" Out of many, one.

Yet even as we speak, there are those who are preparing to divide us, the spin masters and negative ad peddlers who embrace the politics of anything goes. Well, I say to them tonight, there's not a liberal America and a conservative America—there's the United States of America. There's not a black America and white America and Latino America and Asian America; there's the United States of America. The pundits like to slice-and-dice our country into Red States and Blue States; Red States for Republicans, Blue States for Democrats. But I've got news for them, too. We worship an awesome God in the Blue States, and we don't like federal agents poking around our libraries in the Red States. We coach Little League in the Blue States and have gay friends in the Red States. There are patriots who opposed the war in Iraq and patriots who supported it. We are one people, all of us pledging allegiance to the stars and stripes, all of us defending the United States of America.

In the end, that's what this election is about. Do we participate in a politics of cynicism or a politics of hope? John Kerry calls on us to hope. John Edwards calls on us to hope. I'm not talking about blind optimism here—the almost willful ignorance that thinks unemployment will go away if we just don't talk about it, or the health-care crisis will solve itself if we just ignore it. No, I'm talking about something more substantial. It's the hope of slaves sitting around a fire singing freedom songs; the hope of immigrants setting out for distant shores; the hope of a young naval lieutenant bravely patrolling the Mekong Delta; the hope of a millworker's son who dares to defy the odds; the hope of a skinny kid with a funny name who believes that America has a place for him, too. The audacity of hope!

In the end, that is God's greatest gift to us, the bedrock of this nation; the belief in things not seen; the belief that there are better days ahead. I believe we can give our middle class relief and provide working families with a road to opportunity. I believe we can provide jobs to the jobless, homes to the homeless, and reclaim young people in cities across America from violence and despair. I believe that as we stand on the crossroads of history, we can make the right choices, and meet the challenges that face us, America!

Tonight, if you feel the same energy I do, the same urgency I do, the same passion I do, the same hopefulness I do—if we do what we must do, then I have no doubt that all across the country, from Florida to Oregon, from Washington to Maine, the people will rise up in November, and John Kerry will be sworn in as president, and John Edwards will be sworn in as vice president, and this country will reclaim its promise, and out of this long political darkness a brighter day will come. Thank you and God bless you.

Appendix B

FULL TEXT OF SENATOR BARACK OBAMA'S ANNOUNCEMENT FOR PRESIDENT

Springfield, Illinois
February 10, 2007

Let me begin by saying thanks to all you who've traveled, from far and wide, to brave the cold today.

We all made this journey for a reason. It's humbling, but in my heart I know you didn't come here just for me, you came here because you believe in what this country can be. In the face of war, you believe there can be peace. In the face of despair, you believe there can be hope. In the face of a politics that's shut you out, that's told you to settle, that's divided us for too long, you believe we can be one people, reaching for what's possible, building that more perfect union.

That's the journey we're on today. But let me tell you how I came to be here. As most of you know, I am not a native of this great state. I moved to Illinois over two decades ago. I was a young man then, just a year out of college; I knew no one in Chicago, was without money or family connections. But a group of churches had offered me a job as a community organizer for $13,000 a year. And I accepted the job, sight unseen, motivated then by a single, simple, powerful idea—that I might play a small part in building a better America.

My work took me to some of Chicago's poorest neighborhoods. I joined with pastors and lay-people to deal with communities that had been ravaged by plant closings. I saw that the problems people faced weren't simply local in nature—that the decision to close a steel mill was made by distant executives; that the lack of textbooks and computers in schools could be traced to the skewed priorities of politicians a thousand miles away; and that when a child turns to violence, there's a hole in his heart no government alone can fill.

It was in these neighborhoods that I received the best education I ever had, and where I learned the true meaning of my Christian faith.

After three years of this work, I went to law school, because I wanted to understand how the law should work for those in need. I became a civil rights lawyer, and taught constitutional law, and after a time, I came to understand that our cherished rights of liberty and equality depend on the active participation of an awakened electorate. It was with these ideas in mind that I arrived in this capital city as a state Senator.

It was here, in Springfield, where I saw all that is America converge— farmers and teachers, businessmen and laborers, all of them with a story to tell, all of them seeking a seat at the table, all of them clamoring to be heard. I made lasting friendships here—friends that I see in the audience today.

It was here we learned to disagree without being disagreeable—that it's possible to compromise so long as you know those principles that can never be compromised; and that so long as we're willing to listen to each other, we can assume the best in people instead of the worst.

That's why we were able to reform a death penalty system that was broken. That's why we were able to give health insurance to children in need. That's why we made the tax system more fair and just for working families, and that's why we passed ethics reforms that the cynics said could never, ever be passed.

It was here, in Springfield, where North, South, East, and West come together that I was reminded of the essential decency of the American people—where I came to believe that through this decency we can build a more hopeful America.

And that is why, in the shadow of the Old State Capitol, where Lincoln once called on a divided house to stand together, where common hopes and common dreams still [dwell], I stand before you today to announce my candidacy for President of the United States.

I recognize there is a certain presumptuousness—a certain audacity— to this announcement. I know I haven't spent a lot of time learning the ways of Washington. But I've been there long enough to know that the ways of Washington must change.

The genius of our founders is that they designed a system of government that can be changed. And we should take heart, because we've changed this country before. In the face of tyranny, a band of patriots brought an Empire to its knees. In the face of secession, we unified a nation and set the captives free. In the face of Depression, we put people back to work and lifted millions out of poverty. We welcomed immigrants to our shores, we opened railroads to the west, we landed a man on the moon, and we heard a King's call to let justice roll down like water, and righteousness like a mighty stream.

Each and every time, a new generation has risen up and done what's needed to be done. Today we are called once more—and it is time for our generation to answer that call.

For that is our unyielding faith—that in the face of impossible odds, people who love their country can change it.

That's what Abraham Lincoln understood. He had his doubts. He had his defeats. He had his setbacks. But through his will and his words, he moved a nation and helped free a people. It is because of the millions who rallied to his cause that we are no longer divided, North and South, slave and free. It is because men and women of every race, from every walk of life, continued to march for freedom long after Lincoln was laid to rest, that today we have the chance to face the challenges of this millennium together, as one people—as Americans.

All of us know what those challenges are today—a war with no end, a dependence on oil that threatens our future, schools where too many children aren't learning, and families struggling paycheck to paycheck despite working as hard as they can. We know the challenges. We've heard them. We've talked about them for years.

What's stopped us from meeting these challenges is not the absence of sound policies and sensible plans. What's stopped us is the failure of leadership, the smallness of our politics—the ease with which we're distracted by the petty and trivial, our chronic avoidance of tough decisions, our preference for scoring cheap political points instead of rolling up our sleeves and building a working consensus to tackle big problems.

For the last six years we've been told that our mounting debts don't matter, we've been told that the anxiety Americans feel about rising health-care costs and stagnant wages are an illusion, we've been told that climate change is a hoax, and that tough talk and an ill-conceived war can replace diplomacy, and strategy, and foresight. And when all else fails, when Katrina happens, or the death toll in Iraq mounts, we've been told that our crises are somebody else's fault. We're distracted from our real failures, and told to blame the other party, or gay people, or immigrants.

And as people have looked away in disillusionment and frustration, we know what's filled the void. The cynics, and the lobbyists, and the special interests who've turned our government into a game only they can afford to play. They write the checks and you get stuck with the bills, they get the access while you get to write a letter, they think they own this government, but we're here today to take it back. The time for that politics is over. It's time to turn the page.

We've made some progress already. I was proud to help lead the fight in Congress that led to the most sweeping ethics reform since Watergate.

But Washington has a long way to go. And it won't be easy. That's why we'll have to set priorities. We'll have to make hard choices. And although government will play a crucial role in bringing about the changes we need, more money and programs alone will not get us where we need to go. Each of us, in our own lives, will have to accept responsibility—for instilling an ethic of achievement in our children, for adapting to a more competitive economy, for strengthening our communities, and sharing some measure of sacrifice. So let us begin. Let us begin this hard work together. Let us transform this nation.

Let us be the generation that reshapes our economy to compete in the digital age. Let's set high standards for our schools and give them the resources they need to succeed. Let's recruit a new army of teachers, and give them better pay and more support in exchange for more accountability. Let's make college more affordable, and let's invest in scientific research, and let's lay down broadband lines through the heart of inner cities and rural towns all across America.

And as our economy changes, let's be the generation that ensures our nation's workers are sharing in our prosperity. Let's protect the hard-earned benefits their companies have promised. Let's make it possible for hardworking Americans to save for retirement. And let's allow our unions and their organizers to lift up this country's middle class again.

Let's be the generation that ends poverty in America. Every single person willing to work should be able to get job training that leads to a job, and earn a living wage that can pay the bills, and afford child care so their kids have a safe place to go when they work. Let's do this.

Let's be the generation that finally tackles our health-care crisis. We can control costs by focusing on prevention, by providing better treatment to the chronically ill, and using technology to cut the bureaucracy. Let's be the generation that says right here, right now, that we will have universal health care in America by the end of the next president's first term.

Let's be the generation that finally frees America from the tyranny of oil. We can harness homegrown, alternative fuels like ethanol and spur the production of more fuel-efficient cars. We can set up a system for capping greenhouse gases. We can turn this crisis of global warming into a moment of opportunity for innovation, and job creation, and an incentive for businesses that will serve as a model for the world. Let's be the generation that makes future generations proud of what we did here.

Most of all, let's be the generation that never forgets what happened on that September day and confronts the terrorists with everything we've got. Politics doesn't have to divide us on this anymore—we can work together to keep our country safe. I've worked with Republican Senator Dick Lugar to pass a law that will secure and destroy some of the world's deadliest, unguarded weapons. We can work together to track terrorists down with a stronger military, we can tighten the net around their finances, and we can improve our intelligence capabilities. But let us also understand that ultimate victory against our enemies will come only by rebuilding our alliances and exporting those ideals that bring hope and opportunity to millions around the globe.

But all of this cannot come to pass until we bring an end to this war in Iraq. Most of you know I opposed this war from the start. I thought it was a tragic mistake. Today we grieve for the families who have lost loved ones, the hearts that have been broken, and the young lives that could have been. America, it's time to start bringing our troops home. It's time to admit that no amount of American lives can resolve the political disagreement that lies at the heart of someone else's civil war. That's why I have a plan that will bring our combat troops home by March of 2008. Letting the Iraqis know that we will not be there forever is our last, best hope to pressure the Sunni and Shia to come to the table and find peace.

Finally, there is one other thing that is not too late to get right about this war—and that is the homecoming of the men and women—our veterans—who have sacrificed the most. Let us honor their valor by providing the care they need and rebuilding the military they love. Let us be the generation that begins this work.

I know there are those who don't believe we can do all these things. I understand the skepticism. After all, every four years, candidates from both parties make similar promises, and I expect this year will be no different. All of us running for president will travel around the country offering ten-point plans and making grand speeches; all of us will trumpet those qualities we believe make us uniquely qualified to lead the country. But too many times, after the election is over, and the confetti is swept away, all those promises fade from memory, and the lobbyists and the special interests move in, and people turn away, disappointed as before, left to struggle on their own.

That is why this campaign can't only be about me. It must be about us—it must be about what we can do together. This campaign must be the occasion, the vehicle, of your hopes, and your dreams. It will take your time, your energy, and your advice—to push us forward when we're doing right, and to let us know when we're not. This campaign has to be about reclaiming the meaning of citizenship, restoring our sense of common purpose, and realizing that few obstacles can withstand the power of millions of voices calling for change.

By ourselves, this change will not happen. Divided, we are bound to fail.

But the life of a tall, gangly, self-made Springfield lawyer tells us that a different future is possible.

He tells us that there is power in words.

He tells us that there is power in conviction.

That beneath all the differences of race and region, faith and station, we are one people.

He tells us that there is power in hope.

As Lincoln organized the forces arrayed against slavery, he was heard to say: "Of strange, discordant, and even hostile elements, we gathered from the four winds, and formed and fought to battle through."

That is our purpose here today.

That's why I'm in this race.

Not just to hold an office, but to gather with you to transform a nation.

I want to win that next battle—for justice and opportunity.

I want to win that next battle—for better schools, and better jobs, and health care for all.

I want us to take up the unfinished business of perfecting our union, and building a better America.

And if you will join me in this improbable quest, if you feel destiny calling, and see as I see, a future of endless possibility stretching before us; if you sense, as I sense, that the time is now to shake off our slumber, and slough off our fear, and make good on the debt we owe past and future generations, then I'm ready to take up the cause, and march with you, and work with you. Together, starting today, let us finish the work that needs to be done, and usher in a new birth of freedom on this Earth.

http://origin.barackobama.com/2007/02/10/remarks_of_senator_barack_obam_11.php (accessed April 16, 2007).

Notes

CHAPTER ONE

1. Wendy Rahn and R. M. Hirshorn, "Political Advertising and Public Mood: A Study of Children's Political Orientations," *Political Communication* 10 (1999): 387–407; Kim Fridkin Kahn and Patrick J. Kenney, *No Holds Barred: Negativity in U.S. Senate Campaigns* (Upper Saddle River, NJ: Pearson/Prentice Hall, 2004), 105–6.

2. Tammerlin Drummond, "The Barack Obama Story," *San Francisco Chronicle,* April 1, 1990, 5.

3. Barack Obama, *Dreams from My Father: A Story of Race and Inheritance* (New York: Three Rivers Press, 2004), 85.

4. Ibid., 93.

5. Kirsten Scharnberg and Kin Marker, "The Not-So-Simple Story of Barack Obama's Youth," *Chicago Tribune*, March 25, 2007, 1.

6. Obama, *Dreams from My Father*, 120.

7. Ibid., 133.

8. Ibid., 152.

9. Ibid., 231.

10. Ibid., 229.

11. Ibid., 163.

12. Bob Secter and John McCormick, "Portrait of a Pragmatist," *Chicago Tribune*, March 30, 2007, 1.

13. John Coor, "From Mean Streets to Hallowed Halls," *Philadelphia Inquirer,* February 27, 1990, C01.

14. Drummond, "The Barack Obama Story," 5.

15. Terence J. Fitzgerald, "Barack Obama," *Current Biography,* July 2005, 54–63.

16. Vernon Jarrett, "Project Vote Brings Power to the People," *Chicago Sun-Times*, August 11, 1992, 23.

17. David Jackson and Ray Long, "Showing His Bare Knuckles," *Chicago Tribune*, April 4, 2007, 1.

18. Salim Muwakkil, "Candidate Not What He Seems Foes Insist," *Chicago Sun-Times*, February 12, 1996, 29.

19. Joe Frolik, "Chicago: A Newcomer to the Business of Politics," *Cleveland Plain Dealer*, August 3, 1996, 1A.

20. Obama, *Dreams from My Father*, viii.

21. Scott Turow, "The New Face of the Democratic Party—and America," Salon.com (March 30, 2004).

22. William Finnegan, "The Candidate," *New Yorker*, May 31, 2004.

23. Jennifer Allison, telephone interview with Keith Boeckelman, October 12, 2006. (Ms. Allison was a staffer for the Illinois Senate Health and Human Services Committee from 2003 to 2004).

24. Noam Scheiber, "Race against History: Barack Obama's Miraculous Campaign," *New Republic*, May 24, 2004, 21–26.

25. Turow, "The New Face of the Democratic Party—and America."

26. Ibid.

27. Allison, interview 2006.

28. Illinois Legislative Reference Bureau, *Final Legislative Synopsis and Digest of the 93rd General Assembly: 2003–2004* (Springfield: State of Illinois, 2005), 932.

29. Ron Fournier, "State Lawmakers Say Presidency Would Be a Big Leap for Obama," *Quincy (IL) Herald-Whig*, June 27, 2001, 1A.

30. David Joens and Paul Kleppner, *Almanac of Illinois Politics—1998* (Springfield: Institute for Public Affairs, 1998).

31. David Joens, *Almanac of Illinois Politics—2000* (Springfield: Institute for Public Affairs, 2000), 91.

32. Joens and Kleppner, *Almanac of Illinois Politics—1998*.

33. Ibid.

34. Illinois Chamber of Commerce, "2003–2004 Senate Ratings," http://www.ilchamber.org/99/doc/2003-4SenateRatings.xls (accessed September 29, 2006).

35. Fournier, "State Lawmakers Say," 1A.

36. Salim Muwakkil, "Ironies Abound in 1st District," *Chicago Tribune*, March 20, 2000, 17.

37. Scott Fornek, "Running against Rush," *Chicago Sun-Times*, September 29, 1999, 6.

38. Amanda Ripley, "Obama's Ascent," *Time* (November 15, 2004), 74–76, 78, 81.

39. Muwakkil, "Ironies Abound in 1st District," 17.

40. "Our Endorsements," *Chicago Defender*, March 18, 2000, 1.

41. Steve Neal, "Attorney General May Be Obama's Calling," *Chicago Sun-Times*, April 19, 2000, 8.

42. Steve Neal, "A Dozen to Consider if Mayor Skips Race," *Chicago Sun-Times*, May 8, 2000, 8.

43. Barack Obama, *The Audacity of Hope: Thoughts on Reclaiming the American Dream* (New York: Crown Publishers, 2006), 4.

44. Jacob Weisberg, "The Path to Power," *Men's Vogue*, September/October 2006, 224.

CHAPTER TWO

1. Daniel Elazar, *American Federalism: A View from the States* (New York: Harper & Row, 1984).

2. Kevin McDermott, "Obama Defends His Religious Views, Values," *St. Louis Post-Dispatch*, October 6, 2004, B01.

3. U.S. Census Bureau, quickfacts.census.gov/qfd (accessed September 25, 2006).

4. Peter F. Nardulli and Michael Krassa, "Regional Animosities in Illinois: Perceptual Dimensions," in *Diversity, Conflict, and State Politics: Regionalism in Illinois*, ed. Peter F. Nardulli (Champaign: University of Illinois Press, 1989), 264–68.

5. David Kenney and Robert E. Hartley, *An Uncertain Tradition: U.S. Senators from Illinois* (Carbondale: Southern Illinois University Press, 2003), 141, 147.

6. Kenney and Hartley, *An Uncertain Tradition*, 217.

7. Carol Marin, "Looking at Obama in '04 and Seeing Simon in '84," *Chicago Sun-Times*, November 3, 2004, 16.

8. Garance Franke-Ruta, "The Next Generation," *American Prospect* (August 2004), 13–17.

9. Kenney and Hartley, *An Uncertain Tradition*, 236.

10. Thomas Hardy, "Senate Stunner: Braun Wins," *Chicago Tribune*, March 18, 1992, 1.

11. Ibid.

12. Kenney and Hartley, *An Uncertain Tradition*, 205.

13. Ibid., 206–7.

14. Ibid., 232–34.

15. Eric Krol, "Building from the Base," *Illinois Issues*, January 2004, 23.

16. Ibid., 24.

17. Carol Marin, "None of Your Business about My Vote," *Chicago Tribune*, March 3, 2004, 1.

18. Krol, "Building from the Base," 25.

19. Ibid., 24.

20. Ibid., 24.

21. Joshua Green, "A Gambling Man," *Atlantic Monthly*, January/February 2004, 34–38.

22. John Chase, "Pappas Is Picking up One Vote at a Time," *Chicago Tribune*, February 22, 2004, 1 (Metro).

23. Mary Massingale, "Senate Hopeful Uses Props to Illustrate Waste," *Springfield State Journal Register*, February 6, 2004, 16.

24. Mark Brown, "Seems Everyone's Got Latino Endorsements in Dem Race," *Chicago Sun-Times*, February 12, 2004, 2.

25. Peter Savodnik, "Illinois Senate Candidate Compared to Moseley Braun: Barack Obama May Benefit as Top Candidates Vie," *The Hill* (February 10, 2004), http://www.thehill.com/campaign/073003_obama.aspx.

26. Steve Neal, "In the Washington Tradition, Obama Is a Coalition Builder," *Chicago Sun-Times*, March 5, 2003, 55.

27. Perry Bacon, "The Exquisite Dilemma of Being Obama," *Time*, February 20, 2006, 24–28.

28. Caroline Porter, interview with Keith Boeckelman, October 24, 2004. (Ms. Porter was Chair of the Knox County Democratic Party from 2000 to 2004).

29. Krol, "Building from the Base," 24.

30. Laura Washington, "If He Can Turn Out His Black Base, and Build a Coalition of White Progressives and Other People of Color, He's Got It," *Chicago Sun-Times*, September 8, 2003, 39.

31. David Mendell, "Obama Banks on Credentials, Charisma," *Chicago Tribune*, January 25, 2004, 1.

32. Chris Matthews, *Hardball* (New York: Perennial, 1989), 155–56.

33. Noam Scheiber, "Race against History: Barack Obama's Miraculous Campaign," *New Republic*, May 24, 2004, 21–26.

34. Ibid.

35. Mendell, "Obama Banks on Credentials, Charisma," 1.

36. Porter, interview, 2006.

37. John Chase and David Mendell, "Senate Rivals Struggle to Wash Off Mud Stains," *Chicago Tribune*, March 14, 2004, 1.

38. Mike Robinson, "Senate Candidates Aim Their Fire at Bush," *St. Louis Post-Dispatch*, February 5, 2004, B2.

39. Liam Ford, "Democratic Hopefuls Back Tax Increases," *Chicago Tribune*, February 13, 2004, 1.

40. Krol, "Building from the Base," 23.

41. Brian Brueggemann, "Illinois Lawmaker Announces," *Belleville News-Democrat*, December 9, 2003, 3B; Sarah Okeson, "Lawmaker Trying to Be '1 out of 100,'" *Peoria Journal-Star*, November 6, 2003, B3.

42. Daniel Duggan, "One-liners Show Deep Differences with President," *Elgin Courier News*, February 28, 2004, A1; Ron Ingram, "Obama Stakes His Case in Decatur for Senate Nomination," *Decatur Herald and Review*, March 5, 2004, A3.

43. Steve Neal, "What Gives Obama Hope Is That He Is the Clear Favorite of Informed Voters," *Chicago Sun-Times*, August 18, 2003, 41.

44. Scott Fornek, "Obama Takes Jab at Fitzgerald as He Starts Run," *Chicago Sun-Times*, January 22, 2003, 8.

45. Eric Krol, "Democratic Candidate Says Fitzgerald Betrayed State," *Arlington Heights Daily Herald*, January 22, 2003, 11.

46. Jeremiah Posedel, telephone interview with Keith Boeckelman, November 27, 2006. (Mr. Posedel was the downstate coordinator for Barack Obama's 2004 Senate campaign).

47. Steve Neal, "Each Did a Good Job of Outlining Their Legislative Agenda," *Chicago Sun-Times*, October 17, 2003, 47.

48. Neal, "What Gives Obama Hope," 41.

49. John Chase, "TV Spots Pay Off in Ryan, Hull Senate Bids," *Chicago Tribune*, February 23, 2004, 1.

50. Ibid.

51. Rick Pearson and John Chase, "Unusual Match Nears Wire," *Chicago Tribune*, November 2, 2004, 1 (Metro).

52. Eric Krol, "Candidate Refuses to Clear the Air," *Arlington Heights Daily Herald*, February 20, 2004, 15.

53. Eric Zorn, "His Biggest Mistake Isn't in Divorce File," *Chicago Tribune*, February 28, 2004, 18.

54. John Kass, "Hull Learning Nothing Fair in Illinois Politics," *Chicago Tribune*, February 29, 2004, 2.

55. David Mendell and Molly Parker, "Opponents Take Aim at Hull on His Divorce, Other Issues," *Chicago Tribune*, February 24, 2004, 3.

56. Eric Krol, "Hull Responds in Ads About His Divorce," *Arlington Heights Daily Herald*, March 6, 2004, 4.

57. Andrew Herrmann, "New Poll Shows Obama Pulling Ahead of Hull," *Chicago Sun-Times*, February 26, 2004, 30.

58. Rick Pearson, "Obama, Ryan Out Front," *Chicago Tribune*, March 9, 2004, 1.

59. Kristen McQuery, "Obama Surges to Lead in Southtown Poll," *Elgin Courier News*, March 6, 2004, A1.

60. Scheiber, "Race Against History," 21–26.

61. Rick Pearson, "Obama, Ryan Out Front," *Chicago Tribune*, March 9, 2004, 1.

62. Abdon Pallasch, "Hynes Pounces on Obama at Last Debate," *Chicago Sun-Times*, March 11, 2004, 10.

63. John Patterson, "Pro-choice Advocates Defend Obama Votes," *Arlington Heights Daily Herald*, March 10, 2004, 15.

64. Ibid.

65. "Drugs, Divorce Dominate Senate Race," *St. Louis Post-Dispatch*, March 12, 2004, B6.

66. David Mendell, "Obama Routs Democratic Foes," *Chicago Tribune*, March 17, 2004, 1.

67. Don Rose, "Beyond Race ... or Not," *Chicago Tribune*, May 2, 2004, 1 (Perspective).

68. Gary Washburn and H. Gregory Meyer, "Hynes Loss Puts Machine in Doubt," *Chicago Tribune*, March 18, 2004, 1.

69. Debra Pickett, "Sunday Lunch with Dan Hynes," *Chicago Sun-Times*, December 26, 2004, 18.

70. Scheiber, "Race Against History," 21–26.

71. Posedel, interview, 2006.

72. Chase, "TV Spots Pay Off in Ryan, Hull Senate Bids," 1.

73. Posedel, interview, 2006.

74. Monica Davey, "As Quickly as Overnight, a Democratic Star Is Born," *New York Times*, March 18, 2004, 20.

CHAPTER THREE

1. "Senate Race of a Generation," *Chicago Tribune*, March 17, 2004, 28.

2. Lynn Sweet, "Running to the Right," *Illinois Issues*, January 2004, 18.

3. Ibid., 18–21.

4. Kevin McDermott, "Obama, Ryan Will Battle in Key Senate Campaign," *St. Louis Post-Dispatch*, March 17, 2004, A1.

5. Jeff Smythe, "Ryan Describes Three Themes in U.S. Senate Contest with Obama," *Carbondale Southern Illinoisan*, March 20, 2004, 1.

6. Bernard Schoenburg, "Ryan Says Obama Is Seeking Universal Health Care," *Peoria Journal Star*, June 15, 2004, B3.

7. Eric Krol and John Patterson, "GOP, Ryan Begin to Take Aim at Obama," *Arlington Heights Daily Herald*, March 29, 2004, 15.

8. "Jack Ryan Woefully Unprepared for Attack on Obama," *Springfield State Journal Register*, April 18, 2004, 21.

9. Dave McKinney, "Ryan's Chart Is Off—State Jobs Not Off the Chart," *Chicago Sun-Times*, April 16, 2004, 6.

10. "Intrusive Cameraman Raises Questions about Jack Ryan," *Peoria Journal-Star*, June 3, 2004, A5.

11. Tom Polansek, "No Rest for the Winners," *Chicago Sun-Times*, March 18, 2004, 7.

12. Stephen Kinzer, "Illinois Senate Campaign Thrown into Prurient Turmoil," *New York Times*, June 23, 2004, 14.

13. Eric Krol, "Ryan Denies Sex Club Claim," *Arlington Heights Daily Herald*, June 22, 2004, 1.

14. Bernard Schoenburg, "Ryan Still Running: Some in GOP Say They've Been Misled," *Springfield State Journal Register*, June 23, 2004, 1.

15. "Reactions Swirl around 'Ryan Papers,'" *Decatur Herald and Review*, June 23, 2004, A5.

16. Kevin McDermott and Joel Currier, "Illinois GOP Committee Is Divided on Ryan's Future," *St. Louis Post-Dispatch*, June 24, 2004, 1.

17. Eric Krol, "Ryan Gets the Cold Shoulder from GOP Congressmen," *Arlington Heights Daily Herald*, June 25, 2004, 1.

18. Rick Pearson and Rudolph Bush, "With Successor in Mind, GOP Plots Ryan's Exit," *Chicago Tribune*, June 25, 2004, 1.

19. Scott Fornek and Stephanie Zimmerman, "Sex Scandal Drives Ryan from Race," *Chicago Sun-Times*, June 26, 2004, 4.

20. Eric Krol, "Illinois' Bizarre Year in Politics," *Arlington Heights Daily Herald*, December 27, 2004, 1.

21. "News," *Mattoon Journal Gazette*, July 11, 2004, B8.

22. Mei-Ling Hopgood, "Obama the Democrats' Next Big Thing," *Cox News Services*, July 15, 2004.

23. Jim Dey, "Anatomy of an Election Fisaco," *Champaign-Urbana News Gazette*, October 16, 2004, A4.

24. Ed Faneslow, "GOP Left to Grasp Senate Straws," *Aurora Beacon News*, July 16, 2004, A1.

25. Scott Fornek, "Ditka Takes a Pass on Senate," *Chicago Sun-Times*, July 15, 2004, 4.

26. David Mendell, "Running as if He's Got a Rival," *Chicago Tribune*, July 13, 2004, 1.

27. David Mendell, "Political Phenomenon Obama Vaults into National Spotlight," *Chicago Tribune*, July 26, 2004, 1.

28. Monica Davey, "A Surprise Contender Reaches His Biggest Stage Yet," *New York Times*, July 26, 2004, 1.

29. Barack Obama, "The Audacity of Hope: Keynote Address to the 2004 Democratic National Convention," http://www.americanrhetoric.com/speeches/convention/2004/barackobama2004dnc.htm (accessed September 20, 2006).

30. Ibid.

31. Randal C. Archibold, "Day after Keynote, Speaker Finds Admirers Everywhere," *New York Times*, July 29, 2004, 6.

32. Dennis Brody, "Obama's Burden Now Is to Meet High Hopes," *Pittsburgh Post-Gazette*, July 29, 2004, A1; Amanda Ripley, "Obama's Ascent," *Time*, November 15, 2004, 74–76.

33. Nicole Sack, "Edwards Says Kerry Ready to Build One America: Obama Speech Impresses even GOP," *Carbondale Southern Illinoisian*, July 29, 2004, A1.

34. Laura Peterecca, "Bull's Eye," *New York Post*, August 1, 2004, 33.

35. Ann McFeatters, "Obama Wary of Hype He's Spawned" *Pittsburgh Post-Gazette*, July 30, 2004, A9.

36. David Mendell, "Heady Week Yields to Hard Work," *Chicago Tribune*, August 1, 2004, 1 (Metro).

37. Dave McKinney, "Obama Just Can't Help But Shine," *Chicago Sun-Times*, August 4, 2004, 6.

38. Jeremiah Posedel, telephone interview with Keith Boeckelman, November 27, 2006. (Mr. Posedel was the downstate coordinator for Barack Obama's 2004 Senate campaign).

39. Monica Davey, "In a Star's Shadow, Republicans Strain to Find an Opponent," *New York Times*, July 29, 2004, 6.

40. Ibid.

41. Scott Fornek, "Campaign 2004," *Chicago Sun-Times*, July 16, 2004, 3.

42. Eric Krol, "GOP List Down to a Surprising Pair," *Arlington Heights Daily Herald*, August 4, 2004, 1.

43. Mark Brown, "Has GOP Finally Hit Bottom?" *Chicago Sun-Times*, August 5, 2004, 2.

44. "Five Levels Down, " *St. Louis Post-Dispatch*, August 10, 2004, B06.

45. Rich Miller, "Keyes Choice a Major Misstep by State's GOP Leaders," *Daily Southtown*, August 8, 2004.

46. Ed Fansler, "Keyes Brings His Anti-Obama Rhetoric to Aurora," *Elgin Courier-News*, August 15, 2004, A3.

47. Krol, "Illinois' Bizarre Year in Politics," 1.

48. Dey, "Anatomy of an Election Fiasco," A4.

49. "Keyes," *Carbondale Southern Illinoisian*, October 4, 2004, A1.

50. Rick Pearson, "Keyes Says Game Plan Is Controversy," *Chicago Tribune*, September 14, 2004, 1.

51. David Mendell and Liam Ford, "Keyes Derails Obama from Traditional Track," *Chicago Tribune*, September 13, 2004, 1 (Metro).

52. Ibid.

53. Kathy Cichon, "Election 2004: Obama Spreads the Word," *Naperville Sun*, October 6, 2004, 1.

54. Nathaniel Zimmer, "Election 2004: Obama Catching Breaks, Avoiding Liberal Label," *Naperville Sun,* October 6, 2004, 2.

55. John Chase, "Obama, Kees Clash on Terrorism," *Chicago Tribune,* October 11, 2004, 1.

56. Peter Slevin, "Obama Lending Star Power to Other Democrats," *Washington Post,* October 11, 2004, A2.

57. Nicole Sack, "Learning about Obama," *Carbondale Southern Illinoisian,* August 4, 2004, A1.

58. Molly Parker, "Obama Slams 'Say Anything' Politics," *Peoria Journal-Star,* October 23, 2004, B6.

59. Posedel, interview, 2006.

60. Cichon, "Election 2004," 1.

61. Kevin McDermott, "Obama Defends His Religious Views, Values," *St. Louis Post-Dispatch,* October 6, 2004, B01.

62. Maura Kelly Lannan, "Obama Offers Health Plan for Small Firms," *St. Louis Post-Dispatch,* September 8, 2004, B01.

63. Ibid.

64. Dennis Byrne, "A Critical Look at Obama's Politics," *Chicago Tribune,* August 16, 2004, 17.

65. "Dodging Tough Issue Not Good for Obama," *Champaign News-Gazette,* October 11, 2004, A6.

66. Kevin McDermott, "Unlikely Competitors," *St. Louis Post-Dispatch,* October 24, 2004, A01.

67. Hopgood, "Obama the Democrats' Next Big Thing;" McDermott, "Unlikely Competitors," A01.

68. Benjamin Wallace-Wells, "The Great Black Hope," *Washington Monthly,* November 2004, 30–36.

69. William Finnegan, "The Candidate," *New Yorker,* May 31, 2004, 32–39.

70. Doug Finke, "Obama Stars on Governor's Day," *Springfield State Journal-Register,* August 19, 2004, 1.

71. Finnegan, "The Candidate," 32–39.

72. Mike Thomas, "What's Behind Barack's Celebrity," *Chicago Sun-Times,* August 9, 2004, 44.

73. Kevin McDermott, "Obama May Trounce Keyes for Senate," *St. Louis Post-Dispatch,* September 20, 2004, A01.

74. "Illinois Election 2004: Senate Candidates Poll," *Naperville Sun,* October 7, 2004, 18.

75. "Keyes," *Carbondale Southern Illinoisian,* October 4, 2004, A1.

76. Kristin McQueary, "Keyes a Ballotwide Advantage for Dems," *Daily Southtown,* October 24, 2004, 1.

77. Mendell and Ford, "Keyes Derails Obama from Traditional Track," 1 (Metro).

78. Posedel, interview, 2006.

79. Mendell and Ford, "Keyes Derails Obama from Traditional Track," 1 (Metro).

80. Lynn Sweet, "Obama's Sharing the Wealth with Other Dems" *Chicago Sun-Times,* October 7, 2004, 47.

81. Michael Barone and Richard E. Cohen, *Almanac of American Politics* (Washington: *National Journal,* 2006), 560.

82. Lynn Sweet, "Kerry Taps Obama to Court African American Vote," *Chicago Sun-Times*, September 28, 2004, 20.

83. Ibid.

84. Scott Fornek, "Obama to Debut TV Ads Next Week," *Chicago Sun-Times*, August 14, 2004, 6.

85. Scott Fornek, "Keyes Taps National Base to Raise Money for TV Ads," *Chicago Sun-Times*, October 18, 2004, 6.

86. Cheryl V. Jackson, "Rap by Common Plugs a Presidential Bid," *Chicago Sun-Times*, September 18, 2004, 20.

87. Christopher Mills, "Obama Sweeps Newspaper Endorsements in Senate Race," *Mattoon News-Gazette*, October 30, 2004, A8.

88. Eric Krol, "New Ads Criticize Obama's Votes on Crime, Abortion," *Arlington Heights Daily Herald*, October 12, 2004, 1.

89. Scott Fornek, "Keyes Says He Wants to Rumble with Obama," *Chicago Sun-Times*, August 11, 2004, 24.

90. John Chase and Liam Ford, "Obama, Keyes Put on Kid Gloves," *Chicago Tribune*, October 13, 2004, 1.

91. Rich Miller, "Obama Comes Out Firing at Keyes in New Debate Strategy," *Daily Southtown*, October 24, 2004.

92. John Chase and Liam Ford, "Senate Debate Gets Personal," *Chicago Tribune*, October 22, 2004, 1 (Metro).

93. Ibid.

94. Rich Miller, "Obama Comes Out Swinging in Second U.S. Senate Debate," *River Cities Reader*, October 27-November 4, 2004.

95. John Chase and Courtney Flynn, "Keyes, Obama Disagree Sharply," *Chicago Tribune*, October 27, 2004, 1 (Metro).

96. Ibid.

97. Ibid.

98. Illinois State Board of Elections, *Official Vote of the General Election, November 4, 2004* (Springfield: Illinois State Board of Elections, 2004).

99. America Votes—2004. http://www.cnn.com/ELECTION/2004/pages/results/states/IL/S/01/epolls.0.html (accessed November 29, 2006).

100. Kevin McDermott, "Obama Keeps Huge Lead over Keyes in Senate Race," *St. Louis Post-Dispatch*, October 28, 2004, A01.

101. "The Pride of Illinois," *Chicago Tribune*, November 3, 2004, 30.

102. Phillip O'Connor, "Obama Succeeds with Voters of Every Stripe," *St. Louis Post-Dispatch*, November 3, 2004, A01.

103. John Chase and David Mendell, "Obama Sails to Senate Win," *Chicago Tribune*, November 3, 2004, 1.

104. James G. Gimpel and Jason Schuknecht, "Reconsidering Political Regionalism in the American States," *State Politics and Policy Quarterly* 2 (2002): 325–52.

105. Noam Scheiber, "Race against History: Barack Obama's Miraculous Campaign," *New Republic*, May 24, 2004, 21–26.

106. John Chase and David Mendell, "Obama Routs Democratic Foes," *Chicago Tribune*, May 17, 2004, 1.

107. John Chase, "Obama Gets Early Boost from Voters," *Chicago Tribune*, May 31, 2004, 1.

108. Kristen McQueary, "Poll: Obama, Ryan Senate Race Tightens Up," *Waukegan Sun*, May 18, 2004, A1.

CHAPTER FOUR

1. Jesse M. Unruh, 1963, Speaker of the California State Assembly.
2. Paul Merrion, "Obama's Appeal Drives Cash Flow," *Crains's Chicago Business*, September 15, 2003, 3.
3. Jeremiah Posedel, telephone interview with Keith Boeckelman, November 27, 2006. (Mr. Posedel was the downstate coordinator for Barack Obama's 2004 Senate campaign).
4. Rick Pearson and Ray Gibson, "Campaign Fund Law Has Giant Loophole," *Chicago Tribune*, February 5, 2003, 1.
5. Merrion, "Obama's Appeal Drives Cash Flow," 3.
6. David Mendell, "Hull Proves Money No Object in Bid for Senate," *Chicago Tribune*, February 10, 2004, 1.
7. Ibid.
8. Scott Fornek, "Blackjack King Outspends Dem Rival 4–1 in Senate Bid," *Chicago Sun-Times*, July 16, 2003, 1.
9. Ibid.
10. Mendell, "Hull Proves Money No Object in Bid for Senate," 1.
11. Fornek, "Blackjack King Outspends Dem Rival 4–1 in Senate Bid," 1.
12. Ray Gibson and Rick Pearson, "Candidate Hull Spends at Record Pace," *Chicago Tribune*, July 16, 2003, 1.
13. Ken Silverstein, "Barack Obama Inc.," *Harper's Magazine*, November 2006, 34.
14. Matt Adrian and Richard Goldstein, "Senate Candidates Stack up Money," *Herald & Review* (Decatur, IL), July 6, 2003, B4.
15. Merrion, "Obama's Appeal Drives Cash Flow," 3.
16. Ibid.
17. Ibid.
18. Gibson and Pearson, "Candidate Hull Spends at Record Pace," 1.
19. Silverstein, "Barack Obama Inc.," 36.
20. Ibid.
21. Jim Dey, "Cash Makes Candidate a Player in Senate Race," *The News-Gazette (Champaign, IL)*, November 15, 2003, A4.
22. Scott Fornek, "Ryan Spent Less than Dem Obama in Winning GOP Nod," *Chicago Sun-Times*, April 16, 2004, 28.
23. Merrion, "Obama's Appeal Drives Cash Flow," 3.
24. Tamara E. Holmes, "Will Mr. Obama Go to Washington? Illinois State Legislator Seeks to Become Only Black U.S. Senator," *Black Enterprise*, February 2004, 26.
25. David Mendell and Liam Ford, "Keyes Manages to Rake in Cash; Obama So Flush He's Giving It Away," *Chicago Tribune*, October 16, 2004, 1.
26. "U.S. Senate Candidates Seek Younger Voters at Bars, Concerts," *Journal Gazette-Times Courier*, April 21, 2004.

27. Paul Merrion, "Obama Lead Brings Bucks from Biz PACs," *Crain's Chicago Business*, July 12, 2004, 3.

28. Ibid.

29. Lauren W. Whittington, "Obama Endearing Himself with Cash," *Roll Call*, October 7, 2004.

30. "Sector Total," http://www.opensecrets.org (accessed February 22, 2007).

31. John N. Frank, "Green Grasps Inextricable Link Between PR and Politics," *PR Week*, December 13, 2004, 11.

32. Liam Ford and David Mendell, "Senate Race to Hit Airwaves," *Chicago Tribune*, August 16, 2004, 1 (Metro).

33. John Cook, "Political Season a Loser for Local TV," *Chicago Tribune*, August 21, 2004, 1 (Business).

34. Anne E. Kornblut and Mathew Mosk, "Obama's Campaign Takes in $25 Million," *Washington Post*, April 5, 2007, A1.

35. David D. Kirkpatrick, Mike McIntire, and Jeffrey Zeleny, "Obama's Camp Cultivates Crop in Small Donors," *New York Times*, July 17, 2007, A1.

CHAPTER FIVE

1. Gary Washburn and H. Gregory Meyer, "Hynes' Loss Puts Machine in Doubt," *Chicago Tribune,* March 18, 2004, 1.

2. "In Illinois, Political Ads down This Year," *Champaign (IL) News-Gazette*, December 1, 2004, A6.

3. Jim Drinkard and Mark Memmott, "Election Ad Battle Smashes Record in 2004," *USA Today,* November, 26, 2004, 1.

4. John Cook, "Political Season a Loser for Local TV," *Chicago Tribune*, August 21, 2004, 1 (Business).

5. Trevor Jensen, "In Illinois, It's Still Pay to Play," *Adweek*, March 22, 2004.

6. Ibid.

7. Ibid.

8. Ibid.

9. Ibid.

10. Jim Dey, "Cash Makes a Candidate a Player in the Senate Race," *News-Gazette* (Champion-Urbana, IL), November 15, 2003, A4.

11. "Several Senate Candidates on the Air," *Southern Illinoisan,* October 20, 2003, A1.

12. Patrick J. Powers, "Senate Hopeful First to Place Metro-East Ads," *Belleville News Democrat,* June 27, 2003, B1.

13. Rick Pearson, "Not Why, Who," *Chicago Tribune*, March 14, 2004, 1.

14. David Mendell, "Hull Proves Money No Object in Bid for Senate," *Chicago Tribune,* February 10, 2004, 1.

15. Ibid.

16. John Chase, "TV Spots Pay Off in Ryan, Hull Senate Bids," *Chicago Tribune,* February 23, 2004, 1.

17. "Several Candidates on the Air," *South Illinoisan* (Carbondale, IL), October 23, 2003, A1.

18. Ibid.

19. Mendell, "Hull Proves Money No Object in Bid for Senate," 1.

20. "Several Senate Candidates on the Air," *Southern Illinoisan,* A1.

21. John Chase and David Mendell, "Senate Rivals Struggle to Wash off Mud Stains," March 14, 2004, 1.

22. Rick Pearson, "Not Why, Who," 1.

23. Ibid.

24. "Hull Calls Protection Order 'Legal Tactic,'" *Southern Illinoisan* (Carbondale, IL), March 5, 2004, A6.

25. Kristen McQueary. "Obama Surges Past Hull for Democratic Nod," *The Beacon News,* March 6, 2004, A1.

26. David Mendell, "Obama Routs Democratic Foes," *Chicago Tribune*, March 17, 2004, 1.

27. Scott Fornek and Stephanie Zimmermann, "Sex Scandal Drives Ryan from Race," *Chicago Sun-Times*, June 26, 2004, 4.

28. Scott Fornek, "Obama to Debut TV Ads Next Week," *Chicago Sun-Times*, August 14, 2004, 6.

29. Ibid.

30. John N. Frank, "Green Grasps Inextricable Link between PR and Politics," *PR Week*, December 13, 2004, 11.

31. Scott Fornek, "Is Obama Overconfident? Check Out Latest Ad," *Chicago Sun-Times*, October 20, 2004, 22.

32. Ibid.

33. Scott Fornek, "Keyes' First Ad Focuses on Positive Spirit," *State Journal-Register* (Springfield, IL), October 28, 2004, 18.

34. Molly Parker, "Keyes Shrugs Off Polls That Show Him Trailing," *Peoria Journal Star*, October 28, 2004, B2.

35. David Mendell and Liam Ford, "Keyes Manages to Rake in Cash," *Chicago Tribune*, October 16, 2004, 1.

36. Fornek, "Keyes' First Ad Focuses on Positive Spirit," 18.

37. Christopher Wills, "Obama Sweeps Newspaper Endorsement in Senate Race," *Journal Gazette* (Mattoon, IL), October 30, 2004, A8.

38. Molly Parker, "Obama Slams 'Say Anything' Politics," *Peoria Journal Star,* October 23, 2004, B6.

39. Scott Fornek, "A Final Scramble for Votes in Illinois," *State Journal-Register* (Springfield, IL), November 2, 2004, 18.

40. Nathaniel Zimmer, "Group Decries TV Ad as Illegal—Attacks Barack Obama," *Courier News* (Elgin, IL), October 15, 2004, A1.

41. "Anti-Obama Ad Begins on Central Illinois TV," *The Telegraph* (River Bend, IL), October 13, 2004.

42. Press release, "CREW Files FEC Complaint Against US Senate Candidate Alan Keyes, Empower Illinois Media Fund and Jack Roeser," *US Newswire*, October 14, 2004.

43. Jodi Heckel, "Democratic Senate Hopeful Denounces Negative Campaigns," *The News-Gazette (Champaign, IL),* October 12, 2004, B1–B2.

44. Shirley Biagi, *Media/Impact: An Introduction to Mass Media*, 7th Ed. (Belmont, CA: Thomson Wadsworth, 2005), 107.

45. Ibid.

46. David Ellis and Paul R. La Monica, "XM Sirius Announce Merger," *CNN Money*, February 20, 2007, 1.

47. Robert LaRose and Joseph Straubhhar, *Media Now: Understanding Media, Culture, and Technology*, 4th Ed. (Belmont, CA: Thompson Wadsworth, 2004), 144.

48. Ibid., 147.

49. Tom Dobrez, "Radio: The Secret Weapon—Political Campaigns," *Campaigns and Elections*, Gale Group, August 1996, 1–2.

50. Ibid.

51. Ibid.

52. Scott Fornek, "Senate Hopefuls Vie for Black Vote," *Chicago Sun-Times*, August 5, 2003, 8.

53. Ibid.

54. Ibid.

55. Ibid.

56. Fornek, "Senate Hopefuls Vie for Black Vote," 8.

57. Liam Ford and David Mendell, "Senate Race to Hit Airways," *Chicago Tribune*, August 26, 2004, 1.

58. Heckel, "Democratic Senate Hopeful Denounces Negative Campaigns," B1.

59. Robert LaRose and Joseph Straubhaar, *Media Now: Understanding Media, Culture, and Technology*, 4th Ed. (Belmont, CA: Thompson Wadsworth, 2004).

60. Sonya Moore, "Cashing in on Elections," *Editor & Publisher*, February 1, 2004, 53.

61. "Endorsements: U.S. Senate, Democrats—Gery Chico Would Do for Washington What He Did for Chicago's Public Schools," *The Beacon News*, March 7, 2004, D2.

62. Ibid.

63. David Mendell and Jill Zuckman, "Obama to Be Keynote Speaker at Democratic Convention," *Chicago Tribune*, July 14, 2004, 1.

64. Ibid.

65. Ibid.

66. "Obama for U.S. Senate," *State Journal-Register*, October 29, 2004, 8.

67. Wills, "Obama Sweeps Newspaper Endorsement in Senate Race," A8.

68. Ibid.

69. Parker, "Keyes Shrugs Off Polls That Show Him Trailing," B2.

70. Wills, "Obama Sweeps Newspaper Endorsement in Senate Race," A8.

71. Ibid.

72. Ibid.

73. James Wilson and John J. DiIulio Jr., *American Government*, 9th Ed. (Boston: Houghton Mifflin, 2004).

74. Ibid.

75. Lee Raine, Michael Cornfield, and John Horrigan, *The Internet and Campaign 2004*, Pew Internet and American Life Project, http://www.pewinternet.org (accessed February 23, 2007).

76. Clifford A. Jones, "Campaign Finance Reform and the Internet," in *The Internet Election,* eds. Andrew Paul Williams and John C. Tedesco (Lanham, MD: Rowman & Littlefield Publishers, 2006), 5.

77. " '04 Illinois Democratic Senate Candidates," *Campaigns & Elections,* June 2003, 40.

78. Mei-Ling Hopgood, "Obama the Democrats' Next Big Thing," *Cox News Service,* July 15, 2004.

CHAPTER SIX

1. Dawn Turner Trice, "Obama Unfazed by Foes' Doubts on Race Question," *Chicago Tribune,* March 15, 2004, 1.

2. Noam Scheiber, "Race Against History," *The New Republic,* May 31, 2004, 21.

3. Richard Wolffe and Daren Briscoe, "Across the Divide," *Newsweek,* July 16, 2006, 28.

4. Jeff Zeleny, "When it Comes to Race, Obama Makes His Point—with Subtlety," *Chicago Tribune,* June 26, 2005, 18.

5. Wolffe and Briscoe, "Across the Divide," 24.

6. U.S. Census Bureau. http://www.census.gov/prod/2001/pubs/c2kbr01-5.pdf. Accessed July 3, 2007.

7. Garance Franke-Ruta, "The Next Generation," *American Prospect,* August 2004, 13.

8. Ibid.

9. Naftali Bendavid, "Primary Colors," *Chicago Tribune Magazine,* October 24, 2004.

10. Jan Rosenberg and Philip Kasinitz, "Missing the Connection: Social Isolation and Employment on the Brooklyn Waterfront," *Social Problems,* May 1996, 180–196; Marcolm Gladwell, "Blacks Like Them: West Indian Blacks in the U.S.," *The New Yorker,* April 29, 1996.

11. Marcolm Gladwell, "Blacks Like Them: West Indian Blacks in the U.S.," *The New Yorker,* April 29, 1996.

12. Daren Briscoe, "After the Trailblazers," *Newsweek,* July 16, 2006, 29.

13. Franke-Ruta, "The Next Generation," 13.

14. David Bositis, The Black Vote in 2004 (Washington, DC), Joint Center for Political and Economic Studies.

15. Franke-Ruta, "The Next Generation," 13.

16. Ibid.

17. U.S. Census Bureau. Illinois Quickfacts. http://quickfacts.census.gov/qfd/states/17000.html. Accessed July 3, 2007.

18. Dawn Turner Trice, "Democratic Primary Isn't about Skin Color," *Chicago Tribune,* February 11, 2002, 1.

19. Mary Mitchell, "Calling Rivals 'White Boys' Doesn't Negate Burris' Point," *Chicago Sun-Times,* March 1, 1998, 23.

20. Trice, "Democratic Primary Isn't about Skin Color" 1B.

21. Rick Davis, *They Call Heroes Mister: The Jesse White Story* (Richton Park, IL: Lumen-us Press, 2006), 202.

22. "Political Briefs," *Chicago Tribune,* December 6, 1975, S10.

23. Davis, *They Call Heroes Mister*, 196.

24. Scott Fornek, "Burris Posts Race's Smallest War Chest," *Chicago Sun-Times* March 7, 2002, 12.

25. Tatsha Robertson, "Top Elective Spots Eluding Minorities," *Boston Globe*, March 21, 2002, A3.

26. Scheiber, "Race Against History," 21.

27. Ibid.

28. Glenn Jeffers and Rex W. Huppke, "Blacks United Behind Obama; Victory Margin Strong across the Board," *Chicago Tribune*, March 17, 2004, 1.

29. John Chase and David Mendell, "Senate Rivals Struggle to Wash off Mud Stains," *Chicago Tribune*, March 11, 2004, 1.

30. Jeffers and Huppke, "Blacks United Behind Obama," 1.

31. Chase and Mendell, "Senate Rivals Struggle to Wash off Mud Stains," 1.

32. Jeffers and Huppke, "Blacks United Behind Obama," 1.

33. Ibid.

34. William Finnegan, "The Candidate," *The New Yorker*, May 31, 2004, 32.

35. Benjamin Wallace-Wells, "The Great Black Hope," *Washington Monthly*, November 2004, 30–36.

36. David Moberg, "Audacious and Hopeful," *In These Times*, September 20, 2004, 22.

37. Eric Krol, "Jack Ryan Has Uphill Battle for Black Voters," *Daily Herald* (Arlington Heights, IL), March 22, 2004, 1.

38. Ibid.

39. Scott Fornek, "Senate Hopefuls Vie for Black Vote—Hull Takes Heat from Obama for Radio Ads Featuring Rush," *Chicago Sun Times*, August 5, 2003, 8.

40. Salim Muwakkil, "Keyes' Ideological Quest," *In These Times*, September 20, 2004, 13.

41. *The Economist*, "The Politics of Tokenism," August 14, 2004.

42. Dawn Turner Trice, "Obama Unfazed by Foes' Doubts on Race Question," *Chicago Tribune*, March 15, 2004, 1.

43. "This Week," with George Stephanopoulos quoted in Rachel L. Swarns, "'African American' Becomes a Term for Debate," *New York Times*, August 29, 2004, 1.

44. David Mendell, "Key Race May Tip Balance in Senate," *Chicago Tribune*, December 7, 2003, 1.

45. Swarns, "'African American' Becomes a Term for Debate," 1.

46. Ibid.

47. Ibid.

48. Zeleny, "When It Comes to Race, Obama Makes His Point," 18.

49. Kevin McDermott and William Lamb, "Race Matters in Senate Campaign," *St. Louis Post- Dispatch*, October 3, 2004, C1.

50. Editorial, *Peoria Journal Star*, August 27, 2004, 22.

51. Don Terry, "The Skin Game," *Chicago Tribune Magazine*, October 24, 2004, 22.

52. Ibid.

53. Finnegan, "The Candidate," 32.

54. Ibid.

55. Salim Muwakkil, "Shades of 1983," *In These Times*, April 26, 2004, p. 13, The Third Coast.

56. Steve Inskeep, "Obama to Mark Anniversary of Civil Rights March," *National Pubilc Radio*, February 28, 2007.

57. Wolffe and Briscoe, "Across the Divide," 26.

58. Terry, "The Skin Game," 21.

59. Ibid.

60. Wallace-Wells, "The Great Black Hope," 30–36.

61. Wolffe and Briscoe, "Across the Divide," 27.

62. Zeleny, "When it Comes to Race, Obama Makes His Point," 18.

63. Daren Briscoe Alter, "The Audacity of Hope," *Newsweek*, December 27, 2004, 74.

CHAPTER SEVEN

1. Jeff Zeleny, "The First Time Around—Sen. Barack Obama's Freshman Year," *Chicago Tribune*, December 25, 2005, 1 (Perspective).

2. Jeff Zeleny, "New Man on the Hill," *Chicago Tribune*, March 20, 2005, 1.

3. Ibid.

4. Ibid.

5. *Current Biography,* Barack Obama. Cover Biography for July 2005. http://www.hwwilson.com/Currentbio/cover_bios/cover_bio_7_05.htm (accessed 12/04/2006).

6. Ibid.

7. Zeleny, "The First Time Around," 1.

8. Rudolph Bush, "Senators Press on for Vets' Benefits—Durbin, Obama Decry Inaction by VA Official," *Chicago Tribune*, April 15, 2005, 6.

9. Jeff Zeleny, "Voters give Obama, Durbin Good Marks," *Chicago Tribune*, October 16, 2005, 22.

10. Lynn Sweet, "While Obama Basks, Durbin Rises," *Chicago Sun-Times*, January 5, 2005, 6.

11. Scott Fornek, "Obama Is No. 1 Most Popular Senator," *Chicago Sun-Times*, June 17, 2005, 4.

12. Charlyn Fargo, "Tax Credit for E85 Fuel in Energy Bill—Proposal Would Help Put in Station Pumps," *State Journal-Register*, July 28, 2005, 31.

13. Ibid.

14. Charlyn Fargo, "Obama Wants to Give Motorists a Tax Break for Pumping E85," *Peoria Journal Star*, April 19, 2005, C1.

15. Molly Parker, "Obama Touts Ethanol's Use—U.S. Senator Tours Pekin Plant, Urges Congress to Act on Issue," *Peoria Journal Star*, March 15, 2005, 1.

16. "Obama Pushes for More Ethanol Production," *Southern Illinoisan*, March 15, 2005, 7A.

17. Ibid.

18. Zeleny, "Voters Give Obama, Durbin Good Marks," 22.

19. Jacob Weisberg, "The Path to Power," *Men's Vogue*, September/October 2006, 218–23, 247–48.

20. Sweet, "While Obama Basks," 6.

21. Kevin Sampier, "Senator Places Focus on Illinois," *Peoria Journal Star*, May 25, 2005, A17.

22. Ibid.

23. Laura Girresch, "Senators Seek Cooling Funds Grants Help the Needy Pay Energy Bills," *Belleville News-Democrat*, July 28, 2005, 1B.

24. "Senators Get Farmers Relief," *Grayslake Review*, August 4, 2005, 10.

25. Ibid.

26. Jeff Zeleny, "Obama Can't Say No to Farm Aid Invite," *Chicago Tribune*, September 14, 2005, 23.

27. Charles Babington and Shailiagh Murray, "For Now, an Unofficial Rivalry: Possible Clinton–Obama Presidential Clash Has Senate Abuzz," *Washington Post*, December 8, 2006, A01.

28. Kirk Victor, "Reason to Smile," *National Journal*, March 18, 2006, 20–24.

29. Lynn Sweet, "After Cautious Bipartisan Year, Obama Opens New Chapter," *Chicago Sun-Times*, January 22, 2006, A12.

30. Jeff Zeleny, "Senators Ask Why U.S. Paying When Free Ships Offered," *Chicago Tribune*, September 30, 2005, 8.

31. Ibid.

32. Ibid.

33. Jeff Zeleny, "Spending Monitor Urged," *Chicago Tribune*, September 14, 2005, 26.

34. Jeff Zeleny, "Obama on Bush: We Should Trust Although We Should Verify," *Chicago Tribune*, September 18, 2005, 13.

35. Ibid.

36. Clarence Page, "Anti-poverty Victories Have to Begin at Home," *Chicago Tribune*, August 23, 2006, 25.

37. "Obama's 1st Bill Aims to Expand the Pell Grant," *Chicago Tribune*, March 29, 2005, 3.

38. Rummana Hussein, "Obama Fears 'Big Brother' Over Our Shoulders—Says Feds Should Have to Get Search Warrant to See Library Records," *Chicago Sun-Times*, June 26, 2005, 32.

39. "Obama's 1st Bill Aims," 3.

40. Carl Hulse, "By a Vote of 98–0, Senate Approves 25-year Extension of Voting Rights Act," *New York Times*, July 21, 2006, 16.

41. Ibid.

42. "Voter-ID Proposal Opposed by Senators," *San Diego Union-Tribune*, September 21, 2005, A8.

43. Deirdre Shesgreen, "Senate Panel Blocks Bush 'Clear Skies' Proposal," *St. Louis Post-Dispatch*, March 10, 2005, A2.

44. "Murky Forecast for Clear Skies," *Chicago Tribune*, March 9, 2005, 24.

45. Shesgreen, "Senate Panel Blocks," 10.

46. Elizabeth Williamson, "The Green Gripe with Obama: Liquefied Coal Is Still ... Coal," *Washington Post,* January 10, 2007, A11.

47. Ibid.

48. Victor, "Reason to Smile," 20–24.

49. Ibid.

50. Jeff Zeleny, "Obama is Democrats Point Man on Ethics," *Chicago Tribune*, January 18, 2006, 8.

51. Lynn Sweet, "McCain: Obama Is Insincere: Illinois Senator Says He Still Respects Colleague Despite Unusually Harsh Letter," *Chicago Sun-Times*, February 7, 2006, 8.

52. Jeff Zeleny, "Stepping off the Sidelines into the Spotlight," *Chicago Tribune*, February 26, 2006, 4.

53. Weisberg, "The Path to Power," 218–23, 247–48.

54. Ibid.

55. Lynn Sweet and Carol Marine, "Obama, Bush, Lipinski Sworn in Today," *Chicago Sun-Times*, January 4, 2005, 5.

56. Barack Obama, "Upgrading Health Care Technology Would Save Many Lives, Much-Money," *Daily Herald*, July 26, 2005, 10.

57. Lynn Sweet, "Obama Finds Bush's Pitch Offensive," *Chicago Sun-Times*, March 11, 2005, 3.

58. Obama, "Upgrading Health-Care Technology," 10.

59. Ibid.

60. "Senators Worried about Bird Flu Preparedness," *Chronicle*, July 22, 2006, 6.

61. "Senators Pan Voluntary Bird Flu Test," *Press Register*, July 22, 2006, 8.

62. David Goldstein, "Lack of Vaccine Heightens Fear of Potential Bird Flu Pandemic," *Kansas City Star*, May 21, 2005, 1.

63. Barack Obama and Richard Lugar, "Grounding a Pandemic," *New York Times*, June 6, 2005, 19.

64. Michael Lipinsky, *Review of Obama's* "The Audacity of Hope," *The New York Review of Books: The Phenomenon*, http://www.nybooks.com/articles/19651, (accessed 02/22/2007).

65. Ibid.

66. Lynn Sweet, "Obama Heading for Africa 'Because Africa Is Important'," *Beacon News*, August 18, 2006, B1.

67. "Obama Seeks Concrete Results with African Trip—Senator Wants to See What Helps Advance Progress," *Herald Review*, August 20, 2006, B1.

68. Jeff Zeleny and Laurie Goering, "Obama Challenges South Africa to Face AIDS Crisis: Declaring the Matter Urgent, Senator Vows to Get Public HIV Test as Way to Erase Stigma," *Chicago Tribune*, August 22, 2006, 6.

69. Ibid.

70. Lynn Sweet, "Obama Draws on African Roots as He Steps onto Global Stage with Sudan," *Chicago Sun-Times*, July 18, 2005, 30.

71. Jeff Zeleny, "Obama Returns to Africa as Celebrity—But Senator's Agenda is Broad and Serious," *Chicago Tribune*, August 20, 2006, 7.

72. Jeff Zeleny, "Obama-Lugar Proposal Targets Stockpiles of Conventional Weapons," *Chicago Tribune*, November 2, 2005, 15.

73. Ibid.

74. Jeff Zeleny, "U.S. Focuses on Russian WMD—Senators Inspect Weapons Sites," *Chicago Tribune*, August 27, 2005, 3.

75. Jeff Zeleny, "Educating Obama: Foreign Trip with Lugar Teaches Illinois Senator the Ropes," *Chicago Tribune*, October 2, 2005, 5D.

76. Zeleny, "U.S. Focuses," 3.

77. Zeleny, "Educating Obama," 5D.

78. Ibid.

79. *Current Biography,* Barack Obama. Cover Biography for July 2005, http://www.hwwilson.com/Currentbio/cover_bios/cover_bio_7_05.htm (accessed 12/04/2006).

CHAPTER EIGHT

1. Garry Wills, *Lincoln at Gettysburg: The Words that Remade America* (New York: Touchstone, 1992), 145–46.

2. Wayne Fields, *Union of Words: A History of Presidential Eloquence* (New York: Free Press, 1996), 155–56.

3. LeRoy Ashby, *William Jennings Bryan: Champion of Democracy* (Boston: Twanye Publishers, 1987), xiii.

4. Anna Deaveare Smith, "Show and Tell," *New York Times*, July 20, 2004, 19.

5. Quoted in Jennifer L. Hochschild, *Facing up to the American Dream: Race, Class, and the Soul of the Nation* (Princeton: Princeton University Press, 1995), 18.

6. Ray A. Dearin, "The American Dream as Depicted in Robert J. Dole's 1996 Presidential Nomination Acceptance Speech," *Presidential Studies Quarterly* 27 (1997): 699–701.

7. Michael J. Graetz and Ian Shapiro, *Death by a Thousand Cuts: The Fight Over Taxing Inherited Wealth* (Princeton: Princeton University Press, 2005), 120.

8. Mario Cuomo, "1984 Democratic National Convention Keynote Address: A Tale of Two Cities," http://www.americanrhetoric.com/speeches/mariocuomo1984dnc.htm (accessed October 26, 2006).

9. Dennis J. McGrath and Dane Smith, *Professor Wellstone Goes to Washington* (Minneapolis: University of Minnesota Press, 1995), 50–51.

10. Barack Obama, "The Audacity of Hope: Keynote Address to the 2004 Democratic National Convention," http://www.americanrhetoric.com/speeches/convention/2004/barackobama2004dnc.htm (accessed September 20, 2006).

11. Barack Obama, "Remarks at John Lewis's 65th Birthday Gala," http://www.obama.senate.gov (accessed August 25, 2006).

12. Barack Obama, "University of Massachusetts at Boston Commencement Address," http://www.obama.senate.gov (accessed August 25, 2006).

13. Barack Obama, "Remarks at the Knox College Commencement," http://www.obama.senate.gov (accessed August 25, 2006).

14. Barack Obama, "Remarks at the Robert F. Kennedy Human Rights Award Ceremony," http://www.obama.senate.gov (accessed August 25, 2006).

15. Barack Obama, "Statement on Hurricane Katrina Relief," http://www.obama.senate.gov (accessed August 25, 2006).

16. Ibid.

17. John Kingdon, *America the Unusual* (New York: St. Martin's/Worth, 1999), 27–28.

18. Michael Sandel, *Democracy's Discontent: America in Search of a Public Philosophy* (Cambridge: Harvard University Press, 1996), 4–6.

19. Rogers M. Smith, "The American Creed and American Identity: The Limits of Liberal Citizenship in the United States, *Western Political Quarterly* 41 (1988), 247.

20. Barack Obama, *Dreams from My Father: A Story of Race and Inheritance* (New York: Three Rivers Press, 2004), 190.

21. Barack Obama, "Xavier University Commencement Address," http://www.obama.ste.gov (accessed August 25, 2006).

22. Barack Obama, "'Call to Renewal' Keynote Address," http://www.obama.senate.gov (accessed August 25, 2006).

23. Barack Obama, "Remarks of Senator Barack Obama at the 2006 Global Summit on AIDS and the Church," http://www.obama.senate.gov (accessed December 5, 2006).

24. Obama, "Call to Renewal."

25. Ibid.

26. Barack Obama, "Remarks at the NAACP Fight for Freedom Fund Dinner," http://www.obama.senate.gov (accessed August 25, 2006).

27. Barack Obama, "Remarks to the Kaiser Family Foundation on the 'Sex on TV' Report," http://www.obama.senate.gov (accessed August 26, 2005).

28. David Mendell, "Obama Routs Democratic Foes," *Chicago Tribune*, March 17, 2004, 1.

29. Ibid.

30. Obama, "Remarks at the Knox College Commencement."

31. Barack Obama, "Floor Statement on S. 256, the Bankruptcy Abuse and Prevention Act of 2005," http://www.obama.senate.gov (accessed August 26, 2006).

32. Barack Obama, "Remarks at the National Women's Law Center," http://www.obama.senate.gov (accessed August 25, 2006).

33. Obama, *The Audacity of Hope*, 193.

34. Barack Obama, "21st Century Schools for a 21st Century Economy," http://www.obama.senate.gov (accessed August 26, 2006).

35. Barack Obama, "Speech to the Center for American Progress: Teaching Our Kids in a 21st Century Economy," http://www.obama.senate.gov (accessed August 25, 2006).

36. Ibid.

37. Jennifer Hochschild and Natahn Scovronick, *The American Dream and the Public Schools* (New York: Oxford University Press, 2003), 19.

38. Barack Obama, "Remarks at TechNet," (March 8, 2005), http://www.obama.senate.gov (accessed August 25, 2006).

39. Barack Obama, "Remarks at the AFL-CIO National Convention," http://www.obama.senate.gov (accessed August 25, 2006).

40. Barack Obama, "Remarks at Emily's List Luncheon," http://www.obama.senate.gov (accessed August 25, 2006).

41. "Poll: 74 Percent of Americans Say Congress Out of Touch," http://www.cnn.com (accessed October 18, 2006).

42. Hochschild, *Facing up to the American Dream*, 21.

43. Kingdon, *America the Unusual*, 26–27.

44. John Judis, *The Paradox of American Democracy* (New York: Pantheon, 2000), 39–40.

45. Robert D. Putnam, *Bowling Alone: The Collapse and Revival of American Democracy* (New York: Simon and Schuster, 2000), 319–25.

46. Kingdon, *American the Unusual*, 35.

47. Graetz and Shapiro, *Death by a Thousand Cuts*, 119.

48. Samuel Huntington, *American Politics: The Promise of Disharmony* (Cambridge: Harvard University Press, 1981), 337.

49. http://www.obama.senate.gov/blog (accessed Sept 30, 2005).

50. Barack Obama, "Remarks at AFSCME National Convention," http://www.obama.senate.gov (accessed August 25, 2006).

51. Obama, "Remarks at the AFL-CIO National Convention."

52. Barack Obama, *The Audacity of Hope: Thoughts on Reclaiming the American Dream* (New York: Crown Publishers, 2006), 152.

53. Ibid., 247.

54. Ibid., 260.

55. Barack Obama, "Opening Statement for Floor Debate on Ethics Reform," http://www.obama.senate.gov (accessed on August 25, 2006).

56. Barack Obama, "Remarks to Governor's Ethanol Coalition: Energy Security Is National Security," http://www.obama.senate.gov (accessed August 25, 2006).

57. Mike Ramsey, "Keyes Comes Out Swinging," *Springfield State Journal-Register*, August 10, 2004, 1.

58. Barack Obama, "Remarks of Illinois State Sen. Barack Obama against Going to War with Iraq," http://www.barackobama.com (accessed November 11, 2006).

59. Curtis Lawrence, "Rush, Opponents Clash Off the Air," *Chicago Sun-Times*, February 19, 2000, 4.

60. http://www.obama.senate.gov/blog (accessed September 30, 2005).

61. Barack Obama, "Statement of Senator Barack Obama on the Nuclear Option," http://www.obama.senate.gov (accessed August 25, 2006).

62. Obama, "Remarks at Emily's List Annual Luncheon."

63. Barack Obama, "Floor Statement on General Michael Hayden Nomination," http://www.obama.senate.gov (accessed August 25, 2006).

64. Barack Obama, "Remarks at the 2005 Pritzker School of Medicine Commencement," http://www.obama.senate.gov (accessed August 25, 2006).

65. Barack Obama, "Moving Forward in Iraq: Speech to the Chicago Council on Foreign Relations," http://www.obama.senate.gov (accessed on August 25, 2006).

66. Amy Waldman, "In Good Faith," http://www.slate.com (July 3, 2006).

67. "Interview with Barack Obama," http://www.streetprophets.com/story 2006.7/11/2134281301 (accessed September 28, 2006).

68. Barack Obama, "Remarks at the 2006 Lobbying Reform Summit," http://www.obama.senate.gov (accessed August 25, 2006).

69. Obama, "Remarks at Emily's List Annual Luncheon."

70. Obama, *The Audacity of Hope*, 134.

71. Alan Wolfe, *Does American Democracy Still Work* (New Haven: Yale University Press, 2006), 48.

72. Joe Klein, "The Fresh Face," *Time*, October 23, 2006, 46.

73. David Mendell, "Obama Has Center in His Sights," *Chicago Tribune*, April 27, 2004, 1.

74. Ibid.

75. Obama, *The Audacity of Hope*, 32–34.

76. Obama, "The Audacity of Hope: Keynote Address to the 2004 Democratic National Convention."

77. Obama, "Remarks to Governor's Ethanol Coalition: Energy Security is National Security."

78. Jodi Enda, "Great Expectations," *American Prospect*, February 2006, 25–26.

79. Obama, *The Audacity of Hope*, 59.

80. Barack Obama "Remarks at the 2005 Robert F. Kennedy Human Rights Award Ceremony," http://www.obama.senate.gov (accessed August 25, 2006).

81. http://http://www.obama.senate.gov/blog (accessed Sept. 30, 2005).

82. Ibid.

83. Obama, "Remarks at the Robert F. Kennedy Human Rights Award Ceremony."

84. Alexander Cockburn, "Beat the Devil," *The Nation*, April 24, 2006, 10.

85. Ken Silverstein, "Barack Obama, Inc.," *Harper's,* November 2006, 31–40.

86. Perry Bacon, Jr., "The Exquisite Dilemma of Being Obama," *Time*, February 20, 2006, 24–28.

87. Kim Fridkin Kahn and Patrick J. Kenney, *The Spectacle of U.S. Senate Campaigns* (Princeton: Princeton University Press, 1999), 53–61.

88. Barack Obama, "Remarks of Senator Barack Obama: Take Back America," http://www.obama.senate.gov (accessed October 16, 2006).

89. Richard F. Fenno, Jr., *Home Style: House Members in their Districts* (Boston: HarperCollins, 1978), 54–56.

90. Mike Thomas, "What's behind Barack's Celebrity," *Chicago Sun-Times*, August 9, 2004, 44.

91. Smith, "Show and Tell," 19.

CHAPTER NINE

1. "Obama Leads Fundraising for April to June," http://www.msnbc.msn .com/id/18535415. (accessed August 18, 2007).

2. John Samples, *Government Financing of Campaigns: Public Choice and Public Values* (Washington: Cato Institute, 2002).

3. Ken Silverstein, "Barack Obama, Inc.," *Harper's*, November 2006, 36.

4. "2004 Election Outcome: Money Wins," *Open Secrets*, http://www.free-press.net/news/print/5459 (accessed March 13, 2007).

5. Ken Silverstein, "Barack Obama, Inc.," *Harper's,* November 2006, 31–40.

6. Ibid.

7. Barack Obama, *The Audacity of Hope: Thoughts on Reclaiming the American Dream* (New York: Crown Publishers, 2006), 114.

8. Richard R. Lau et al., "The Effects of Negative Political Advertisements: A Meta-Analysis Assessment," *American Political Science Review* 93 (1999): 851–75.

9. Kim Fridkin Kahn and Patrick J. Kenney, "Do Negative Campaigns Mobilize or Suppress Voter Turnout? Clarifying the Relationship between Negativity and Participation," *American Political Science Review* 93 (1999): 877–89.

10. E. J. Dionne, Jr., *Why Americans Hate Politics* (New York: Simon & Schuster, 1991), 12–13; Alan Wolfe, *Does American Democracy Still Work* (New Haven: Yale University Press, 2006), 4–7.

11. Morris Fiorina, *Culture War: The Myth of a Polarized America* (New York: Pearson/Longman, 2006), 167–82.

12. Neal Peirce, "Minorities Slowly Gain State Offices," *National Journal*, January 5, 1991, 33.

13. "Did You Know," *Essence*, June 2004, 38.

14. Nelson Polsby, *Consequences of Party Reform* (New York: Oxford University Press, 1983), 169–70.

15. John B. Judis and Ruy Teixeira, *The Emerging Democratic Majority* (New York: Scribner, 2002), 39–66.

16. http://www.cnn.com/ELECTION/2004/pages/results/states/IL/S/01/epolls.0.html, (accessed November 29, 2006).

17. Glenn Thrush, "Clinton's Camp Fires First Salvo," *Newsday*, January 22, 2007, 1.

18. Maureen Dowd, "The Year of the Furies," *Fort Worth Star-Telegram*, November 14, 2006, B11.

19. http://www.pollingreport.com (accessed August 19, 2007).

20. http://www.presidentpolls2008.com (accessed August 19, 2007).

21. David Mendell, "Looking beyond Obama-mania: Is He Ready Yet?" *Chicago Tribune*, September 24, 2006, 1 (Perspective).

22. Howard Kurtz, "The Obama Swoon," *Washington Post*, October 30, 2004, http://www.washingtonpost.com (accessed October 30, 2004).

23. Sunil Garg, "A Profile in Discouragement," *Chicago Tribune,* March 24, 2006, http://www.chicagotribune.com (accessed March 27, 2006).

24. Eric Zorn, "Letter to Voters a Letdown for Obama Idealists," *Chicago Tribune* November 2, 2006, 7.

25. Jeremiah Posedel, telephone interview with Keith Boeckelman, November 27, 2006. (Mr. Posedel was the downstate coordinator for Barack Obama's 2004 Senate campaign).

26. Mark Halperin and John F. Harris, *The Way to Win: Taking the White House in 2008* (New York: Random House, 2006).

27. http://www.Techpresident.com (accessed April 23, 2007).

28. "Senator Obama's Office Responds to Misleading Harper's Magazine Story," http://www.obama.senate.gov (accessed November 5, 2006).

29. Maureen Dowd, "Haunted by the Past," *New York Times,* November 1, 2006, 23.

30. Jeff Zeleny, "As the Skeptics Ask Why, Obama Asks Why Not," *New York Times*, http://www.nytimes.com (accessed January 18, 2007).

31. Mickey Kaus, "Obama—Too Reflective," http://www.slate.com (accessed December 21, 2006).

32. Jacob Weisberg, "Obama's New Rules," http://www.slate.com (accessed October 26, 2006).

33. Barbara A. Bardes and Robert W. Oldendick, *Public Opinion: Measuring the American Mind*, 3rd ed. (Belmont, CA: Thomson-Wadsworth, 2006), 186–87.

34. Drew Westen, "Gut Instincts," *American Prospect*, December 2006, 30–31.

35. David C. Wilson, "Prospective Presidents or Long Shots? Political Optimism Toward Black Candidates and Racial Realities" (paper presented at the Annual Meeting of the American Political Science Association). (Philadelphia, PA, September 1, 2006).

36. Fred I. Greenstein, *The Presidential Difference: Leadership Style from FDR to Clinton* (New York: Free Press, 2000), 194–200.

37. Newton Minow, "Why Obama Should Run for President," *Chicago Tribune*, October 26, 2006, A27.

38. Tammerlin Drummond, "The Barack Obama Story," *San Francisco Chronicle,* April 1, 1990, 5.

39. Greenstein, *The Presidential Difference*, 197–98.

40. Sebastian Mallaby, "The Decline of Trust," *Washington Post*, October 30, 2006, A17.

41. David Sirota, "Mr. Obama Goes to Washington," *The Nation*, June 7, 2006, http://davidsirota.com/index/php/mr-obama-goes-to-washington (accessed December 5, 2006).

42. Silverstein, "Barack Obama, Inc.," 40.

43. Greenstein, *The Presidential Difference*, 195–97.

44. Posedel, interview, 2006.

45. David Brooks, "Run, Barack, Run," *New York Times* October 19, 2006, 27.

46. Howard Kurts, "Headmaster Disputes Claim that Obama Attended Islamic School," *Washinton Post*, January 23, 2007, C7.

47. Barack Obama, "The American Moment—Remarks to the Chicago Council on Global Affairs," April 23, 2007, http://www.barackobama.com (accessed April 28, 2007).

Selected Bibliography

Alter, Jonathan. "Is America Ready?" *Newsweek*, December 25, 2006/January 1, 2007, 28–36, 38–40.

Bacon, Perry. "The Exquisite Dilemma of Being Obama." *Time*, February 20, 2006, 24–28.

Chicago Tribune. "Barack Obama: Making of a Candidate." (Thirteen part series), http://www.chicagotribune.com/news/politics/chi-obama-life-story-gallery.0,1773480.storygallery.

Dougherty, Steve. *Hopes and Dreams: The Story of Barack Obama.* New York: Black Dog and Leventhal Publishers, 2007.

Enda, Jodi. "Great Expectations." *American Prospect*, February 2006, 25–26.

Finnegan, William. "The Candidate." *New Yorker*, May 31, 2004, 32–39.

Fitzgerald, Torence J. "Barack Obama." *Current Biography,* July 2005, 54–63.

Franke-Ruta, Garance. "The Next Generation." *American Prospect,* August 2004, 13–17.

Gray, Kevin A. "The Packaging of Obama." *The Progressive*, February 2007, 41–44.

Green, Joshua. "A Gambling Man." *Atlantic Monthly*, January/February 2004, 34–38.

Hirsch, Michael. "No Time to Go Wobbly, Barack." *The Washington Monthly,* April 2007, 26–29, 31–36.

Klein, Joe. "The Fresh Face." *Time,* October 23, 2006, 28–33, 102–3.

Krol, Eric. "Building from the Base." *Illinois Issues*, January 2004, 23–25.

Lizza, Ryan. "The Agitator." *The New Republic*, March 19, 2007, 22–26, 28–29.

MacFarquhar, Larissa. "The Conciliator." *The New Yorker,* May 7, 2007, 46–57.

"Obama's Fire Ignited By Political Heroes." *Jet,* November 13, 2006, 28, 30, 36, 44.

Obama's Senate website, http://www.obama.senate.gov.

Obama, Barack. *The Audacity of Hope: Thoughts on Reclaiming the American Dream.* New York: Crown Publishers, 2006.

———. *Dreams from My Father: A Story of Race and Inheritance.* New York: Three Rivers Press, 2004.

Ripley, Amanda. "Obama's Ascent." *Time,* November 15, 2004, 74–76, 78, 81.

Savadnik, Peter. "Illinois Senate Candidate Compared to Moseley-Braun: Barack Obama May Benefit as Top Candidates Vie." *The Hill,* February 10, 2004. http://www.thehill.com/campaign/073003_obama.aspx

Scheiber, Noam. "Race against History: Barack Obama's Miraculous Campaign." *New Republic*, May 24, 2004, 21–26.

Senior, Jennifer. "Dreaming of Obama." *New York,* October 2, 2006, 28–33, 102–103.

Shapiro, Walter. "Barack Obama's Quiet Rebellion." *Salon,* May 30, 2007, http://www.salon.com.

Silverstein, Ken. "Barack Obama Inc." *Harper's,* November 2006, 31–38, 40.

Sirota, David. "Mr. Obama Goes to Washington." *The Nation,* June 7, 2006, 20–23.

Sweet, Lynn. "Running to the Right." *Illinois Issues,* January 2004, 18–20.

Tumulty, Karen. "The Candor Candidate." *Time,* June 11, 2007, 32–35.

Turow, Scott. "The New Face of the Democratic Party—and America." *Salon,* March 30, 2004, http://www.salon.com.

Victor, Kirk. "Reason to Smile." *National Journal,* March 18, 2006, 20–24.

Wallace-Wells, Benjamin. "Destiny's Child." *Rolling Stone,* February 22, 2007, 48–50, 52–54, 57.

Wallace-Wells, Benjamin. "The Great Black Hope." *Washington Monthly,* November 2004, 30–36.

Weisberg, Jacob. "The Path to Power." *Men's Vogue,* September/October 2006, 224.

Williams, Patricia J. "L'Etranger." *The Nation,* March 5, 2007, 11, 13–15.

Index

Abortion, 8, 22, 32–34, 37, 38, 54, 55, 64, 67, 71, 85, 106, 112, 119, 121, 123
AFL-CIO, 14
AIDS, 97, 105, 121
Allen, George, 29
Ashcroft, John, 74
Axelrod, David, 57, 62, 63

Bean, Melissa, 37
Blackwell, Kenneth, 75
Blagojevich, Rod, 15, 45
Booker, Cory, 77
Borling, John, 26, 27
Bositis, David, 13, 77
Brooke, Edward, 73
Brooks, David, 119
Brown, Anthony, 77
Brown, Steve, 59
Bruce, Blanche Kelso, 73
Bryan, William Jennings, 101
Bunning, Jim, 94
Burris, Roland, 13, 78–80
Bush, George W., 13, 67, 96

Cain, Herman, 75
Capparelli, Ralph, 64
Cardin, Benjamin, 75
Chaffee, Lincoln, 94
Cheney, Dick, 33, 123

Chicago vote, 80
Chico, Gery, 14, 16, 46, 60, 61, 68, 70
Chisholm, Shirley, 124
Clinton, Bill, 5, 9, 30, 55, 71, 74, 82, 83, 106, 121
Clinton, Hillary, 55, 120
Coburn, Tom, 92
Cockburn, Alexander, 114
Coffey, Thomas, 47
Collins, Earlean, 78
Communitarianism, 104
Cooperative Threat Reduction Program, 98
Corzine, Jon, 46, 52, 59
Craig, Gregory, 49
Cross, Tom, 29
Cuomo, Mario, 30, 102

Daily Show, 123
Daley, Richard J., 12, 79
Daley, Richard M., 6, 12, 16, 79
Davis, Danny, 17, 19, 81
Davis, Jeff, 64
Day, Dorothy, 106
DePriest, Oscar, 8
Developing Communities Project, 4, 126
Dillard, Kirk, 6, 28, 29, 31, 76
Ditka, Mike, 29, 63
Dixon, Alan, 13, 16
Douglas, Paul, 12

Douglass, Frederick, 105
Dukakis, Michael, 115
Dunne, George, 79
Durbin, Dick, 91, 92

Edgar, Jim, 27, 29
Education, 16, 29, 34, 37, 61, 68, 69,
    78, 85, 87, 92, 93, 97, 100, 104,
    107–109, 134
Edwards, John, 55, 130, 131
Environmental Protection Agency, 90
Erkes, Jason, 46
Evans, Lane, 17, 19

Farm Aid, 91, 101
Fenno, Richard, 115
Fenty, Adrian, 77
Finnegan, William, 86
Fitzgerald, Patrick, 29
Fitzgerald, Peter, 31, 46, 59, 63
Ford, Harold, 75, 88
Franke-Ruta, Garance, 76, 77

Gantt, Harvey, 74
GI Bill, 30, 107, 127
Giannoulias, Alexi, 123
Gibbs, Robert, 62, 63, 65
Gidwitz, Ron, 29
Gore, Al, 13, 78
Gorman, Elizabeth Doody, 29
Green, Julian, 53, 63, 91

Hairston, Leslie, 17
Halperin, Mark, 123
Harris, John F., 123
Hastert, Dennis, 14, 28, 32, 91
Health care, 9, 15, 22, 26, 32–35, 37,
    40, 45, 47, 59, 60, 62, 66, 68, 69,
    83, 85, 93, 95, 96, 100, 104,
    107–109, 111, 119
Helms, Jesse, 14, 74
Hofeld, Al, 13, 16
Hope Fund, 55
Hull, Blair, 14–16, 20, 23, 42, 44–46,
    59, 60, 66, 67, 70, 82, 83
Hurricane Katrina, 88, 91, 92, 103
Hyde, Henry, 63
Hynes, Dan, 14–17, 20, 2, 22, 23, 60,
    61, 70, 83, 120
Hynes, Thomas, 14

Illinois Chamber of Commerce, 8
Illinois Farm Bureau, 8
Internet, 31, 54, 55, 65, 66, 69,
    70–72, 104, 117, 123
Iraq War, 19, 35, 110, 114, 121, 125

Jackson, Jesse, Jr., 17, 19, 77, 83
Jackson, Jesse, Sr., 75
Jefferson, Thomas, 107
Jones, Emil, 6, 19, 83
Jordan, Vernon, 49

Kennedy, Robert, 112, 114
Kennedy, Ted, 91, 114
Kerry, John, 13, 40, 67, 129, 130, 131
Keyes, Alan, 2, 25, 29, 31, 40, 41, 51,
    63, 68, 69, 71, 83, 84, 110, 112,
    119, 124
King, Martin Luther, Jr., 81

Lagana, Susan, 46, 67
Lampe, Kevin, 58
Lazio, Rick, 46
Lieberman, Joe, 114
Limbaugh, Rush, 37, 63
Lincoln, Abraham, 106, 109, 112, 124,
    135

Madigan, Michael, 14, 59
Majette, Denise, 75
Malcolm X, 5
Mather, Chris, 46
Matthews, Chris, 18
McAuliffe, Mike, 64
McCain, John, 94, 95, 124
McCain-Feingold Bipartisan Campaign
    Reform Act, 44
McCall, Carl, 74
McKenna, Andrew, 26
Mendell, David, 45
Mfume, Kweisi, 75
Miller, Rich, 38
Miller, Zell, 75
Morrison, David, 58
Moseley-Braun, Carol, 5, 13, 16, 19,
    23, 24, 73, 74, 78, 82, 124
Muwakkil, Salim, 83, 86, 87

National Abortion and Reproductive
    Rights Action League, 45

No Child Left Behind, 16, 19
Noble, Larry, 44
Nugent, Ted, 29

Oberweis, James, 26

Palmer, Alice, 5
Pappas, Maria, 14, 15, 21, 61, 71
Partee, Cecil, 78, 79
Pataki, George, 74
Patrick, Deval, 75, 77, 119
Pearson, Rick, 61
Pew Internet and American Life
    Project, 70
Powell, Colin, 87
Preckwinkle, Toni, 17
Progressive Movement, 108, 112
Project Vote, 5

Racial discrimination, 76, 84
Rauschenberger, Steve, 26,
    29, 113
Reagan, Ronald, 63, 112
Reed, Rick, 59
Reid, Harry, 94
Revels, Hiram Rhodes, 73
Rezko, Tony, 123
Richards, Ann, 30
Roeser, Jack, 64, 65
Roosevelt, Franklin, 101
Rove, Karl, 92, 110
Rumsfeld, Donald, 123
Rush, Bobby, 8, 15, 17, 42, 66, 67, 83,
    88, 103, 110
Ryan, George, 6, 11, 13, 22
Ryan, Jack, 2, 25–28, 37, 41, 49, 51, 53,
    58, 60–62, 64, 65, 82, 83, 113, 119
Ryan, Jeri, 27

Saltzman, Bettylu, 44
Salvi, Al, 66
Schakowsky, Jan, 17, 18
Scheiber, Noam, 18, 75
Schock, Aaron, 64
Scott, William, 79
Serdiuk, Claire, 43, 47
Sharpton, Al, 124
Simmons, John, 59
Simon, Paul, 7, 12, 21, 23, 24, 36, 61,
    78, 82, 111
Sloan, Melanie, 65
Steele, Michael, 75
Stroger, John, 83
Swann, Lynn, 75
Swarns, Rachel, 85

Teixeira, Ruy, 120
Thomas, Clarence, 13
Topinka, Judy Baar, 27, 28, 33

Vallas, Paul, 78
Voting Rights Act, 93

Wallace-Wills, Benjamin, 87
Warfel, Justin, 27
Washington, Harold, 4, 8, 12,
    81, 82
Wellstone, Paul, 102, 110, 114
West, Cornel, 76
Wheat, Alan, 74
White, Jesse, 13, 78–80
Wilder, Douglas, 74, 88
Williams, Alvin, 85
Williamson, Richard, 13
Winfrey, Oprah, 119

Zeleny, Jeff, 89

About the Authors

MARTIN DUPUIS is Assistant Dean of the Burnett Honors College and Associate Professor of Political Science at the University of Central Florida. He received his Ph.D. from the University of Southern California and his J.D. from the American University.

KEITH BOECKELMAN is Associate Professor of Political Science and Research Fellow of the Illinois Institute for Rural Affairs, Western Illinois University. He received his Ph.D. from the University of Illinois-Urbana.